Geography for CCEA GCSE

Geography for CCEA GCSE

SECOND EDITION

- Petula Henderson
- Stephen Roulston
- Peter Corr

Editor: Kay Clarke

HODDER EDUCATION
AN HACHETTE UK COMPANY

Introduction

Introduction for students

'Geography is the subject which holds the key to our future.'

Michael Palin, CBE, President of the Royal Geographical Society

The study of Geography fosters an understanding of the world and its people. It encourages an appreciation of the relationships between physical and human processes in varied places and environments. It enhances your knowledge of the world around you, raises awareness of the environment and develops your problem-solving skills. Through studying the subject you will have opportunities to develop an understanding of your responsibility as a global citizen, and develop your awareness of different cultures and therefore become environmentally and socially more aware.

I trust that you find the book informative and thought provoking and hope that you will enjoy following the GCSE course as much as the specification writers have enjoyed developing a relevant, engaging and contemporary specification, and the authors enjoyed writing this supporting text.

It is my wish that the knowledge and understanding gained and skills developed, will stimulate your interest and encourage you to continue to develop your appreciation of geography as a dynamic subject, perhaps even to an advanced level of study and through your lifelong learning.

Introduction for teachers

Geography for CCEA GCSE is intended for 14–16-year-old GCSE geography students preparing for the CCEA GCSE specification in Geography (first assessment in summer 2010). The book provides a comprehensive class text and equips students with the knowledge and resources needed to succeed in GCSE Geography.

The content is presented following the thematic structure of the CCEA specification, but this does not necessarily imply a proposed teaching order. The CCEA Geography specification is now offered as a unitised course. This means that students have the opportunity to sit Unit 1 or Unit 2 in the first year of teaching. This development increases flexibility and choice for teachers and learners. Teachers wishing to follow the course in a unitised manner will therefore need to opt to teach either Unit 1 or Unit 2 in a particular year to enable the material to be fully covered in adequate detail for the unitised assessment. Both Unit 1 'Understanding Our Natural World' and Unit 2 'Living in Our World', will be available for assessment in each examination series. Teachers can organise the teaching of the content of each unit as they consider appropriate and should attempt to emphasise the interrelationship of the different themes. In covering the two units of the specification, the book addresses the key aspects of the curriculum through six themes: 'The Dynamic Landscape', 'Our Changing Weather and Climate', 'The Restless Earth',

'People and Where They Live', 'Contrasts in World Development' and 'Managing Our Resources'.

Different spatial contexts are used to illustrate the specification content at a range of scales from local to global. Concepts of sustainable development, the interrelationships between people and the natural environment, the need to manage both physical and human resources, interdependence between countries and international co-operation to tackle global issues are addressed throughout the book.

The authors have included theoretical information on each topic, a glossary of key ideas and appropriate case study material. The book is supplemented with learning outcomes, active learning activities, extension work, weblinks, GIS activities and exemplar examination questions for both foundation and higher tier students. The book affords teachers the opportunity to integrate a wide variety of skills and techniques such as reading plans and maps, interpreting patterns on maps, satellite images and photographs, using a variety of methods to present geographical information and to investigate patterns between variables incorporating tables, graphs, diagrams, maps and text using ICT where appropriate, e.g. GIS.

When using the book it should be noted:

- The websites specified are usually but not always associated with identified activities, but rather, in some cases are included to give students a starting point for further research and to provide sources of further information that could be used to generate additional student activities and discussion. At the time of publication all the websites mentioned are active and accurate.
- Students need to demonstrate a strong knowledge of place, particularly exemplified through case studies. The authors have selected certain case studies required by the specification. However, information for all case studies is contained within the book and students could use the information provided to develop their own case study notes. Although material has been included for the case studies, this is not intended to be prescriptive, as other examples you may develop will equally be valid in the examination. In fact, the dynamic nature of the subject is such that you will probably wish to develop alternative areas of interest to maintain the vibrancy and topical nature of the subject. Where a case study is not required by the specification, the authors have attempted to enhance the learning outcomes by reference to places for illustration purposes.
- As the controlled assessment tasks are replaced by CCEA each year, the authors have chosen not to include detailed exemplification of the same in the book. However, the content will support controlled assessment of a wide variety of topics from both the physical and human themes as required.

Kay Clarke
Editor

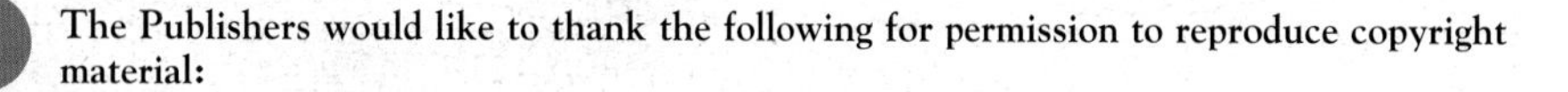

The Publishers would like to thank the following for permission to reproduce copyright material:

Photo credits

p.1 © NASA/Corbis; p.6–7 © Crown Copyright 2009; p.11 © Charles E. Rotkin/CORBIS; p.12 © NASA/JPL; p.15 © Jack Fields/CORBIS; p.18 © Apex News and Pictures Agency/ Alamy; p.20 © Peter Titmuss/Alamy; p.21 *t* © Nigel Bell/Alamy; p.21 *b* © Geogphotos/ Alamy; p.22 © Google Earth; p.23 © Nagelestock.com/Alamy; p.24 © Crown Copyright 2009; p.27 Cranfield University, www.soil-net.com (2009); p.31 Panoramic Images; p.32 *t* © Jim Laws/Alamy; p.32 *b* © Frank Naylor/Alamy; p.33 *t* © Stockbyte/Alamy; p.33 *br* © Klaus Hackenberg/Corbis; p.34 *t* © Neil Holmes Freelance Digital/Alamy; p.34 *b* Jason Edwards/National Geographic/Getty Images; p.36 © Ken Welsh/Alamy; p.37 © Stephen Saks/Alamy; p.38 *t* © Jon Sparks/Corbis; p.38 *b* HR Wallingford; p.39 *t* © Andrew Stacey; p.41 *t* Courtesy of the National Library of Ireland; p.41 *b* © JoeFoxCountyDown/Alamy; p.45 © Justin Kase zonez/Alamy; p.47 © David R. Frazier Photolibrary, Inc./Alamy; p.48 Jerry Mason/Science Photo Library, Sam Ogden/Science Photo Library, Cape Grim B.A.P.S./Simon Fraser/Science Photo Library, © Paul Seheult/Eye Ubiquitous/Corbis, © Ashley Cooper/Corbis, © Douglas Schwartz/Corbis, © Philippe Giraud/Sygma/Corbis; p.50 © David Howells/Corbis; p.52 © Dennis Cox/Alamy; p.53 *tr* © David R. Frazier Photolibrary, Inc./Alamy; p.53 *mr* © Michael Dwyer/Alamy; p.53 *br* © David L. Moore/Alamy; p.53 *l* © NASA; p.59 © Crown Copyright 2009; p.60 *l* © Scenicireland.com/Christopher Hill Photographic/Alamy; p.60 *r* © JoeFox/Alamy; p.61 © Crown Copyright 2009; p.62 © Crown Copyright 2009; p.64 © Crown Copyright 2009; p.73 © LH Images/Alamy; p.75 © Crown Copyright 2009; p.76 *t* Gill Massey, Otter Wrought Iron, www.weathervanes.co.uk; p.76 *m* Jerry Mason/Science Photo Library; p.76 *b* © Paul Seheult/Eye Ubiquitous/Corbis; p.79 © Michael S. Yamashita/Corbis; p.81 Dirk Wiersma/Science Photo Library, E.R. Degginger/Science Photo Library, Aaron Haupt/Science Photo Library, Mark A. Schneider/Science Photo Library, Joyce Photographics/Science Photo Library, © WILDLIFE GmbH/Alamy; p.91 *t* © JoeFoxBelfast/Alamy; p.92 *l* © Blend Images/Alamy; p.92 *m* © Astock/Fotolia; p.92 *r* © Andres Rodriguez/Fotolia; p.93 *l* © Image Source/Corbis; p.93 *tr* © David Kneafsey/Fotolia; p.93 *br* © nyul/Fotolia; p.96 © Michael S. Yamashita/CORBIS; p.97 © Pacific Press Service/Alamy; p.100 © Google Earth; p.101 Romeo Gacad/AFP/Getty Images; p.102 Gregory Bull/AP/Press Association Images; p.103 © Rungroj Yongrit/epa/ Corbis; p.104–5 © NASA; p.109 © Ed Kashi/Corbis; p.111 www.cartoonstock.com; p.114 © Crown Copyright 2009; p.117 © Elmtree Images/Alamy; p.131 *tl* © Robert Gray/ Alamy; p.134 *t* © Crown Copyright 2009; p.134 *b* © Crown Copyright 2009; p.135 *t* © Crown Copyright 2009; p.135 *b* © Crown Copyright 2009; p.139 © EmmePi Travel/Alamy; p.140 *tl* © Thierry Prat/Sygma/Corbis; p.140 *bl* © Thierry Prat/Sygma/Corbis; p.140 *tr* © Thierry Prat/Sygma/Corbis; p.140 *br* © Earl & Nazima Kowall/CORBIS; p.141 *l* © Frédéric Soltan/Sygma/Corbis; p.141 *r* © Ed Kashi/Corbis; p.142 *b* © CivicArts/Eric R Kuhne & Associates, www.civicart.com; p.147 © Reuters/CORBIS; p.150 © Crown Copyright 2009; p.152 © Reuters/CORBIS; p.155 © Polyp www.polyp.org.uk; p.161 Bryan Bedder/Getty Images for IMG; p.164 © NASA; p.165 © Avalon Guitars; p.167 © Amit Bhargava/Corbis/Corbis; p.168 © Parth Sanyal/Reuters/Corbis; p.174 © George Steinmetz/Corbis; p.176 *l* Robert Churchill/Getty; p.176 *tr* © Frédéric Soltan/Sygma/Corbis; p.176 *mr* The Hindu Photo Archives; p.176 *br* Dinodia Photo Library; p.179 *t* © David Turnley/Corbis; p.179 *bl* © Owen Franken/Corbis; p.179 *br* © Owen Franken/Corbis; p.180 © Robert Gray; p.181 © Greg Wright/Alamy; p.182 Dave Hogan/Getty Images; p.183 © Danita Delimont/Alamy; p.191 Sarah Leen/Getty; p.193 © Ed Kashi/Corbis; p.196 © Superclic/Alamy; p.200 © Bob Sacha/Corbis; p.201 © Lou-Foto/Alamy; p.202 © Colin Garratt; Milepost 92½/Corbis; p.203 *t* © Michael Reynolds/epa/Corbis; p.203 *b* Shi Wei/ChinaFotoPress/Getty Images; p.204 *t* © Liu Liqun/Corbis; p.204 *b* © Keren Su/Corbis; p.205 *t* © John Holmes; Frank Lane Picture Agency/Corbis; p.205 *b* © Chan Yat Nin/Redlink/Corbis; p.207 Sarah Leen/Getty; p.210 © Photoshot Holdings Ltd/Alamy; p.217 Randy Olson/National Geographic/Getty Images; p.218 © Gideon Mendel/Corbis; p.219 *t* © Frans Lemmens/Alamy; p.219 *b* © Gideon Mendel/Corbis; p.221 © Gideon Mendel/Corbis; p.223 © Chris Madden http://www.chrismadden.co.uk.

Text credits

NICCEA GCSE Geography past paper compendium, © 2003–2008. p.15 Borough of Telford & Wrekin www.taw.org.uk; p.35 The Christian Science Monitor www.csmonitor.com; p.59 Met Office © Crown Copyright; p.65 Nelson Thornes for a text extract from *Cut, Paste & Surf* by Philip Webster, 2002; p.65, p.153 N.I. Education Boards for an extract from *Thinking Through Geography Material*, November 2009; p.68 Met Office © Crown Copyright; p.72 *China Today* for an extract from 'Rich Nations Urged to Transfer Green Tech' by Fu Jing, 8 November 2008; p.143 © CivicArts/Eric R Kuhne & Associates, www.civicart.com; p.165 © Avalon Guitars.

Every effort has been made to trace all copyright holders, but if any have been inadvertently overlooked the Publishers will be pleased to make the necessary arrangements at the first opportunity.

UNIT ONE

Understanding Our Natural World

The Dynamic Landscape

Learning outcomes

In this theme you will learn:

- what a drainage basin is
- what changes occur along the long profile of a river
- how waterfalls, meanders and floodplains are formed
- how the coast is shaped by waves
- how coastal landforms are formed
- why floods occur
- how rivers can be managed
- how to evaluate a river management scheme
- why coastal defences are needed
- to evaluate the coastal management strategies used in an area of the British Isles.

The Dynamic Landscape

The drainage basin: a component of the water cycle

The characteristics of a drainage basin

Water is a critical resource. The water that is most useful to humans is fresh water, although this only makes up 2.8% of all the water on the planet, and only 0.1% is stored in rivers and lakes. The rest of the water on land is stored in ice sheets and glaciers, or in the soil and deeper down in the ground. The total amount of water on our planet never changes: in other words, none arrives from space, and none is lost to space. This is called a closed system. The water on Earth circulates between the sea, land and air (stores), being recycled in a natural process known as the hydrological cycle (**water cycle**).

On the land the water is stored on the surface as lakes and rivers. Each river is contained within its own **drainage basin** – the area of land drained by a river and its **tributaries**. The boundary of a drainage basin follows a ridge of high ground, known as the **watershed**. This and other features of the drainage basin are summarised in Figure 1.

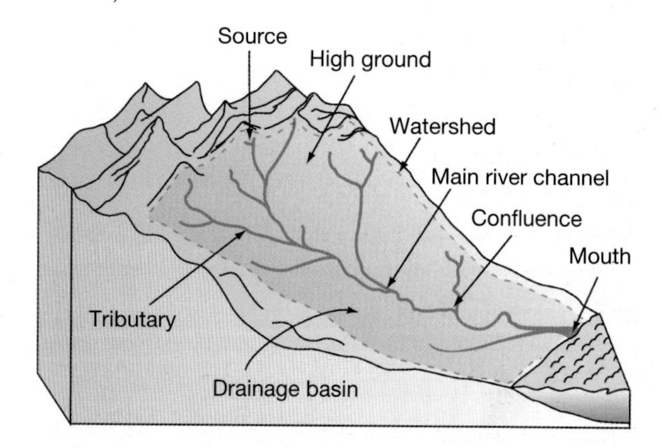

▲ **Figure 1** A generalised drainage basin

The components of the drainage basin cycle and their interrelationships

The amount of water within a single drainage basin can vary, as it has inputs (from precipitation) and outputs (from evapotranspiration). So this is an open system.

Simple open system of the drainage basin:

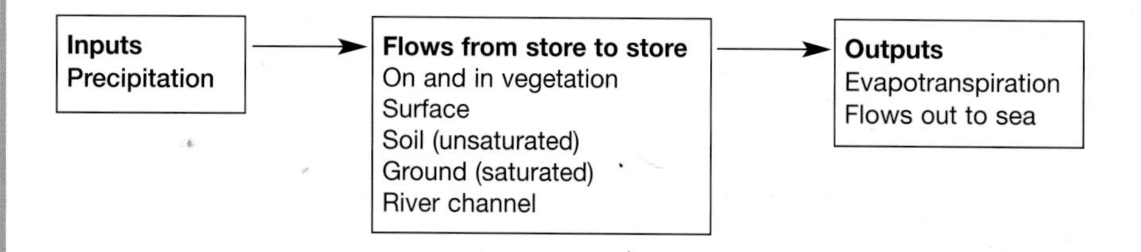

Water enters the drainage basin system as precipitation. This may be any form, such as snow or rain. Most drainage basins have some vegetation. The precipitation may be caught on the leaves of plants. This is called **interception**. Generally, it is greatest in summer. From the surface of the plant, the water may be evaporated back into the air, or flow down the stem of the plant to reach the ground. At this point the water has moved from the store in the vegetation to be part of the surface storage. If conditions are right, it will then seep into the soil. This process is called **infiltration**. Soil normally has small pockets of air called pores, which allow the water to get into it. Once in the soil, gravity will pull the water downwards and it will move down through the soil as **through-flow**, until it reaches the water table, where all the pores in the soil, or rock, are already full of water, so it cannot move any further downwards. Instead it now flows laterally (sideways) into the nearest river as groundwater flow.

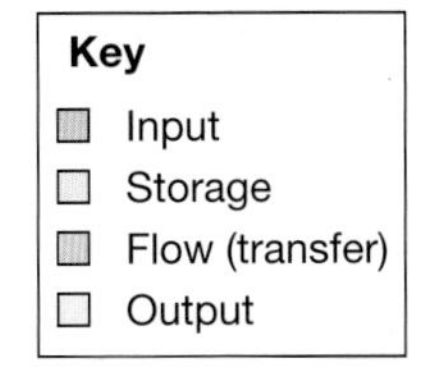

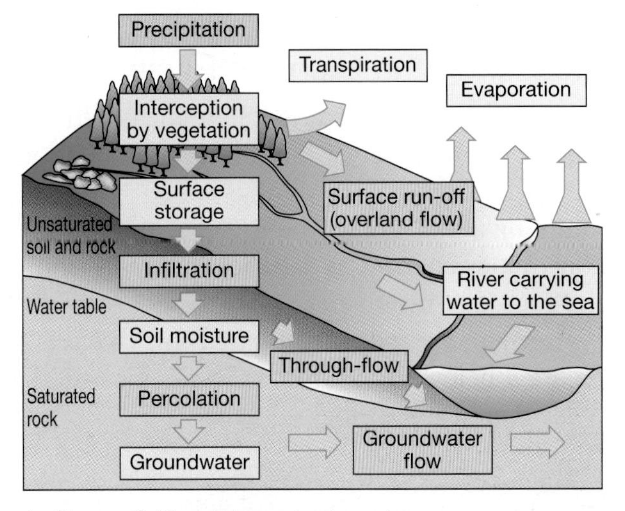

▲ **Figure 2** The drainage basin system

Any water that hits an impermeable surface, with no pores, such as tarmac, cannot infiltrate the soil below. It simply flows over the surface as **surface run-off** into the nearest river.

Although some precipitation can fall directly into the river, most water reaches a river by a combination of surface run-off, through-flow and groundwater flow. It takes water the longest time after falling to reach the river by groundwater flow, since it has had to flow through so many stores to get to the river channel.

Get Active

1. In your own words, define the following river basin terms: drainage basin, watershed, **source**, tributary, **confluence**, river channel, mouth. You can get some useful help at: www.revisioncentre.co.uk/gcse/geography/drainage_basins.html.
2. Draw a flow diagram that shows one input, two stores and two flows within the drainage basin system. Check out: www.bbc.co.uk/scotland/education/int/geog/rivers/drainage/index.shtml.
3. Why does the total amount of water falling as precipitation never reach the river channel? Give two reasons.
4. Why are environmentalists strongly against polluting rivers and lakes?
5. What effect might the building of urban areas have on the drainage basin cycle?

Glendun River

To investigate how a river can change downstream, it is possible to examine a local river like the Glendun River in Co. Antrim. The location of this river is shown in Figures 4 and 5 on pages 6–7. Any river may be divided into upper, middle and lower courses.

Measuring the Glendun River

Various fluvial characteristics are measured at regular points (every 1 km) along the Glendun River. This type of sampling is called systematic sampling and it allows the investigation of continuous changes as distance increases from the source of the river.

A group of pupils investigated this river. Figure 3 below shows what students measured.

How are these things measured?

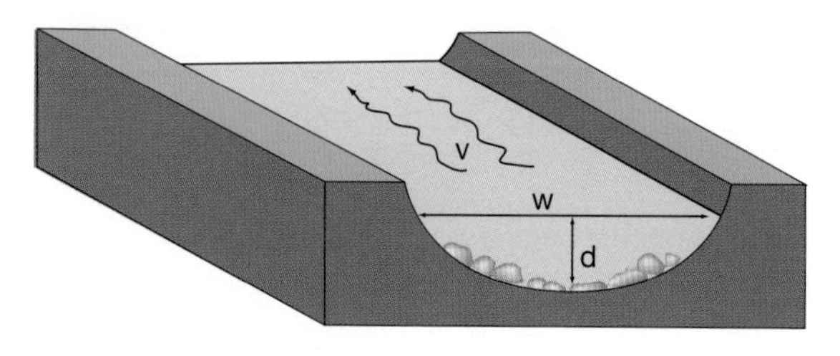

w = width v = velocity d = depth

width × depth = cross-sectional area
velocity × cross-sectional area = discharge area

▲ **Figure 3** Aspects of a river that can be measured

Width

This is measured by placing one end of a measuring tape at one side of the river channel, then pulling it out to the other side of the channel. The distance is the width of the river.

Depth

This is completed using a metre stick. The stick is lowered into the water every 10 cm, and the distance from the top of the water to the river bed gives the depth of water. An average of all these readings is taken.

Discharge

Discharge is the amount of water passing any point in a river in a certain time, normally given as cubic metres of water per second (cumecs). It is calculated by multiplying the cross-sectional area of a river channel at a certain point by the speed (velocity) of the river at the same point.

The cross-sectional area is obtained by multiplying the width of the river by the average depth. The speed (velocity) of the river is recorded using a flow metre that when dipped into the river gives a digital reading of the speed of flow in metres per second.

Load

The load of a river is the material it is carrying, ranging from small sediment to large boulders. It is very hard to measure the size of the load in **suspension**, so instead, we can concentrate on the load lying on the channel bed – called bed load. This load is measured for size and roundedness. By measuring the longest axis of 15 random samples at each point an idea of the size of the load is obtained. Each stone is then given a rating for roundedness.

What were the results?

To help see the overall trends, here is a selection of results obtained from the Glendun. They represent the three courses of this river:

	Upper course (Station 1)	Middle course (Station 11)	Lower course (Station 16)
Width (m)	2.7	10.4	14.2
Depth (m)	0.14	0.33	0.46
Discharge (cumecs)	0.08	0.2	5.1
Load long axis (cm)	26	12	7
Load – roundedness	angular	sub-angular	rounded

To help understand and explain the results collected read the information about the processes a river carries out – **erosion**, **transportation** and **deposition**, pages 9–10.

Going downstream from source to **mouth**, it appears that the Glendun River gets wider. At Station 16 (16.5 km from the source) the river is just over five times the width it is at station 1, only 1.5 km from the source.

The river also appears to get deeper. At the station in the lower course the river is 32 cm deeper than it is in the upper course.

This can be explained by the fact that there is more lateral erosion and vertical erosion occurring downstream from the source.

The enlarged river channel size downstream relates well to the pattern of increasing discharge. Because discharge is calculated by multiplying the cross-sectional area of the channel by the river's velocity, then it follows logically that as cross-sectional area increases so does the discharge. The river is receiving additional water from the tributaries that are entering it at regular intervals within the Glendun valley: these will also cause the discharge to be greater downstream. In the upper course very few tributaries have contributed to the flow. Finally, the velocity of the river is also greater as the water flowing in the river channel in the lower course does not have to overcome as much friction as that in the upper course, which has angular rocks and a shallow channel.

Most of the weathering of bare rock happens in mountain areas, where it is exposed. This material can then fall down the steep valley sides into the upper course of the river. It is still very angular, as the results show. As it moves downstream it hits the sides of the river bed, and also other rocks that make up the load. This knocks the sharp edges off the material, smoothing its sides and making it rounded. The load of the river, therefore, is noticeably more angular in the upper course, but becomes rounded in the lower course – even on a relatively short river such as the Glendun.

Get Active

1. Draw *scattergraphs* (use a suitable spreadsheet package) to show the relationship between distance from the source of the Glendun River and:
   a. Width (m).
   b. Depth (m).
   c. Discharge (cumecs).
   d. Long axis of load (cm).
2. Quoting actual figures, describe the results.
3. Do you observe any trends in the results? How can you explain these results?
4. What are the advantages of using scattergraphs to show these results as opposed to other types of graphs such as line graph, bar graph, pie chart, etc.?
5. What do the results tell you about the Glendun River?
6. How accurate do you think these results might be? What factors might contribute to their degree of accuracy?
7. Why do you think systematic sampling was used in this little investigation?
8. What other types of sampling might have been used?
9. What would be the effect of having fewer recording sites along the Glendun River?

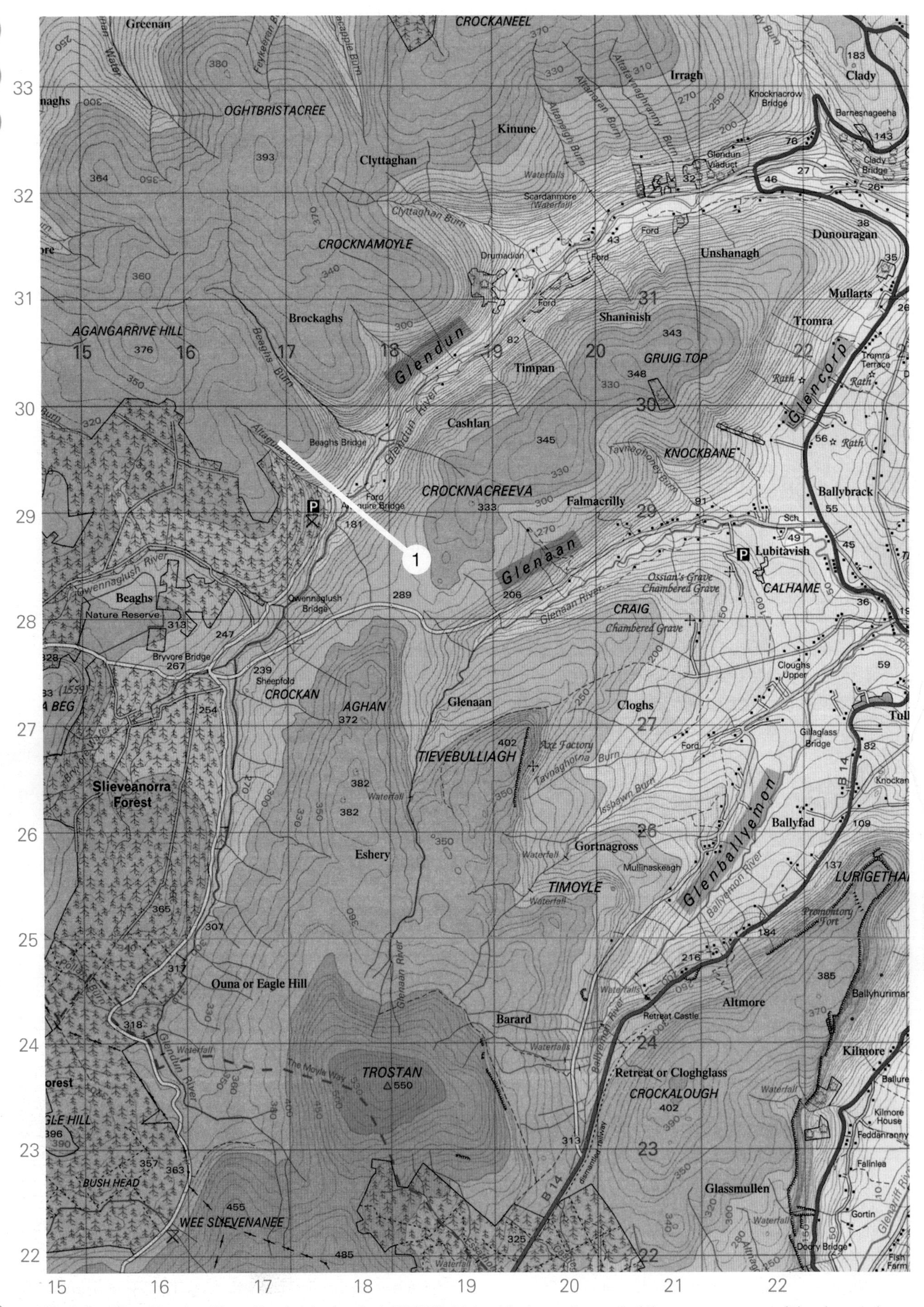

▲ **Figure 4** The Glendun River, Co. Antrim (scale 1:50,000). Note: (1) shows the end of the upper course of the river and (2) shows the end of the middle course

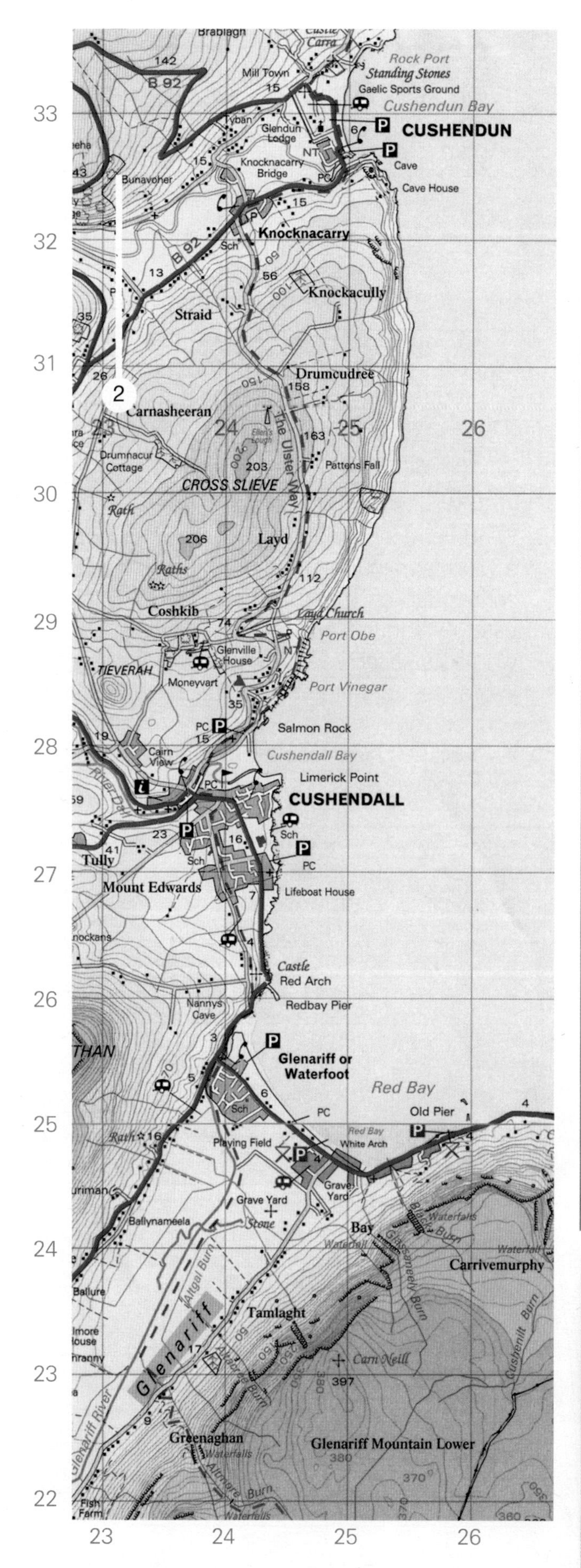

Get Active

1. What evidence can you find on the Ordnance Survey (OS) map to support the view that tourists visit this area? State your evidence from the map, draw the relevant OS map symbols and give the six-figure grid references.
2. Calculate the distance the river covers in its middle course. Give your answer in kilometres. (Tip: be sure to check out the scale of this map. How many centimetres on the map represent a kilometre on the ground?)
3. Look carefully along the course of the Glendun River and you will see the word 'Ford'. Give the six-figure grid reference for one of these fords.
4. What is a 'ford'? Who might use these 'fords' and for what reason?
5. In the upper course of the Glendun River there is a waterfall. Give its four-figure grid reference.
6. How would you describe the valley sides of the Glendun in grid square 1830? What is the evidence from the OS map to support your opinion?
7. Give at least four pieces of evidence from the map (name and grid reference) to support the view that settlement dates back a very long time in this area.
8. Why would much of the land in this area be of limited use to farmers? How could farmers make best use of the land?
9. How would you describe Slieveanorra Forest?
10. How would you describe the coastline south of Cushendun?

▲ **Figure 5** Measurements being taken on the Glendun River

Extension Activity

Living Map Exercise: Life in the Glens

Part 1

a The location of each of the people described in the table below can be found on the map on pages 6–7. Work in pairs and use the details written about them to decide where you think they are. There may be more than one possibility for some of them. Think carefully about why you have chosen each location. For each one, give a grid reference, and be prepared to explain your choices to the rest of the class.

b Now imagine two more characters that you could ask the rest of the class about. Think what clues you could give about what they are doing and where. Make sure you know where you think they would be found and why.

c Working in small groups, agree where you would site one of the following:
- café
- bird-watching lookout
- shopping centre.

1 Give your location (quoting grid square).
2 State your reasons.
3 Note the clues or evidence from the map.

Part 2: Can you help?

Frank and Sharon have brought their children, Jack aged 7 and Amy aged 11, to their caravan in Cushendun on holiday. Working in small groups, plan two days out for the family; one for a rainy day, and one for a sunny day.

Part 3: Where would you site …?

a Wind Farms International PLC want to locate a wind farm in the Glens of Antrim and have sent you to choose the best location. Think carefully about all the reasons why this area would be suitable for a wind farm. Working in groups, agree the best location and justify your choice.

b As a whole class decide which group proposal would be the best site.

Tom parks his car in a car park where he can see a church with a tower GR	Peter buys a house in the village close to the school GR	Ciara rides her horse across fields and over a stream GR
Mary takes her children to their caravan overlooking the sea GR	Jonathan is taking photos to illustrate a book on the history of the Glens GR	Paul is at his work as a caretaker at a National Trust property GR
Alice has brought her American cousins to watch the local hurling team play a game GR	Driving along the Glendun the O'Neill family stop to have a picnic close to a forest GR	At the end of the public walkway Alan stops to make a call from a public phone box GR
From the top of this hill Julie can see a telecommunications mast to the north-east GR	Billy books into a youth hostel GR	Amy spots an information sign along the road directing her to an old castle nearby GR

Get Active

1 Use the OS map extract in Figure 4 on pages 6–7 to draw your own annotated sketch map to show the course of the Glendun River. Your map should show:
  a the course of the Glendun River
  b the Glendun valley
  c major tributaries
  d the upper, middle and lower courses of the river
  e a V-shaped valley
  f wide floodplain
  g land over 300 m above sea level
  h Crocknamoyle, Crocknacreeva, Gruig Top and Wee Slievenanee
  i Slieveanorra Forest
  j roads
  k Knocknacarry and Cushendun
  l a waterfall
  m at least one ford.
2 Devise a suitable key for your sketch map.
3 Give your sketch map an appropriate title.

Processes carried out by a river: erosion, transportation and deposition

Erosion

When rivers have a large bed load made up of coarse materials these scrape or rub against the channel bed, eventually lowering the level of the bed, creating steep valley sides. This is vertical (downwards) erosion.

In sections of the river channel where the river is flowing especially fast, the water itself has enough energy to wash away the bank of the river, leading to undercutting and collapse. As this is a sideways motion, it is called lateral erosion.

Abrasion is the grinding of rock fragments carried by the river against the bed and banks of the river. This action causes the channel to widen and deepen. This grinding is most powerful in flood time when large fragments of rock are carried along in the river bed.

Solution is the process by which river water reacts chemically with soluble minerals in the rocks and dissolves them.

Attrition is the collision of rock fragments in the water against one another. The rock particles are broken into smaller pieces and become smoother the longer the process continues.

Hydraulic action is a form of mechanical weathering caused by the force of moving water. It can undermine the river banks on the outside of a meander, or force air into cracks within exposed rock in waterfalls.

Transportation

All rivers contain minerals and solid material: this is known as the load of the river. Weathered material falling into the river from the valley sides forms 90% of the load. The remaining 10% is the result of erosion caused by the river on its own banks and bed.

Rivers move their load in four ways:

1 **Traction** – the rolling of large rocks along the river bed. This requires a lot of energy, and the largest bed load will only be moved like this in times of severe flood.
2 **Saltation** – the bouncing of medium-sized load along the river bed.
3 **Suspension** – the smallest load, like fine sand and clay, is held up continually within the river water. This makes the water appear opaque. Some rivers carry huge quantities of suspended material, for example the Yellow River in China has enough sediment suspended in its flow at any one time to bury the city of London a metre deep.
4 **Solution** – soluble minerals dissolve in the water and are carried in solution. This may also colour the water, for example water in the rivers of the Mournes often appears yellow/brown as it is stained from iron coming off the surrounding peat bog.

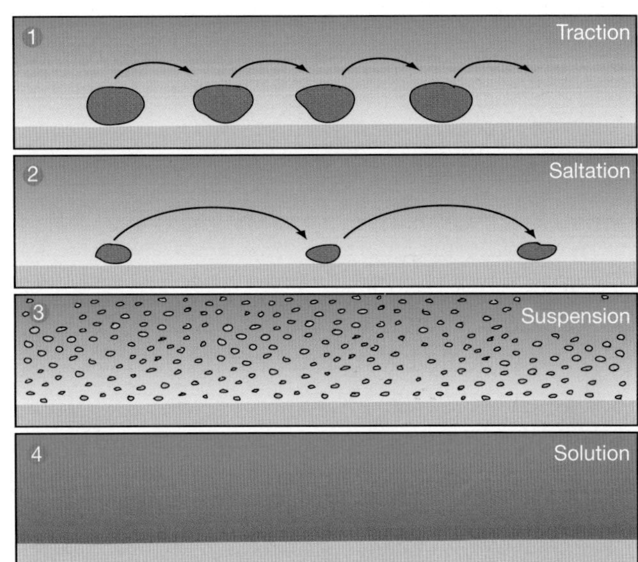

▲ **Figure 6** Methods that a river uses to move its load

Deposition

When the velocity of the river is reduced, its energy falls, and it can no longer erode or transport material instead, the load is dropped, starting with the largest, and therefore heaviest, particles. This process is called deposition.

Conditions when deposition is likely:

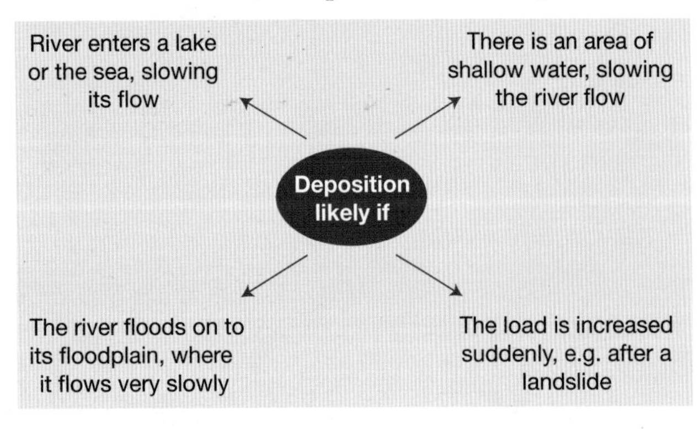

It is the combination of erosion, transportation and deposition that creates the general landforms seen along a river channel.

Get Active

1 With the aid of annotated diagrams, name and describe four methods that rivers use to move their load. Check out: www.geography.ndo.co.uk/animations.htm and http://cgz.e2bn.net/e2bn/leas/c99/schools/cgz/accounts/staff/rchambers/GeoBytes%20GCSE%20Blog%20Resources/Animations/rivererosion_njenkins.swf.
2 Explain why rivers move more load in the winter time than the summer time.
3 Using Figure 4, draw a cross-section of the river in its upper course in grid square 1625 and in its lower course in grid square 2332. Use these to help you describe and explain whether the river is eroding vertically or laterally at these points.

Formation of fluvial features

Waterfalls

Waterfalls are generally found in the upper course of a river, near its source area, where the landscape is still quite mountainous. They form where a layer of hard rock lies on top of a layer of softer rock. As the river passes over the soft rock, it is able to erode it at a faster rate than the harder rock, so a step in the river's bed develops. The force of hydraulic action and abrasion deepens this step until a waterfall is formed. Eventually erosion makes a deep pool under the waterfall called a plunge pool and the hard rock will begin to hang over this pool. When it becomes too unstable, the hard rock overhang collapses and the waterfall retreats backwards, leaving a gorge.

One of the most famous waterfalls is Niagara; here hard limestone lies over softer shale.

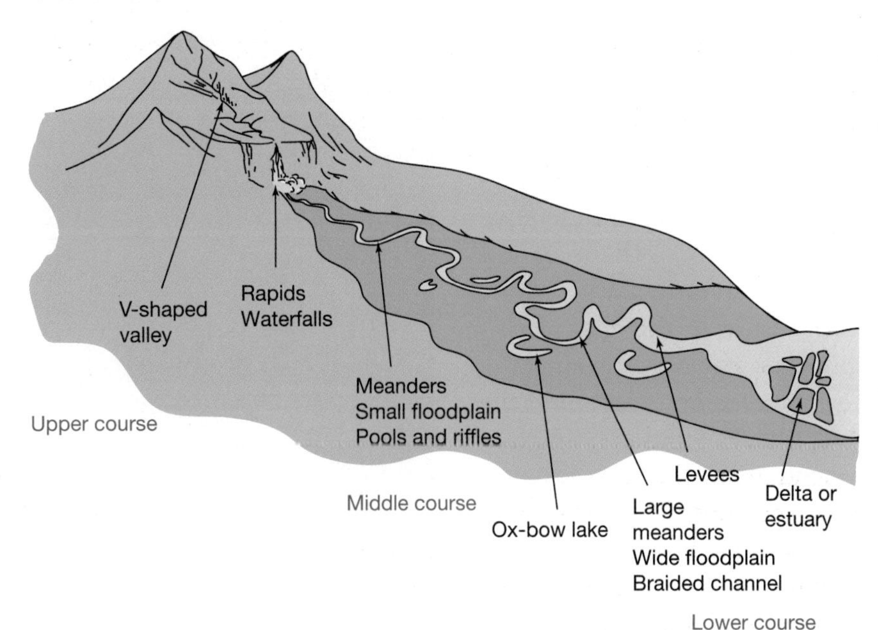

▲ **Figure 7** Landscape features in a drainage basin

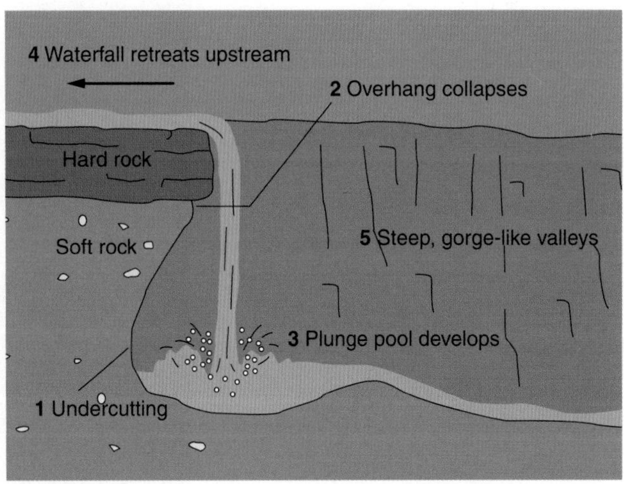

▲ **Figure 8** Formation of a waterfall (cross-section)

▲ **Figure 9** Niagara Falls

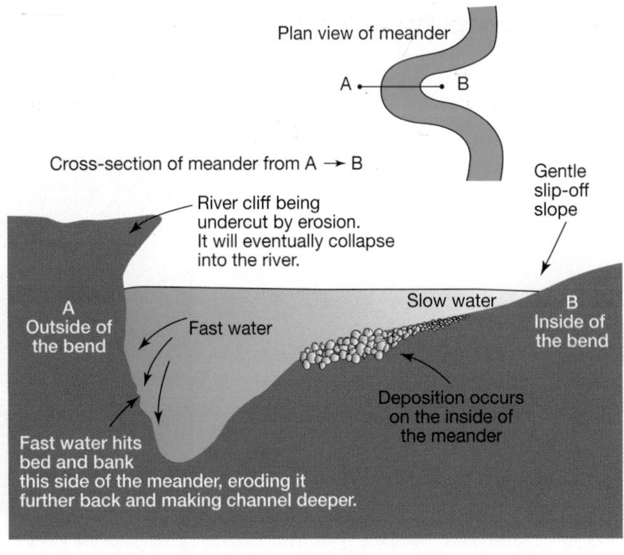

▲ **Figure 10** Plan and cross-section of a meander

Meanders

Meanders are bends that develop in a river channel as the gradient (slope) of the river evens out. They are continuously changing features that are the result of differences in the velocity of the river across its channel. Where water flows fastest in the channel it spirals downwards, causing vertical erosion, deepening the river channel and creating a river cliff on the bank. Opposite this, water flows very slowly and does not have enough energy to erode. It cannot even hold up the load it is carrying, so it drops (deposits) the heaviest material first, then the next largest and so on, until only the smallest clay particles may be left in suspension. This leads to a lop-sided cross-section through a meander – see Figure 10.

In the middle and lower courses of a river, meanders are constantly being formed and reformed. The bends can get bigger and sometimes they can even be cut off altogether, and an ox-bow lake is formed. A very good example of a river that has clear ox-bow lakes and meanders is the Mississippi River in the USA. This can be seen at http://photojournal.jpl.nasa.gov/catalog/PIA01311 and is shown in Figure 11.

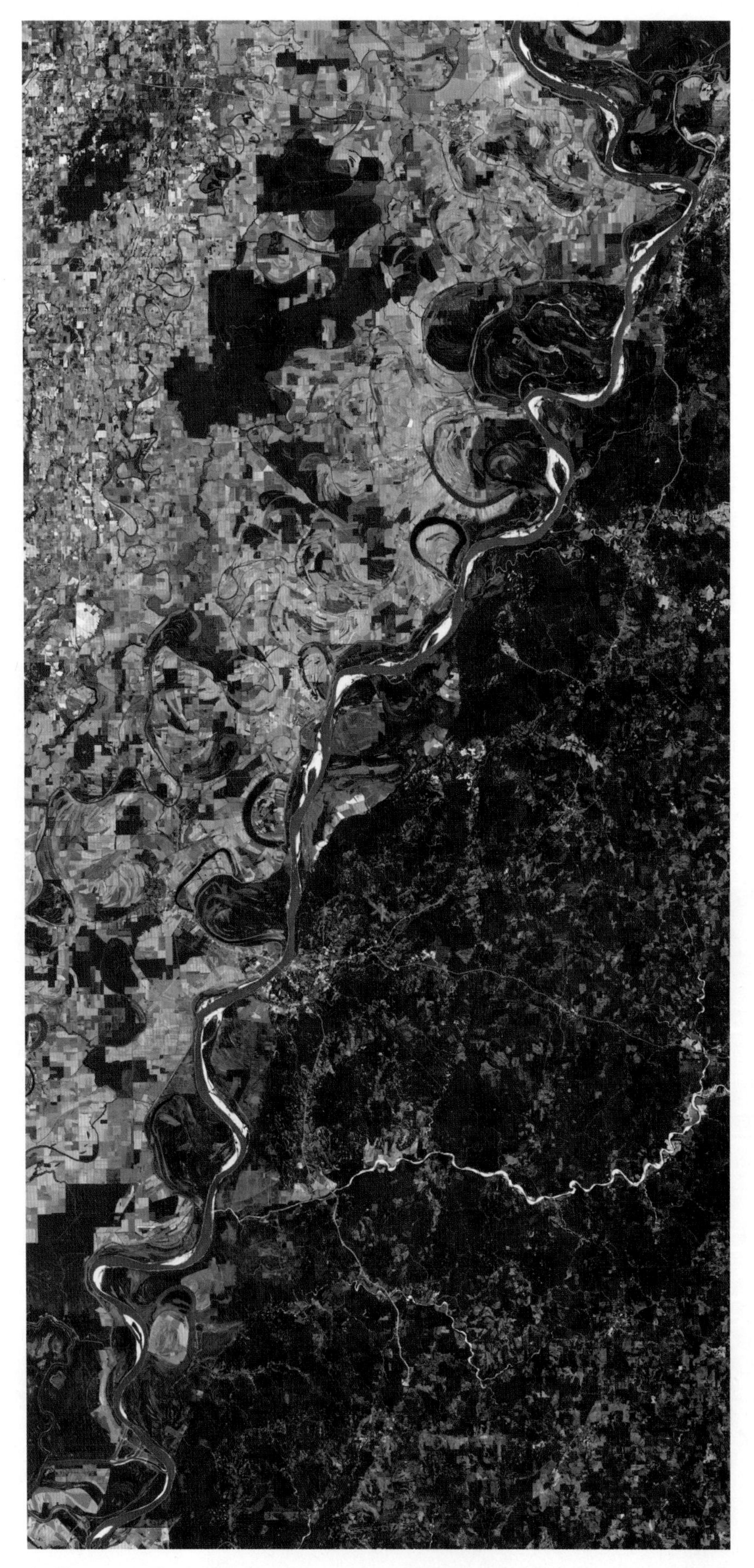

▲ **Figure 11** The Mississippi River: a good example of a river with ox-bow lakes and meanders

Floodplain

As the river meanders back and forth it flattens the land around it creating a floodplain either side of the river in its valley. The floodplain is covered in sediments that have been deposited by the river in times of flood. This material is called alluvium, and is very fertile, which is why river valleys make good places to grow crops. Floodplains can be easily recognised on maps. Look out for the features shown in Figure 12 on OS maps.

When the river does overflow its banks, it quickly loses energy and so must deposit much of its load on to the floodplain. As the largest load is deposited first it quickly builds up to form natural embankments called levees. During low flow, the river may also deposit material on its bed, if the velocity becomes very slow as the amount of water in the river falls. The river might even dry up altogether. If load is deposited on to the river bed, and not washed away later in the season, the river bed can be raised and in some cases the river may end up flowing above the level of the floodplain.

Levees can be artificially strengthened and raised to protect the floodplain from **flooding**.

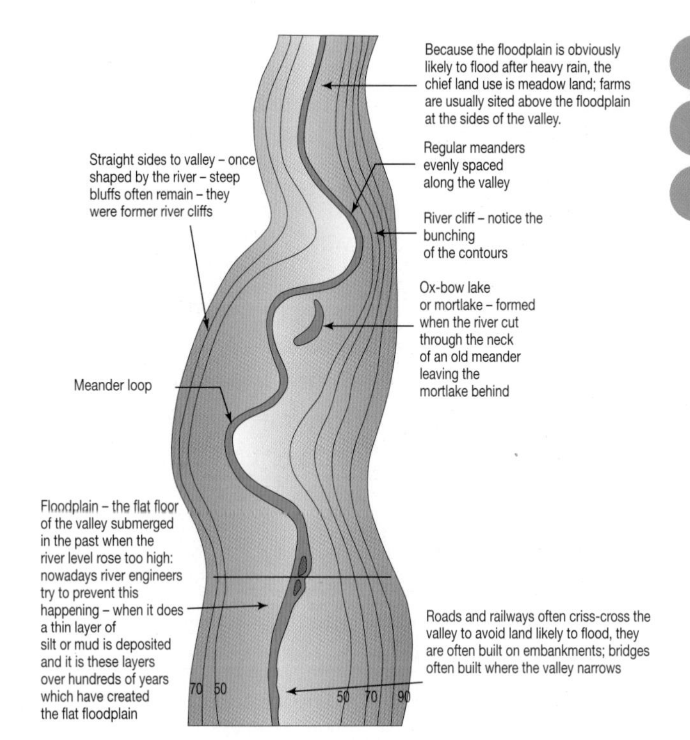

▲ **Figure 12** Features of a floodplain

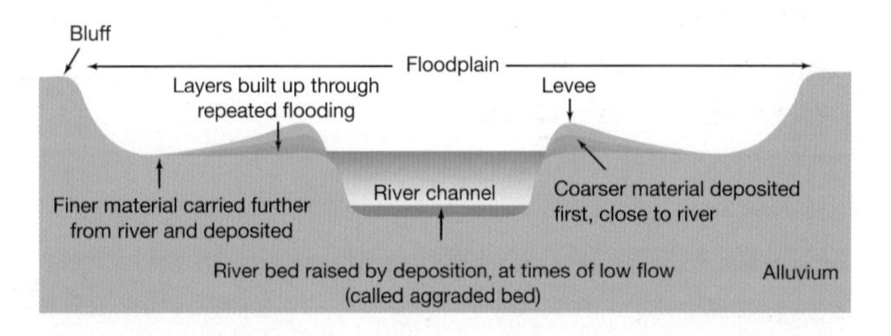

▲ **Figure 13** Levees

Get Active

Work in groups of three.

1 Individually, make notes to describe and explain the formation of *one* of the following fluvial features:
- waterfall
- meander
- floodplain.

2 Give feedback on what you have learned to your two group members.

3 Listen to their descriptions and explanations of their fluvial features.

4 Make your own notes based on what you learn from the other members of your group. Check out the following website to view helpful animations of the processes at work: http://highered.mcgraw-hill.com/sites/0072402466/student_view0/chapter10/animations_and_movies.html.

● weblinks

Review your learning on rivers:

www.sciencecourseware.org/VirtualRiver/Files/page01a.html – Try out the interactive quiz.

www.georesources.co.uk/darentintro.htm – Go on a virtual fieldtrip.

http://cgz.e2bn.net/e2bn/leas/c99/schools/cgz/accounts/staff/rchambers/GeoBytes/GeoGames/geogames.htm – Try out the quizzes and games on rivers.

www.bbc.co.uk/schools/gcsebitesize/geography/riverswater/ – For the key things you need to know about rivers and test questions.

Using photographs

If you are investigating rivers in your project work try using photographs to bring life into the project, but it is important to use them appropriately.

When using photographs:

- Only photograph what is relevant to the project – give it a full title.
- Focus in on the important feature or building you want. Annotate the photograph in the final project.
- Include an object such as a metre rule to give an idea of scale.

Remember to keep a record of what each photograph shows. In this case it was Station 1 on the Glendun River. Field sketches are another method of illustrating project work. Here you draw a simplified picture of the geographical feature or area you are studying. Each field sketch should then be given an appropriate title and be fully labelled (see Figure 14).

First stage:

Draw a frame the size you want your field sketch to be, then add the main lines, separating different land uses, water from land, or important buildings

Second stage:

Add colour to clarify features

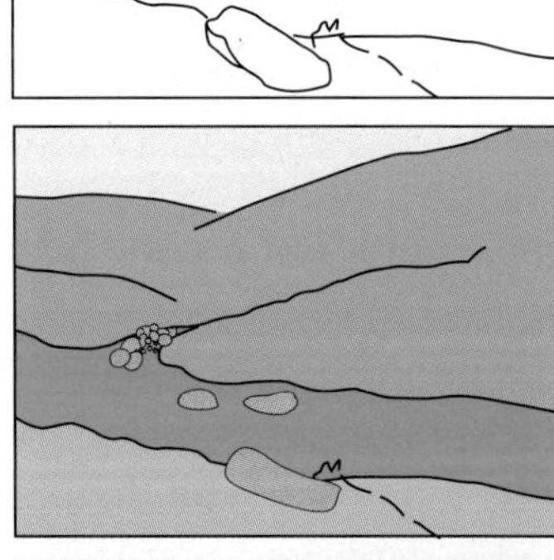

Third stage:

Add annotation

Steep sides of V-shaped valley

Narrow river channel

Grasses on valley sides

Large bed load

Rapids with 'white water'

▲ **Figure 14** Drawing a field sketch of Station 1 of the Glendun River

▲ **Figure 15** Station 1 on the Glendun River

Land uses near rivers

Humans have found many uses for both rivers and the land next to them. In more economically developed countries (MEDCs), cattle may be grazed on damp floodplains, or factories, which need water for cooling, might locate next to a river. Housing has also been built on floodplains. In less economically developed countries (LEDCs), floodplains make good natural paddy fields for growing rice and provide fertile land for many other crops.

In many places, settlements have grown up next to the mouth of rivers to take advantage of trading opportunities.

▲ **Figure 16** A boy working in a paddy field in Indonesia

Get Active

What are the reasons for developing land on a floodplain?

In groups, read and discuss each of the statements below that outline reasons for developing land and living next to a river that could, at some time in the future, flood. Some of the statements are true but others are false. One or two may be partly true and partly false. Can you decide which ones are which?

Sort the statements into the three categories:

- true
- false
- partly true/partly false.

1. Most lowland river floodplains are flat.
2. Despite flooding dangers, riverside building plots are very expensive. Only very large executive style housing over £300,000 can therefore be built, helping to pay for the high cost of land.
3. Heavy industrial developments in the 1990s were built next to rivers to allow easy import of bulk raw materials.
4. Housing estates can be built next to rivers, provided adequate flood protection schemes are constructed beforehand.
5. Factory developments have been built on river floodplains because there is plenty of room to expand if factory extensions are needed in the future.
6. Only expensive housing is built next to rivers, as buyers with money like beautiful scenery and country views.
7. New housing developments are often built next to rivers so that river sand and gravel can be used in construction. It reduces transport costs.
8. Development on floodplains is far easier because the land is flat, and the construction of buildings is so much easier.
9. New housing development next to rivers is far too risky, and insurance companies will not insure against flood damage.
10. The only use for floodplain land, next to a river, is for the grazing of livestock (cows and sheep). Animals can be moved if there is a danger of flooding. The land is therefore very cheap to buy for alternative property development.
11. Houses in Britain are often built next to rivers to supply a reliable and cheap supply of drinking water.
12. The demand for new housing is increasing, and we are running out of flat land to develop. The only cheap option is to build on floodplains, and hope there are few serious floods.
13. Houses can no longer be built on flood plain sites, liable to flooding, due to new government building regulations.
14. Local authorities and building companies will build on any available land, even if it is liable to flooding, if they can make large amounts of money from a deal.
15. New housing and factory developments, with linking roads, are still being built next to rivers that may flood, because it gives a choice of routes reducing traffic congestion in the rush hour.

Source: Based on an idea from www.taw.org.uk.

Coastal processes and features

We gained our 10,000-mile long coastline following the end of the Ice Age when the British Isles obtained its familiar shape as lowland areas filled with melt water to form the Irish Sea, North Sea and English Channel. The Irish Sea was filled first, cutting Ireland off from mainland Europe, which is why Ireland only has 20 native species of mammals.

The sound of the waves crashing on to a shore evokes a strong reaction within a person's spirit. We are an island, so a stretch of coastline is never more than a few hours' drive away.

Waves

Waves themselves are the main force of coastal change. Waves are caused by wind blowing over a stretch of open water, called the fetch. The greater the fetch, the larger the wave. This is why the Atlantic coastline of Northern Ireland has better surf conditions than the more sheltered eastern coastline bordering the Irish Sea. Although fetch is important, wind speed can greatly affect wave height. The stronger the wind, the bigger the waves.

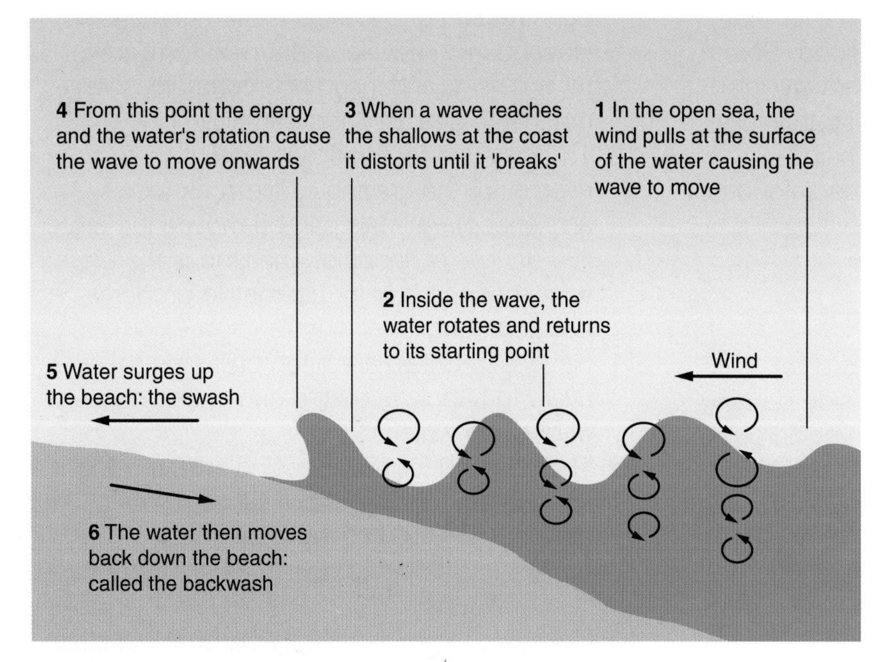

▲ **Figure 17** Coastal erosion

As a wave approaches the coast, its lower section is slowed more than the upper sections due to friction from the beach or seabed. The upper section of the wave reaches a crest then topples over (breaks) and either hits a cliff face or surges up a beach as the swash of a wave. As the wave retreats back it creates a backwash. Waves with a strong swash and weak backwash are the constructive waves and they push material up a beach. Waves with a strong backwash pull material out to sea, and are therefore **destructive waves** that erode coasts.

Characteristics of destructive waves

- They have a strong backwash compared to their swash.
- They are high in relation to their length.
- They are frequent waves (break at a rate of close to 15 per minute).

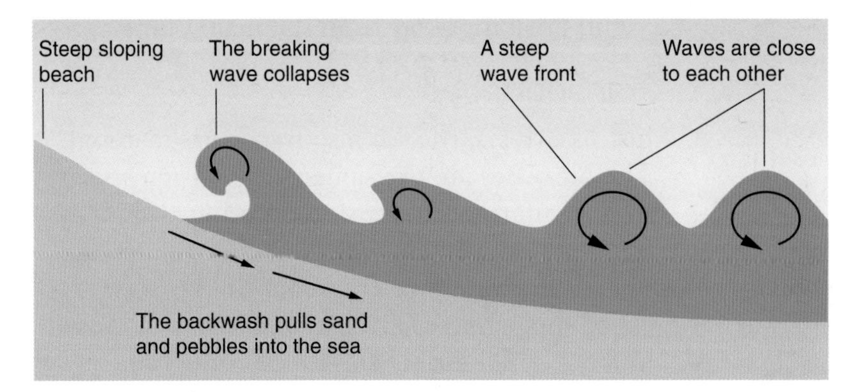

▲ **Figure 18** Destructive waves

Characteristics of constructive waves

- They have a weak backwash compared to their swash.
- They are long in relation to their height.
- They are gentle (break at a rate of 6–9 waves per minute).

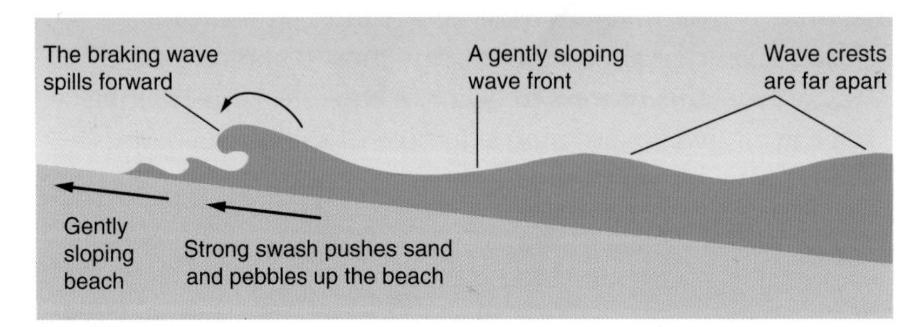

▲ **Figure 19** Constructive waves

Coasts are amazing places that seldom remain the same shape for long. This constant changing makes them one of our most dynamic landscapes.

Get Active

Reinforce your knowledge of waves.

1 Check out the diagrams and short video clip at: www.geography.learnontheinternet.co.uk/topics/waves.html.

2 Listen to a podcast on 'Energy at the coast – waves and wave formation' (made by St Ivo's School Geography Department): http://cgz.e2bn.net/e2bn/leas/c99/schools/cgz/accounts/staff/rchambers/GeoBytes/GCSE%20Revision/Podcasts/Coasts%20Podcast/Coasts_part1.mp3.

3 With the aid of diagrams explain the difference between constructive and destructive waves.

Coastal processes

As with rivers, the sea also erodes, transports and deposits material. Unlike a river, however, the sea has a much greater force and can move material all around the globe! Coconuts from the Caribbean may be found on the beaches of south-west Ireland and Cornwall.

Erosion

When we think of coastal erosion it is useful to think of the acronym C-A-S-H.

- **Corrasion** – when a wave hits the coast, it throws sand and pebbles against the cliff face. These knock off small parts of the cliff and cause undercutting. Another word for this is abrasion.
- **Attrition** – particles being transported by the sea hit against one another, reducing their size and making them more rounded, just like in rivers.
- **Solution** – seawater can dissolve away the rocks from the seabed or cliffs. This process is especially effective on limestone coasts, and can create spectacular caves. It is also known as corrosion.
- **Hydraulic action** – the power of the sea can physically wash away soft rocks like boulder clay. Under storm conditions with strong waves, hundreds of tonnes of seawater can be hitting the coast. Also air can be trapped in small cracks within a cliff when a wave breaks against it. This compressed air can widen the cracks, eventually leading to a large section of cliff breaking away from the main cliff face.

Transportation

Just like rivers, the sea also transports material. The processes are the same as fluvial transport: that is saltation, suspension, solution and traction. On a beach, waves can move material in one direction more than another; this is called **long-shore drift**. This process is discussed in more detail during the explanation of spit formation on page 22.

Deposition

When the load of the seas and oceans builds up on the coastline it forms beaches, spits and sand dunes. This material is added by **constructive waves**. Deposition occurs during periods of light winds. This means that the summer is the most common period for this process to occur in the UK. Constructive waves are most effective in sheltered coastal locations such as bays.

▲ **Figure 20** A destructive wave hits Cornwall in March 2008. The hydraulic power of this wave is huge

Coastal landforms and erosion

Cliffs and wave cut platforms

A cliff is a vertical rock face along the coast. The shape of the cliff is determined by the nature of the geology. The type of rock the cliff is made from determines how resistant it is to erosion, and the way the layers (strata) of the rock are angled can determine the shape of the cliff. Where the rock is hard, dramatic tall cliffs can form, but with weaker rocks, like the boulder clays of the Holderness coast in England, then erosion is faster, but the cliffs are less dramatic.

A wave cut platform is the narrow flat area often seen at the base of a cliff. It is caused by erosion. First a notch is formed at the base of the cliff due to corrosion and hydraulic action, serving as a point of weakness. The upper cliff face is undercut and eventually collapses. This happens again and again, until a new landform, called a wave cut platform is created at the base of the cliff. It is only fully exposed at low tide.

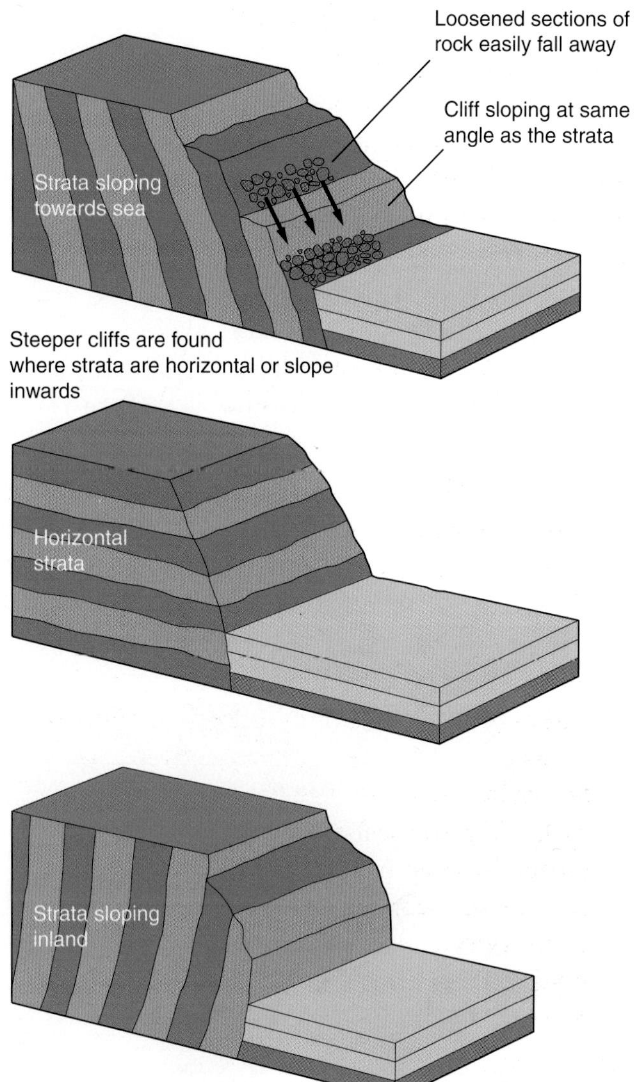

▲ **Figure 21** A schematic showing how coastal erosion occurs

▲ **Figure 22** Wave cut notch visible on the Ballintoy coast

Get Active

Explain the formation of a cliff and wave cut platform.

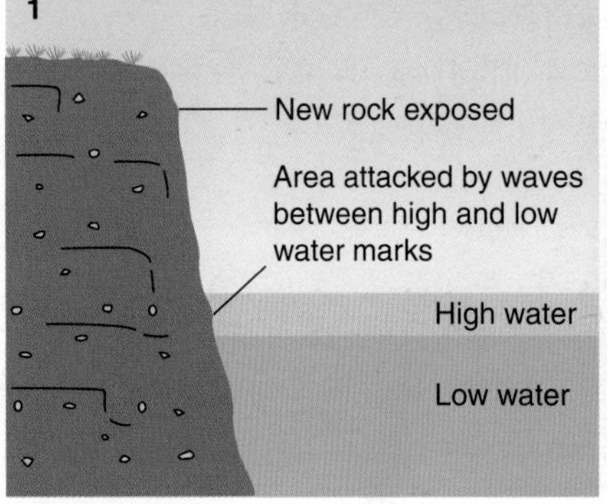

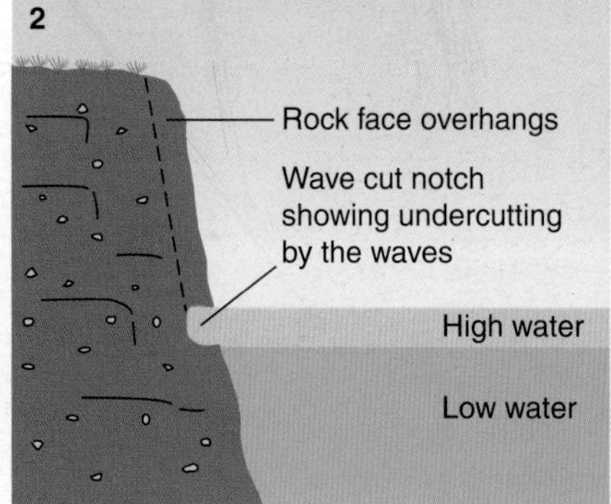

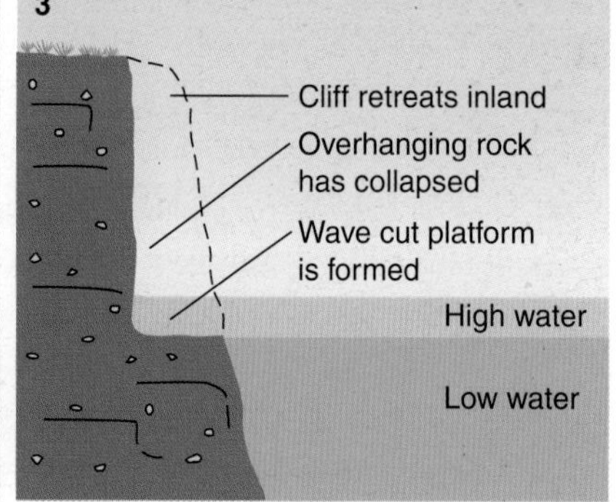

▲ **Figure 23** Formation of cliff and wave cut platforms

Caves, arches and stacks

A wave cut notch may enlarge into a cave. Following further erosion, the cave erodes through the headland to form an arch. The waves and weathering from the elements undermine the upper portion of the arch until it cannot hold its own weight up, and collapses to leave a stack.

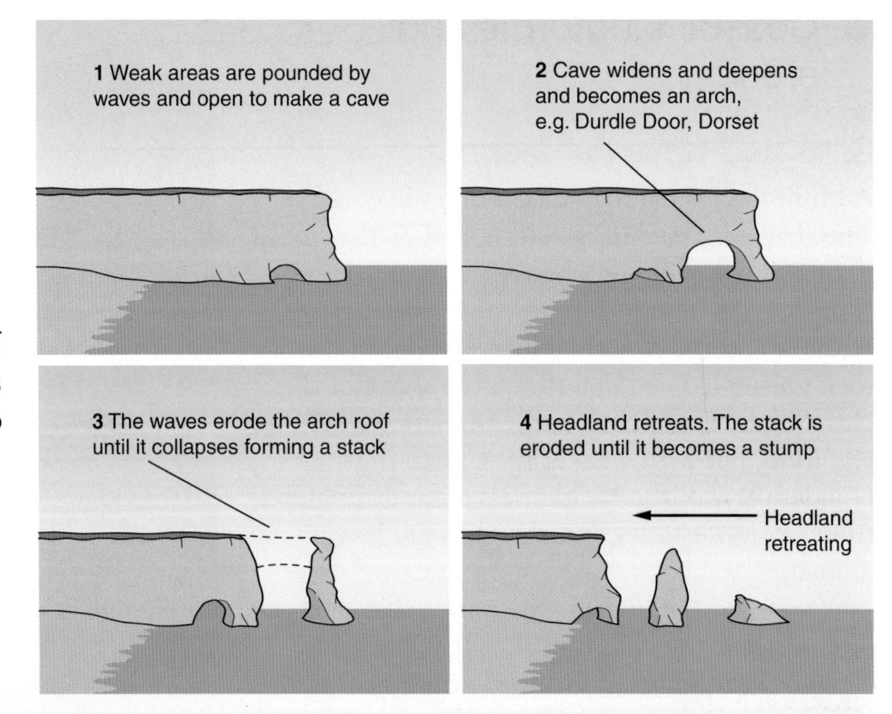

► **Figure 24** Erosion of a headland

▲ **Figure 25** Old Harry Rocks, Studland, Dorset: an example of an eroded headland

Get Active

1. As a class, watch the video at this link so that you are able to identify the coastal landforms described above from their distinctive features: http://geobytesgcse.blogspot.com/2007/08/coastal-erosion-landforms-features-and.html.
2. In small groups read and discuss the section headed 'Coastal Erosion Landforms – Features and Formation' on the website.
3. Working individually, your task is to prepare a short presentation using Photo Story 3 to explain the formation of one of the following coastal landforms: cliff, wave cut platform, cave, arch, stack, stump.
   - Start by carrying out an internet search to find an example of your feature.
   - Continue your internet search to find at least two good photographs of your example.
   - Import your photographs into Photo Story 3.
   - Add your own narration, saying what your feature is, its name, its location, what it is like and how it was formed.
   - Watch all the presentations.

Landforms of coastal deposition

Beaches

Beaches are the most familiar coastal landform created by deposition. They are formed in the intertidal area between high and low tide where constructive waves push material like sand, shingle and pebbles on to the coast. Over time this material can build up and be blown inshore by wind to create a beach. The supply of beach material depends on erosional rates further up the coast. On sandy beaches, the backwash of the waves still removes material, forming a gently sloping beach. On shingle beaches the energy of a wave is reduced because the large particle size allows **percolation**, so the backwash is not very powerful, and a steep beach is created.

Get Active

1. Why are shingle beaches steeper than sandy beaches?
2. What type of waves form beaches?

▲ **Figure 26** A sandy beach – Whitepark Bay, Co. Antrim

▲ **Figure 27** A shingle beach – Bawdsey Beach, Suffolk

Spits

These are depositional features made of sand that look like beaches and extend out from the mainland into the sea. They form if the following conditions are met:

- There is a constant supply of sand or other material from erosion further up the coast.
- Long-shore drift operates most of the time.
- The coastline has a sudden change in direction to leave a sheltered bay area.
- The sea is quite shallow.

The end of a spit may be curved if it grows far enough out into the sea to meet more powerful waves or waves from a different direction. New land can be established behind a spit on the coastal side where mud accumulates to create salt marshes which will eventually become useable land.

One famous example of a spit is Spurn Head in northern England. Erosion of boulder clay from the Flamborough Head region and a southerly long-shore drift direction has created this landform. It is not fully permanent as maps of the area show that it has been destroyed by storms four times in the last six hundred years. The most recent was in 1996. Each time it has slowly been rebuilt by long-shore drift.

A local example is in Dundrum Bay, where sand and shingle from Newcastle have built up a small spit. New coastal defences in Newcastle and sea level rises forecast for the region have jeopardised its future survival.

▲ **Figure 28** Google Earth image of Spurn Head

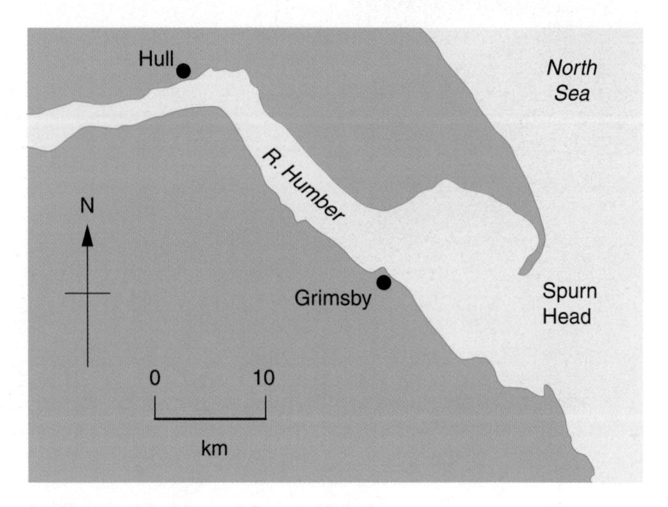

▲ **Figure 29** Map of Spurn Head

Get Active

1. Carry out an image search on the internet to find a photograph of Spurn Head. Print out a copy of what you consider to be the best image of this coastal feature. Use the map extract and the aerial photograph to draw an annotated sketch map showing the location of the spit at Spurn Head.
2. Describe what the spit looks like today.
3. Describe the process that led to the formation of the spit at Spurn Head.
4. What is the direction of the long-shore drift here?
5. Use the map to calculate the approximate length of the spit.
6. Will this spit keep the shape it has today? How might it change in the future?
7. What processes might change Spurn Head in the future?

Coastal land use

Coasts are used for many purposes. In the past, cliffs made excellent defence sites for castles or larger settlements. Today they see many tourism uses, such as car parks, caravan parks, nature reserves, golf courses and walks. Some spits and coastal areas are used for agriculture and of course fishing and trade. Many of these uses can be seen in Figure 30.

▲ **Figure 30** A defensive site on the coast: Dunluce Castle in Co. Antrim

Get Active

In pairs, create a colourful and informative poster to illustrate different coastal land uses (e.g. residential, industry, business, leisure, sport, etc.). Think in terms of past, present and the future; things you like or dislike; things that threaten or preserve the coastline; things for people of different ages:

- Carry out an image search on the internet.
- Save the photographs that you both like.
- Print out the photos.
- Arrange on a large flipchart sheet.
- Add appropriate labels.
- Display finished poster in the classroom.

Complete a *Two Stars and a Wish* activity on the posters by writing down on sticky labels two things that you like (Stars) and one thing that you think would enhance/improve the posters (Wishes). Individually, describe coastal land use in Northern Ireland.

weblinks

www.georesources.co.uk/recintro.htm – Go on a virtual tour about coastal management in south-east England.

www.fife-education.org.uk/inspiration/coasts/coastal_processes_menu.htm – For active board users there are interactive quizzes.

http://geobytesgcse.blogspot.com/2007/08/coastal-processes-erosion-transport-and.html – For revision notes

www.wellingtoncollege.org/page.aspx?id=6740 – For PowerPoints and useful information.

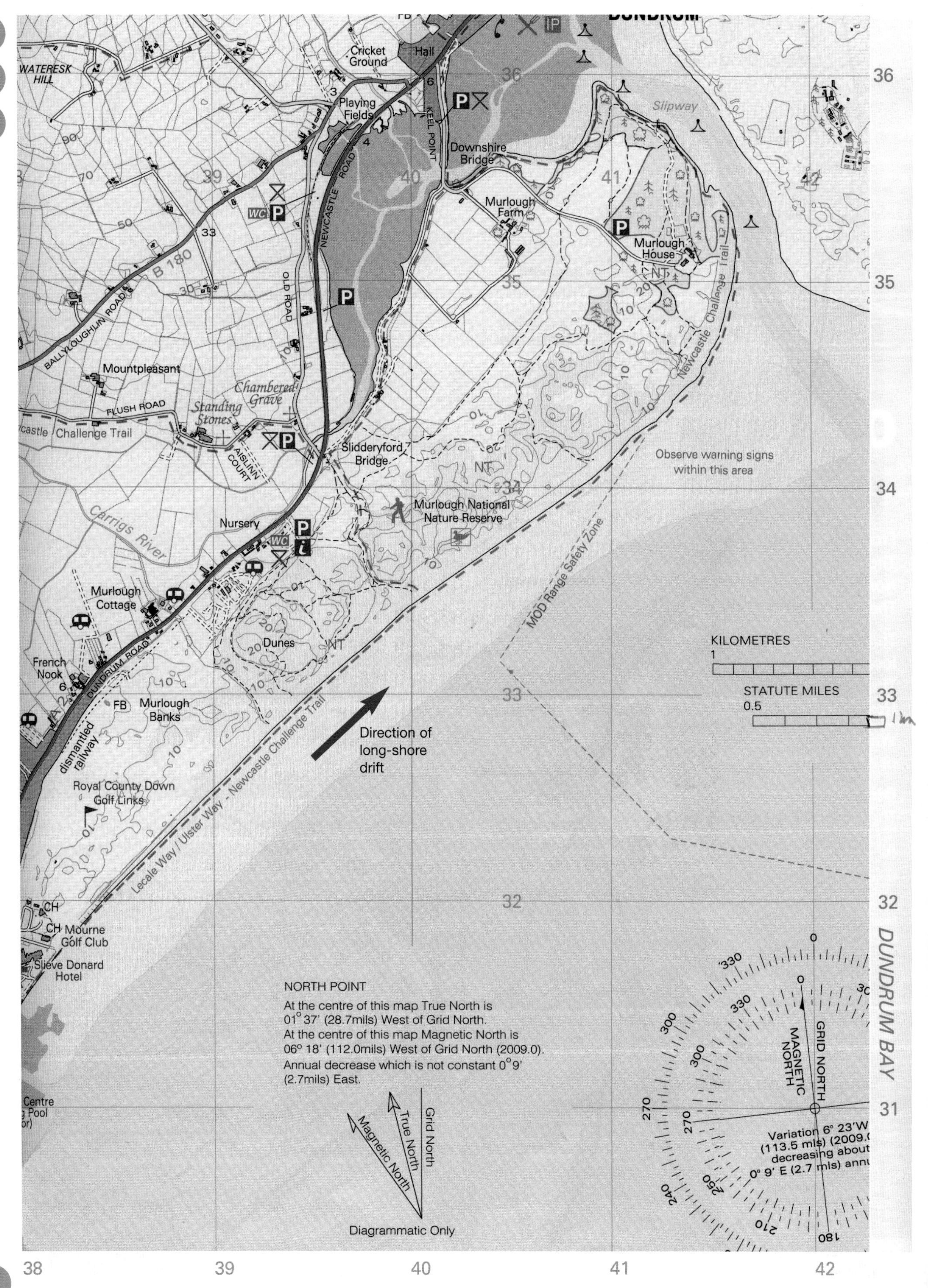

▲ **Figure 31** Murlough National Nature Reserve. Scale 1: 25,000

Get Active

Part A

Take a virtual visit of Murlough Bay, Co. Down (www.virtualvisit-northernireland.com/gallery.aspx?dataid=49754&id=869&title=Nature%20and%20Wildlife) and then answer the following questions:

1. Describe the sand dunes at Murlough Bay Nature Reserve. What words would you use to describe the terrain, the vegetation cover? Why has the boardwalk been laid on the dune? Is there any evidence of human activity on the dune? How does human activity threaten a fragile ecosystem like a coastal sand dune?
2. Describe the beach at Murlough Bay Nature Reserve. What does it look like? What is it made up of? Is it narrow or wide? Is the slope of the beach gentle or steep? Is there any evidence of human activity on the beach?
3. Are there any questions you wish to ask about this place?

Part B

Look carefully at Figure 31 showing Murlough Bay Nature Reserve and the spit and answer the following questions:

1. What is the scale of this OS map?
2. How wide is the spit at its widest point?
3. Who owns the land on the spit? What is the evidence for your answer?
4. What is the name of the large home on the spit?
5. Which sport could be played in grid square 3932? What is the evidence for your answer?
6. Along which famous pathway can one walk on the spit?
7. Which river flows into Dundrum Bay in grid square 3934?
8. What is the direction of the long-shore drift along this part of the County Down coastline?
9. Give the six-figure grid reference of the chambered grave.
10. What evidence is there on the map to suggest that visitors may come to the area?
11. Giving evidence from the OS map extract, name three sporting activities young people could engage in if visiting this area.
12. Use *NI maps* (accessible in the links area of Learning NI) to look at recent aerial photographs of Murlough Bay. What does it show?

Sustainable management of rivers

Rivers are an important resource to people, so any changes made to them need to be sustainable. Future generations will need these rivers just as much as we do today.

Uses of rivers

- A source of water – irrigation and water supply.
- A source of power – hydroelectricity or water mills.
- A waste outlet – used as a drain taking effluent out to sea.
- A routeway – roads and rail links follow valleys, river traffic and shipping.
- A source of food – fish makes up the main source of protein in many LEDCs.

Causes of flooding

Floods are temporary excesses of water that cover areas that are usually dry.

Physical causes

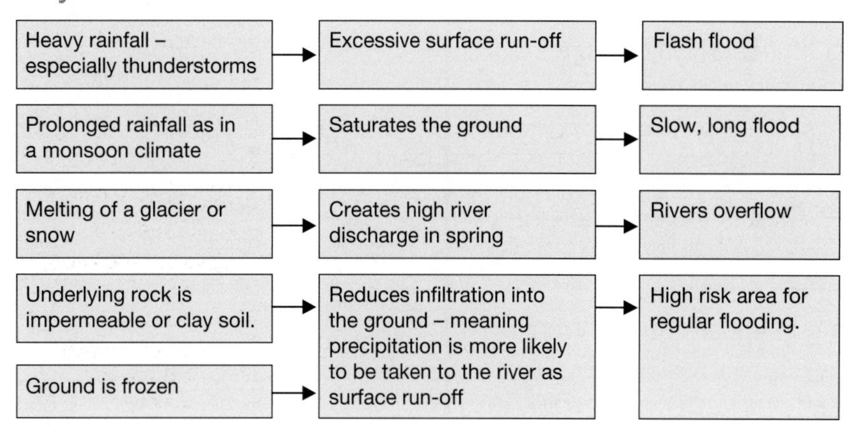

Human causes

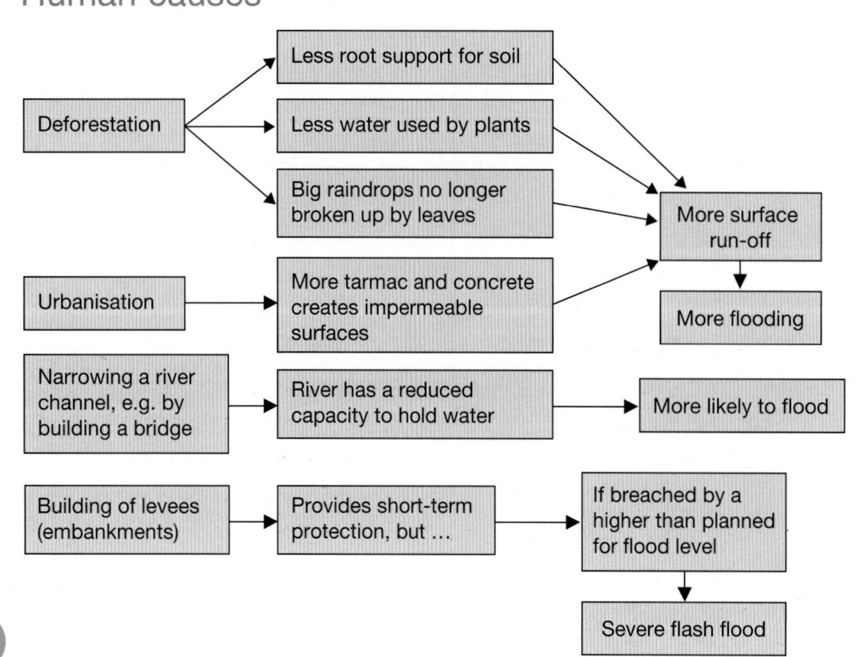

case study

The causes of flood in the British Isles: the River Derwent in 1999

In March 1999 people living near the River Derwent, Yorkshire, experienced its worst flooding in 70 years. Places nearby were flooded up to 1.5 m deep and two main roads had to be closed.

Some causes of the flood

Physical

- Heavy rainfall – between 28 February and 11 March over 250 mm of rain fell on the North York moors.
- Lack of infiltration – this rainfall fell on to ground that was almost saturated from previous rainfall events.
- Time of year – there was snow melt adding to the discharge from the North York moor source region.

Human

- Peat removal – the extraction of peat in the source area lowered the soil storage capacity there, as peat acts like a sponge.
- New building – areas of the floodplain were being urbanised, such as the new estate built at Malton. This reduces infiltration but increases surface run-off.

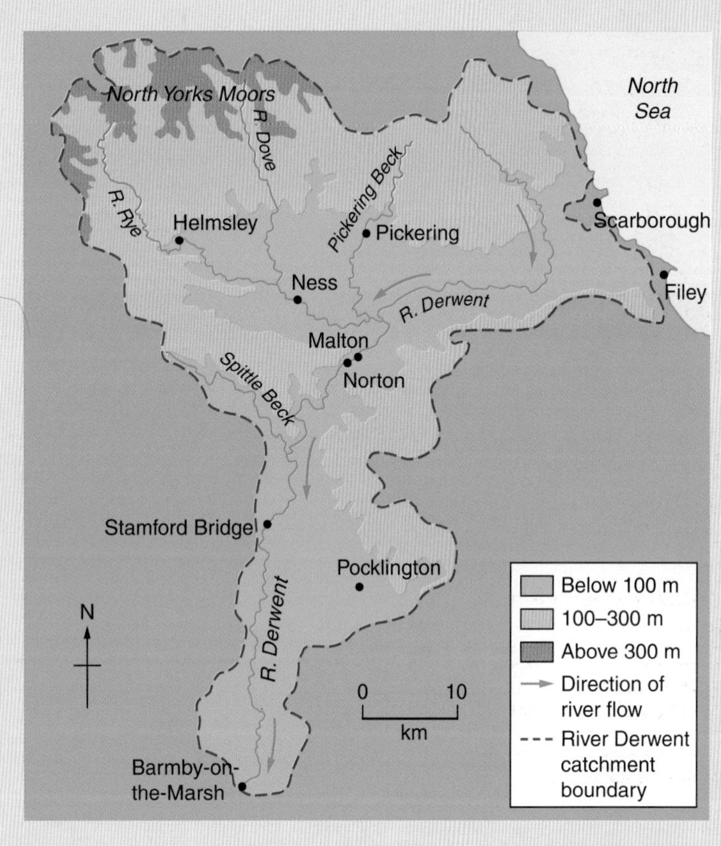

▲ **Figure 32** Map showing the drainage basin of the River Derwent

▲ **Figure 33** Stamford Bridge under water following the Derwent flood in 1999

Get Active

Find out about more recent flood events in the UK. You can get some idea of the extent of one flood by looking at the aerial photographs at: www.webbaviation.co.uk/gallery/v/greatfloods/.

Your task is to produce a PowerPoint presentation on this event. It should outline the factors that contributed to the severity of the flooding (both physical and human), describe how the flood affected people and the environment (natural and built) and include a location map, photographs and any relevant diagrams. Your presentation should have a maximum of 10 slides. You could add your own narration or music soundtrack.

Share the presentations.

Impacts of flooding

On people

Positive impacts	Negative impacts
• Replenishes drinking water supplies, especially wells. • Provides sediment (other terms are silt or alluvium) that naturally fertilises the soils of the floodplain. • Countries such as Bangladesh and Egypt rely on floods.	• Spreads waterborne diseases. • People and animals can be made homeless or even drown. • Buildings and infrastructure (roads and railways) can be damaged or destroyed. • Crops grown on fertile floodplains can be washed away in a flash flood.

On the environment

Positive impacts	Negative impacts
• Fish benefit as they can breed in the standing floodwater. • In dry areas, floods bring relief from drought, providing drinking water for wild animals.	• Flooding can wash chemicals or sewage into the local rivers and so pollute them. • Wild animals may drown or lose their habitat during a flood.

Get Active

1. Working in groups of three or four, you are going to think about flooding in terms of *cause and effect* by completing an *Analysis Tree* activity. Your group needs a large sheet of flipchart paper and some coloured markers.
2. On your page draw a tree with branches and roots like the one below.

3. On your tree the roots represent the causes of flooding and the branches represent the effects of flooding.
4. Talk about the causes of flooding (physical and human) and add the points that you agree on to the roots of the tree.
5. Talk about the effects of flooding (positive and negative) and add the points that you agree on to the branches of the tree.
6. Select a reporter to give feedback to the rest of the class.
7. Use the analysis trees from the different groups to make revision notes on the topic.
8. Individually, reflect on what you liked/disliked about this activity and how useful you found it. Did using the tree help you to clarify your thinking?

River management strategies

River management schemes aim to control rivers and reduce the risk of unwanted flooding. Planners can respond to the flood hazard by changing the river through engineering. They might implement hard or soft flood control measures.

Soft engineering flood controls

Soft engineering flood controls are generally sympathetic to the natural landscape, so tend not to damage the river for future generations, making them more sustainable than hard flood control measures. They may involve:

- Planting trees (afforestation) in the upper course of the river.
- Land use zoning – when areas most likely to be flooded are protected from urban development.
- Washlands – these are parts of the river floodplain in the lower course, into which the river can flood temporarily. They are one kind of flood storage area.

Hard engineering flood controls

Hard engineering flood controls often involve making large artificial structures to control the river, breaking its natural cycle of flood and subsidence. These measures are not sustainable in the long term. They may involve:

- Building a dam or reservoir in the upper course. The resulting reservoir can be used for leisure and hydroelectricity, but can flood good farmland and displace local people and destroy habitats.
- Changes to the river channel. By deepening and widening the river channel, they increase its cross-sectional area, allowing it to contain more water, meaning the discharge has to be greater to create a flood.
- Building high embankments along the sides of the river to contain any floodwater.

Get Active Extension

You have learned how river management schemes aim to control rivers and reduce the risk of flooding. In the case of the Mississippi River, USA, numerous hard and soft flood control measures had been implemented by planners to protect the inhabitants of cities such as New Orleans.

Part A

Working in groups, consider the following questions. You will need to use a search engine such as Google (www.google.co.uk) or BBC News (www.bbc.co.uk/news) on the internet to find appropriate information on Hurricane Katrina:

1 Why did Hurricane Katrina have such a devastating effect on New Orleans?
2 In what ways were the flood control measures that were already in place before this particular hurricane ineffective?
3 Copy a photograph from the internet that shows the extent of the flooding in New Orleans. If possible, highlight (by adding labels to the photo) any of the hard or soft flood control measures that had been put in place but which had failed in their intended purpose.
4 In the future what hard and soft flood control measures might be put in place by the city authorities to better protect the people that live there?
5 Should the city of New Orleans be rebuilt to its former glory? What are the arguments for and against such a proposal?
6 Should new housing developments in the UK and Ireland be allowed on floodplains where there is a history of flooding?
7 Can planners in the UK and Ireland learn anything from the New Orleans experience?

Part B

Appoint a representative from each group to give feedback to the rest of the class.

Part C

Make notes on what has been learned in this case study.

case study

A river management scheme outside the British Isles: the Mississippi River

Background

The Mississippi River has one of the largest drainage basins in North America – it drains water from a third of the USA and part of Canada. It is located in the south-east of the USA. When it flooded in 2001 some 4400 people had to move and the damage cost $13 million.

Management response to the flooding

Hard engineering

1. Raised levees. Levees were raised to 15 m and strengthened to enclose the river channel for a stretch of 3000 km.
2. Straightening the river channel – meanders were cut through over a stretch of 1750 km, creating a fast-flowing straight river channel.
3. Dams – the flow of the main tributaries, e.g. Ohio River, has been controlled by 100 dams.

Soft engineering

1. Afforestation in upper course – trees have been planted in areas such as the Tennesse Valley to intercept some of the rainfall and stabilise soil.
2. Safe flood zones – building has been restricted in many of the floodplain areas, and in areas like Rock Island where housing had already been built on the floodplain, the housing has been bought by the county and demolished.

Evaluation of such measures

Remember that to manage a river sustainably the needs of the present generation must be met without endangering the ability of future generations to meet their needs.

The Mississippi River is very important to the USA since 18 million people rely on it for their water supply – so carefully co-ordinated management decisions need to be made as each decision in one state may affect millions of people's water supply in another state.

Current hard engineering methods have proven neither totally effective nor sustainable.

The river still floods, and indeed the dangerous flash flood nature of the 2001 floods has been partly blamed on the artificial levees failing. Also, as the river silts up along the levees, river beds rise and the floodplain ends up below the river level, e.g. New Orleans where some areas are 4.3 m below river level.

For current and future generations, the lack of silt reaching the land means that fertility of the soil is no longer being naturally completed during the deposition of alluvium in the floods. Eventually more and more artificial fertilisers will have to be added to the soil.

For wildlife, the draining of wetland and lack of silt to maintain the delta is destroying valuable habitats. This means that birds like the heron are becoming endangered in that area.

● weblinks

www.big-river.com/ – A good general site on the Mississippi.

http://floodsim.com/ – Try saving millions of people in a flood management simulation game.

http://news.bbc.co.uk/1/hi/uk/292691.stm – Study the effects of the Derwent flood.

www.dartmouth.edu/~floods/Archives/1999sum.htm – Compare the Derwent flood to others of 1999.

Get Active

1 How successful do you judge the Mississippi River management scheme to have been?
2 Working in groups, complete a *PMI analysis* (plus = a benefit; minus = a downside; and interesting = an interesting point stemming from the topic under discussion) on each of the soft and hard engineering flood control measures implemented in the Mississippi scheme. Record the views of the group using a table like this one:

Flood control measure: Building dams		
Plus	**Minus**	**Interesting**
•	•	•
•	•	•
•	•	•

You will need to create a table for each of the flood control measures (hard and soft) implemented on the Mississippi River.
3 List the ways the Mississippi river management scheme has had an impact on:
- people
- the environment.

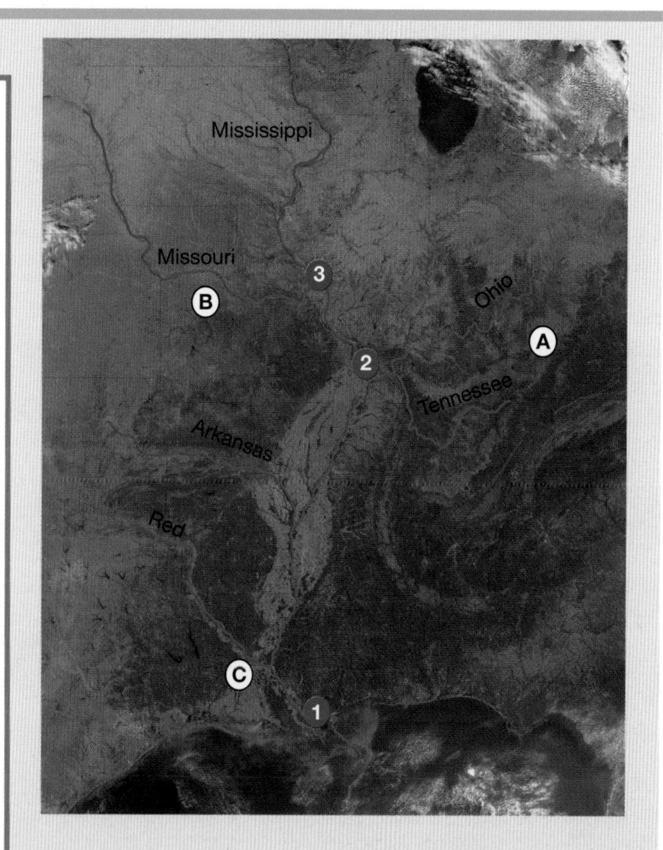

Ⓐ Ohio–Tennessee rise in the Appalachians which receive heavy cyclonic rainfall between January and May. Flood risk increases following snow melt.
Ⓑ Right-bank tributaries drain relatively dry. Mid-west rainfall mostly falls in summer when evaporation is at its highest.
Ⓒ Lower Mississippi usual and most frequent floods.

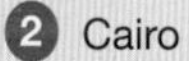

❶ New Orleans
❷ Cairo
❸ St Louis

▲ **Figure 34** Main features of the Mississippi River

▼ **Figure 35** An example of a hard engineering project – Fontana Dam, North Carolina, USA

Sustainable management of coasts

Human activity on coasts

Figure 36 shows a hard coastal engineering strategy – a stone sea wall. This makes the sea hard to reach for tourists. Figure 37 is evidence of a conflict between transport and tourism when a boat carrying wood crashed and spilled its load over a tourist beach in Sussex.

▲ **Figure 36** A stone sea wall in Sea Palling, Norfolk

▲ **Figure 37** A boat spilled its load on to the beach at Worthing, Sussex

The conflicting nature of human activity on coasts

There are four main land uses seen in coastal zones.

Residential

A sea view is very desirable; many people want to see the sea from their house. This means that there is great pressure on local landowners and councils to develop housing or hotels in coastal locations, which may ruin their natural landscape value forever. The second problem is that demand is greater than supply, so coastal homes can prove to be too expensive for some local people in local towns to afford. Also it has led to some homes being built in locations which are threatened by coastal flooding and sea level rise. This is the case on the Florida coast and in Bangladesh.

▲ **Figure 38** Unsuitable housing near the coast of Bangladesh

Tourism

Almost everyone enjoys a beach holiday, and this can cause conflict with residential land use and industry. In Jamaica there is a three-storey height restriction law for housing and hotels, so the skyline does not become as blighted by tall hotels as in some Spanish and American resorts. Tourism does bring money into the economy, but it can be hard to make it sustainable. This is a current issue for the north coast of Northern Ireland, where people are slowly eroding away the very Giant's Causeway which they came to see.

▲ **Figure 39** Tourists on the Giant's Causeway, slowly wearing it away

▲ **Figure 40** The unnatural seafront in Miami, Florida, USA

Transport

Road and railway lines that follow coastlines cost more money to maintain and some need special planning to ensure they can remain open. Others are sacrificed to the sea, as on the Holderness coastline in England. Coastal transport also includes ships, and natural harbours have been managed for generations to allow the safe passage of boats from the open waters of seas or oceans. Today, in order to accommodate the newest large ships, called supertankers, many ports are having to relocate to deeper water or dredge to increase their depth. This is a pressure from industries who want products moved faster and more cheaply.

▲ **Figure 41** A road now going nowhere, but disappearing at the rate of 2 m per year in Holderness, Yorkshire

Industry

As oil supplies can be extracted from underwater locations, the North Sea coastline of Scotland has seen dramatic changes due to oil extraction. In Aberdeen alone, 100,000 people are employed by the oil industry.

Offshore, the main industrial activities are fishing and commercial shipping, and there is also some dredging for marine sediment.

Shipbuilding and ship-breaking are also commonly seen on coasts. The negative impacts of the creation of the Alang-Sosiya Ship-Breaking Yard (ASSBY) in a sensitive coastal area in the state of Gujarat, India, present many challenges and lessons for practitioners of integrated coastal management.

▲ **Figure 42** Alang-Sosiya ship-breaking yard in India. To investigate the Alang-Sosiya ship-breaking yard go to: http://unesdoc.unesco.org/images/0013/001375/137515e.pdf

Spain 2008

Rampant development has turned much of Spain's Mediterranean coast into concrete jungles. Now, the country's environment ministry is determined to fight back, taking on the unchecked and frequently illegal construction that has threatened to overwhelm Spain's shores – causing erosion rates of up to 1 metre per year. The environment ministry had 665 buildings demolished and more are planned. Adapted from www.csmonitor.com/2008/0117/p13s01-woeu.html

AFRICA 2009: 70% OF CORAL REEFS COULD BE GONE IN 40 YEARS

Coastal erosion

Human activities are eroding close to 70% of the world's beaches at greater than natural rates. Coastlines in developing countries are suffering from serious erosion problems due to unplanned coastal construction, dredging, mining for sand, harvesting of coral reefs for building material and other activities. Erosion is particularly severe along the coasts of Nigeria, Sierra Leone, Liberia, Gambia, Benin and Togo in West Africa. Hundreds of coastal villages have been moved inland as the sea advances. In the Niger River Delta, for instance, erosion claims 400 hectares of land a year and 40% of the inhabited delta could be lost in three decades.

▲ **Figure 43** Headlines on coastal development

Get Active

Look at the photo below showing the seafront in Torremolinos, a popular sunshine destination in Spain for holidaymakers from the UK and Ireland.

You could also do an internet search on Torremolinos to further your knowledge and understanding of the impact mass tourism has had on this part of the Spanish coast.

1. With a partner, discuss and note the competing demand for land in a place like Torremolinos.
2. What are the advantages and disadvantages of such development in coastal areas?
3. In your opinion, do the advantages of such development outweigh the disadvantages? Give detailed reasons.
4. What, if any, different approach could have been taken to the development of this coastal area?

▲ **Figure 44** Torremolinos, Spain

The need for coastal defences

The protection of coasts is important as just over half the world's population – around 3.2 billion people – live within 200 km of the sea. In all continents, except Africa, the majority of people live near coasts.

Coastal zones include waters and shores of coastal lands as well as islands, salt marshes, wetlands and beaches. The use of the shoreline has a direct and significant impact on the coastal waters and the large numbers of people that inhabit the areas. Geographical information systems (GIS) are used to understand and control those areas that are likely to be affected by or are vulnerable to rising sea levels or coastal erosion.

Global warming is making the need for coastal defences a pressing issue for many low-lying coastal regions and countries. The average predicted rise in sea level due to the thermal expansion of water is about 48 cm, although it could be up to almost 90 cm by the end of the century. The World Bank estimates that a 1-m rise in sea level would flood half of Bangladesh's rice fields and force the migration of millions of people. The European city of Amsterdam is already mostly below sea level, and relies on sea defences to protect it from flooding. The islanders of Tuvalu, in the Pacific Ocean, have already made plans to abandon their homeland as it is now regularly being flooded by rising tides.

Coasts are economically important to many countries as the main ports are the centre of commerce, trade and investment. The marsh areas provide natural areas for waste assimilation and detoxification. The income generated from fishing can be vital and tourism can be very lucrative. As much as 60% of Majorca's gross national product (GNP) is generated by tourism, which is centred around the beaches.

Coastal management strategies

Coastal areas need management to:

- keep the sea out
- retain cliffs and beaches.

Sea walls

The most common way to keep the sea at bay is to build sea walls. These look like tall concrete walls built at the back of beaches. They may have a curved shape which is designed to deflect the erosive energy of the wave and add extra protection against waves topping the wall.

▲ **Figure 45** The sea wall in Portrush, Co. Antrim

Retaining cliffs and beaches

Sea walls are expensive to build and the need for constant maintenance means costs continue. They can be economically acceptable if they are needed to protect many people and properties, like in Portrush.

Cliffs can be difficult to retain, but recently gabions have been used successfully as a short-term measure to stabilise cliff bases. A gabion is a metal cage, measuring about 1 m by 1 m, that is built on site from six metal mesh sides and then filled with local rocks. As gabions rust and can be damaged during severe storms, they do not provide a long-term solution to coastal management. Such damage is seen in Figure 47, where the nearby gabion baskets on Chilling Cliff in Hampshire have been damaged by a storm. The main advantage they have is their low cost.

Beaches are essential natural coastal protection and are a main tourist attraction to any coastal area, so many resorts are keen to ensure they are conserved.

When long-shore drift is displacing sand from a beach, then groynes or beach replenishment are strategies used to ensure beach survival.

Groynes are often made of hard wood and look like low fences stretching seawards out along a beach at intervals of about 50 m. They slow down long-shore drift and promote the deposition of sand, building up the beach. The wood will eventually weather down and so groynes have a lifespan of 20 years. Modern construction techniques favour rock groynes which have a much longer life span than wooden ones. They can cause problems of public access along a beach and can lead to extra erosion further down the coast as beach material cannot move naturally by long-shore drift.

Beach nourishment is sometimes called beach recharging. Sand is dredged from the seabed and added to an eroded beach, or even brought in as lorry loads to add extra material along a stretch of coastline. It is very expensive, costing about £1 million per mile and is not a permanent fix. Nourished beaches erode faster then natural ones because the sand is not as tightly packed. As it costs so much, the economic returns, generally through tourism, must be great.

Get Active

Figure 46 shows a curved sea wall. Why is it effective at keeping the sea at bay? Why would a sea wall that is more vertical be less effective in keeping the sea at bay?

▲ **Figure 46** A curved sea wall in Blackpool

● weblinks

www.snh.org.uk/publications/on-line/heritagemanagement/erosion/sitemap.shtml – A guide to managing coastal erosion in beach/sand dune systems from the Scottish Natural Heritage.

▲ **Figure 47** Collapsed gabions near Aberdeen

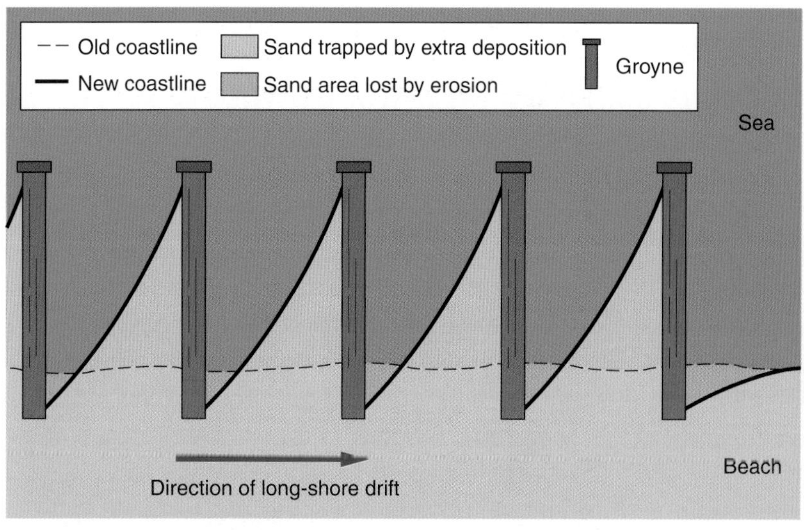

▲ **Figure 48** How groynes can change the shape of a beach

▲ **Figure 49** Beach nourishment: before and after photos of beach restoration efforts of the Florida coastline in 1972

case study

Coastal Management in the British Isles: Newcastle, Co. Down

Tourism has been the major cause of coastal pressure in Newcastle, Co. Down. The opening of a rail link between Belfast and the town in 1869 meant that the seaside resort was just an hour's journey from the city. The town is set in a bay, which boasts 8 km of beach that attracts tourists. Boarding houses were built as close to the sea as possible. Even today Newcastle is a popular day or weekend destination, with thousands packing the beach and main streets on bank holidays. It has been estimated that the population of Newcastle rises by 15,000 in the summer months, and it's all down to tourism.

Evaluation of coastal defences

Background

Newcastle sits in Dundrum Bay, which has a 20-km long beach running between St John's Point and Newcastle Harbour. Waves are the most important driving force controlling the natural coastal system here. These waves are gentle, as there is a limited fetch area, and approach from the south-east. The shallow and wide beach dissipates wave energy, meaning constructive waves dominate, except during storm times. The sediment which makes up the beach was washed down from the mountains after the last Ice Age. A wave cut notch in Dundrum Village at 14 m above the current sea level is believed to mark the maximum height of the sea during the late glacial period 15,000 years ago. There have been many attempts to control the coast at Newcastle using hard engineering methods.

Groynes

The old urban council created concrete groynes near the Newcastle centre section of the beach in the 1980s, to trap and hold sand that was drifting north-east. Since they have now decayed, they can no longer perform this function and may have contributed to sand loss at Newcastle.

The present council is carrying out a study to see if a new set of wooden groynes could stabilise sand on the beach. Each would be 20–30 m long and would cost £1250 per metre.

Gabions

Gabions have been used to protect the recreation ground built over the beach at the mouth of the Shimna, where it enters Dundrum Bay in Newcastle. The first set had badly decayed and were no longer proving effective, so in the regeneration programme during 2006 they were replaced and a new footbridge built on the stabilised coast to allow unrestricted pedestrian access along the promenade. Gabions are more sustainable than rock armour or a sea wall as they allow water to enter each cage and slowly dissipate the energy rather than deflecting it back outwards.

Rock armour

Rocks may be used to control erosion by armouring a dune face. They dissipate the energy of storm waves and prevent further recession of the backshore if well designed and maintained. Rock armour is used widely in areas with important backshore assets subject to severe and ongoing erosion where it is not cost-effective or environmentally acceptable to provide full protection using sea walls. This has been used along various sections of Dundrum Bay. In the late 1990s, extensive rock armouring was constructed to protect the Royal County Down Golf Course. This has proved unsustainable, as it is reducing the sediment supply for Murlough Bay, an Area of Special Scientific Interest (ASSI).

Sea wall

The need for a sea wall came when Newcastle experienced urban growth and the boarding houses were built close to the coast for the sea views. These new buildings at the time needed protection from the high tides and waves. The sea wall constructed in Newcastle is used as support for the pedestrian walkway called a promenade.

The promenade in Newcastle therefore doubles as a sea wall to protect the town. Following a severe storm in 2002, when the old wall was partially washed away, the promenade and wall have been rebuilt and extended at a cost of £4 million. The wall was raised by 1 m from the old Victorian level and now has a curved, wave return design to stop water splashing over the wall.

Although this wall protects the built environment, refracted waves appear to be increasing beach erosion. Combined with a lack of material coming from further up the coast, this means that Newcastle is losing beach sand. So it is unsustainable. Indeed, studies show that north of the Shimna River, the high tide beach has been reduced due to promenade construction.

The future

Although Newcastle's beach has been badly eroded over the past 50 years, it remains popular with locals and visitors from other parts of Northern Ireland. Each of the hard engineering measures is not singularly to blame for this erosion, but such inappropriate and uncoordinated development along the coast has increased problems. It is no longer a naturally functioning zone, where erosion and deposition are in balance. The Department of the Environment has recently announced an Integrated Coastal Zone Management Strategy for Northern Ireland that applies for 20 years (2006–26). In this groups are encouraged to work together towards a more sustainable approach to coastal management. Down Council is considering building new groynes and even beach nourishment in order to maintain a wide and sandy stretch of beach at Newcastle to satisfy the demands of tourists.

▲ **Figure 50** This photograph of Newcastle harbour was taken in 1880

▲ **Figure 51** Newcastle as it is today

Get Active

1 Draw a *timeline* to show attempts to manage the coastline at Newcastle in Co. Down from Victorian times to the present day. On your line mark specific dates and note the coastal management scheme implemented.
2 Even with these various coastal management schemes the beach at Newcastle has been badly eroded in the past 50 years. Why do you think this has been the case?
3 Could the coastal management schemes implemented at Newcastle have been improved? What else could have been done?

Get Active

The big task

You are going to work in groups to solve a mystery. The question is: 'Where has our beach gone?'

1 Read the statements on page 43.
2 Access some photos and maps on the following websites:
   - http://news.bbc.co.uk/1/hi/in_pictures/5246638.stm
   - http://picasaweb.google.com/olkenimages42/NewcastleCountyDownNIreland#5235467851927876258
   - http://www.google.co.uk/maps and search for "Newcastle, County Down".
3 Make some predictions as to what the answer to the question might be.
4 Read the statements and consider each piece of information carefully. Ask for clarification if there is anything you do not understand.
5 Look at and talk about the photos and the map.
6 Use the statements to come up with an extended answer to the original question (Remember, all the information may not be relevant. Some 'red herrings' may have been included to confuse you.) You can use any other knowledge you have acquired in the study of this topic to piece together a convincing explanation.
7 Pay attention to the time you have been given to complete the task.
8 Agree on a 'best' group answer.
9 Select a group member to report the fully agreed answer to the rest of the class in the feedback session.
10 Individually, write an answer to the original question.

Unusual happenings at Dundrum Bay, County Down, have been puzzling local residents for some time. Reports of the beach at Newcastle disappearing while sand dunes at Ballykinler, across the bay, were getting bigger and bigger, had locals and Down County Council stumped.

The beach in Newcastle is disappearing because of global warming and climate change.

Dr Andrew Cooper and Dr Fatima Navas, from the Centre for Coastal and Marine Research at the University of Ulster, have discovered that natural forces on the seabed are responsible for the previously unexplained changes.

'In the 1970s, our family spent many sunny Sunday afternoons on the sandy beach in Newcastle. It was like a second home to our children.' – Portadown resident.

Navigation charts from the nineteenth and twentieth centuries show a substantial build-up of sand offshore.

Computers have been used to simulate waves moving across the seabed. As sand builds up off shore, a marked change in how waves approach the shoreline can be observed.

In the mid-nineteenth century waves carried sand to both ends of the bay, sustaining beaches at Newcastle and Ballykinler but now, the change in wave movement means that the sand is being carried away from Newcastle and toward Ballykinler instead.

Tourism has led to the eroding of Newcastle beach.

The result is the obvious physical changes that local people have noticed on their coastline: healthy, growing sand dunes at Ballykinler but diminished volumes of sand at Newcastle.

The sandy beach at Newcastle is really quite a thin veneer and a slight loss of sand exposes the underlying glacial pebbles. This has a dramatic effect on the appearance of the shoreline.

'Could the Minister of the Environment detail the steps he is taking to prevent further erosion of Newcastle beach.' – Jim Wells, local MLA.

'My wife and I have bought a new apartment close to the seafront for our retirement. Our beautiful beach needs to be saved and fully restored.' – A retired lawyer.

Experts believe the natural changes on the beaches of Dundrum Bay are not a cause for concern. There is plenty of sand in the system as a whole; the waves have simply moved it away from Newcastle under the present conditions.

Air photographs of Newcastle beach taken in the 1970s show a much greater covering of sand.

The area of beach in Newcastle has been reduced by the construction of the promenade, the sea wall in front of the Slieve Donard Hotel grounds and the rock-armour revetments in front of the Royal County Down Golf Club.

The amount of sand cover on the beach at any given time reflects the balance between onshore sediment transport and sediment dispersal by long-shore drift and river currents.

A relatively wide beach has occurred at different periods in time adjacent to the mouth of the Shimna River.

'Our beach is useless for holidaymakers and day trippers as it has become narrow, pebbly and poorly maintained.' – Owner of amusement arcade in Newcastle.

'I am appalled to see the way the sea defences in Newcastle have been neglected over the years.' – Local environmentalist.

There is evidence that the seafloor changed substantially enough over a 150-year period for it to alter the wave patterns and for them to cause changes in the shoreline over the same timescale.

Most of the sand lost from Newcastle beach has been blown away by strong coastal winds in the winter months.

Following a severe storm in 2002, when the old sea wall was partially washed away, the promenade and wall were rebuilt and extended. The wall was raised by 1 m from the original Victorian level and now has a curved, wave return design to stop water splashing over the wall. Although this wall protects the built environment, refracted waves appear to be increasing beach erosion.

'I have no powers to prevent the erosion of Newcastle beach. I understand that studies commissioned by Down District Council have indicated that much of the erosion of sand from the beach at Newcastle has been caused by the progressive rock armouring of the sea front. Although theses measures provide flood protection to the promenade and the Newcastle centre, they are thought to have contributed to the problems of sand erosion.' – Sam Foster, Minister of the Environment.

Sample examination questions

1 The drainage basin: a component of the water cycle

Foundation Tier

(i) Complete the following sentences by writing in one of the words from the list below.

Soil	Input	Mouth	Tributary	Source

The start of a river is called the ________________.

Precipitation is an ____________ to a drainage basin.

Water which is moving through ______________ is called through-flow.

A small river that joins the main river is called a ________________. [4]

(ii) Classify the following components of a drainage basin. One has been completed for you.

STORE IN THE DRAINAGE BASIN

TRANSFER IN THE DRAINAGE BASIN

Surface runoff

Interception by vegetation

Percolation

Through-flow

Infiltration →

[4]

Higher Tier

(i) Explain how rainfall becomes part of the groundwater flow within a drainage basin. [5]

(ii) State the meaning of the following terms:

- Watershed [2]
- Confluence [2]

2 River processes and features

Foundation Tier

(i) State if the following sentences about river processes are true or false.

Sentence	True/False
Attrition is an erosional process	
Deposition is more likely if the river's load is small in size	
Large rocks are mostly moved by suspension	
Erosion means a river gets wider moving from source to mouth	

[4]

(ii) Complete the key below with the labels on the diagram opposite to fully label a waterfall. [4]

Key	
Hard rock	
Soft rock	
Overhang	
Plunge pool	

Higher Tier

(i) Describe two ways a river erodes. Choose from the list below. [4]

Attrition Abrasion
Hydraulic action Solution

(ii) Explain the formation of floodplains. [4]

3 Coastal processes and features

Foundation Tier

(i) Explain the difference between constructive and destructive waves. [2]

(ii) State the meaning of the term long-shore drift. [2]

(iii) Put the following coastal features into the order in which they would form from one another.

One has been done for you.

Feature	Order
Stack	
Crack	1
Arch	
Cave	

[3]

Higher Tier

(i) With the aid of a diagram, explain how long-shore drift works [6]

(ii) Explain the formation of stacks, like those shown in the picture to the right. [6]

4 Sustainable management of rivers

Foundation Tier

(i) For a named river you have studied, explain one reason why it flooded.

River ________________ [1]
Cause of flood [3]

(ii) Describe how flooding might affect people. [4]

(iii) Write out four types of hard engineering which might be used to reduce flooding. Choose your answers from the list below. [4]

Washlands Dams Levees Afforestation Flood walls

Straightening the river Land use zoning Storage areas

Higher Tier

(i) For a named river you have studied, identify and explain two reasons it flooded. [6]

(ii) Describe the possible impacts flooding could have on people and the environment. [6]

(iii) Evaluate the flood management strategies used on one river which you have studied. Remember this river must be from outside the British Isles. [7]

5 Sustainable management of coasts

Foundation Tier

(i) Suggest two problems caused by a large number of visitors to a beach. [2]

(ii) Describe how these problems could be solved. [4]

(iii) Explain why sea walls are not always built to protect an area of coastline. [3]

Higher Tier

(i) Describe and explain two measures which might be used to retain cliffs and beaches. [6]

(ii) Evaluate the extent to which a coastal management strategy, which you have studied, is sustainable. [9]

UNIT ONE

Understanding Our Natural World

Our Changing Weather and Climate

Learning outcomes

In this theme you will learn:

- how elements of the weather are measured and what sources weather forecasters use
- about the characteristics of the air masses that affect the British Isles
- to explain the weather patterns and the changes associated with depressions and anticyclones
- to interpret synoptic charts and satellite images
- to debate the causes and effects of climatic change at a global scale.

Our Changing Weather and Climate

Measuring the elements of the weather

What is the difference between weather and climate?

The word **weather** is used to describe the day-to-day changes in the conditions of the atmosphere – that is the weather elements. **Climate** is the average conditions of the weather taken over a long period of time – usually 35 years. The climate of Northern Ireland, for example, is described as mild and damp with few extremely low or high **temperatures** or large amounts of rain.

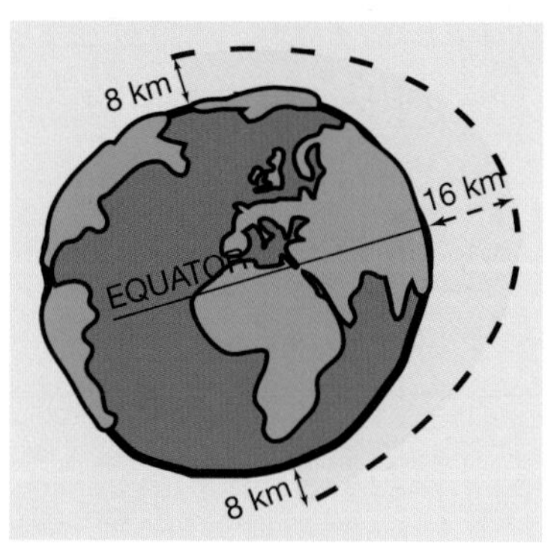

◄ **Figure 1** Weather takes place in the lowest layer of the atmosphere

Elements of the weather

Weather conditions change every day and can vary over short distances even within Northern Ireland. For example, Belfast can have very different weather to Enniskillen or Coleraine.

Element	Unit	Instrument
Temperature	degree centigrade (°C)	Maximum–minimum thermometer
Precipitation	millimetres (mm)	Rain gauge
Wind speed	knots per hour (kph)	Anemometer
Wind direction	8 compass points	Wind vane
Pressure	**millibars** (mb)	Barometer

▲ **Figure 2** Table showing some weather elements, their unit of measurement and the instrument used to record the weather.

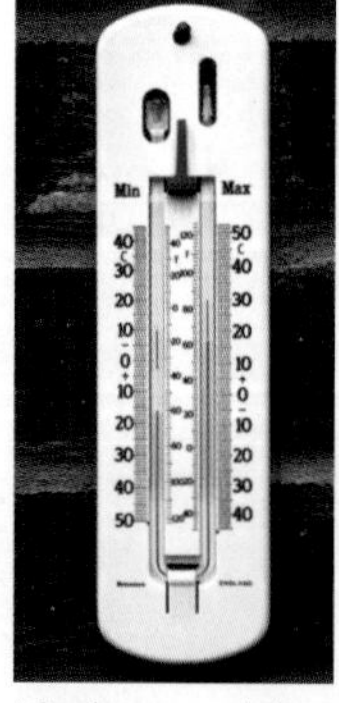

Maximum–minimum thermometer

Barograph

Stevenson's screen stores instruments

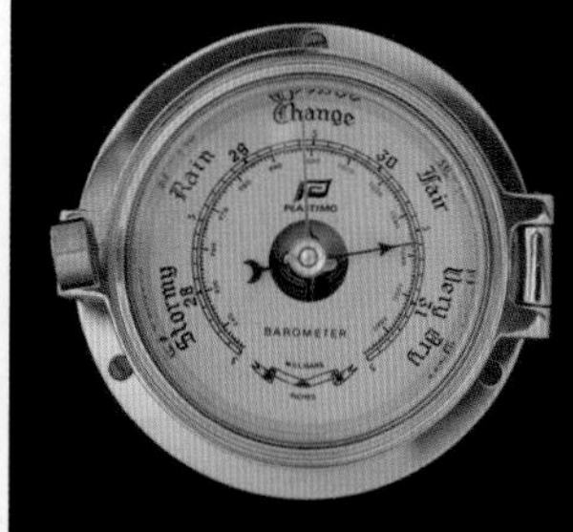

Barometer

Rain gauge

Wind vane

Anemometer

▲ **Figure 3** Recording weather

Clouds

Cloud watching can be fun, especially in Northern Ireland, where we get a wide variety of cloud types. Look out the window. What cloud type is outside today?

There are three basic types of clouds:

- Cirrus clouds. These are the whitest, highest clouds made of tiny ice crystals. They are often wispy in appearance.
- Cumulus clouds. They are often low in the air and look like cotton wool or like cauliflower on top with a flat base. Cumulus is the Latin word for 'heap'. Clusters of small, white cumulus clouds are usually a sign of fine weather. Sometimes, cumulus clouds develop into the storm cloud cumulonimbus, which brings lightning and thunder. Cumulonimbus clouds are called 'the king of clouds'. The base of a cumulonimbus cloud is often low but it may be as high as 10 km.
- Stratus clouds. These appear as light grey clouds that look like even sheets and cover all or part of the sky. They are composed of fine water droplets that become larger as they collide with each other and are often very low in the air.

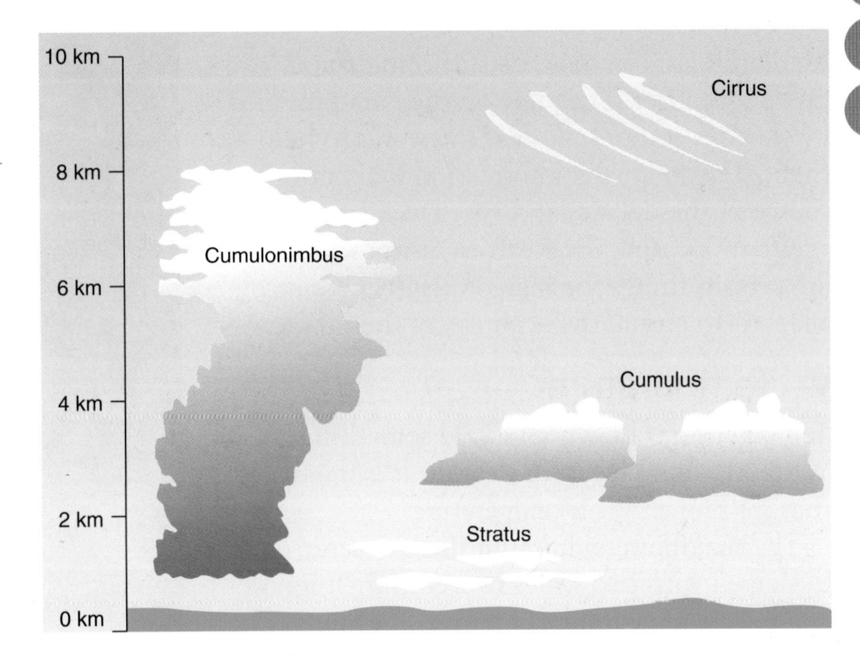

▲ **Figure 4** The main cloud types

Nimbus refers to any cloud that is rain-bearing. You can tell this by the grey colour of the cloud.

You can identify clouds by looking at their shape and height above the Earth. **Cloud cover** is measured in oktas or eighths of the sky covered with cloud.

Get Active

1 How well do you think you know your clouds? You can find out by completing an online cloud observation quiz at the following website: www.globe.gov/sda-bin/m2h?gl/clouds.men (click on 'Take the Cloud Quiz!').
2 Note your score in the quiz.
3 How well did you do? Which clouds did you find easy/difficult to identify?

Tip to succeed: before taking this online quiz, you can view a cloud-type tutorial at: http://asd-www.larc.nasa.gov/SCOOL/cldtype.html.

Why does a weather station look like it does?

Meteorologists are scientists who study and predict weather. They rely on the data provided by weather stations all over the world to help them. The following information is about one source of these data: land-based weather stations.

When locating the weather instruments there are certain things the meteorologists take into account to ensure the accuracy of their data.

Temperature

Temperature is how hot or cold something is. When trying to measure weather it is important that we know the air temperature.

The **maximum–minimum thermometer** is U-shaped with two scales to record the highest and lowest temperatures for every 24 hours. The maximum thermometer is filled with mercury. It has a constriction in the thread so that once the mercury rises to record a high temperature it cannot return to the bulb. The minimum thermometer is filled with pure alcohol. A metal pin is pulled downwards towards the bulb as the alcohol contracts when cooled. The small metal pins are reset using a magnet or reset button after each reading.

As temperature varies depending on the type of surface or exposure to sunlight, meteorologists have agreed to standardise the measuring of temperature to allow for comparison. The shade temperature is the agreed correct measure. In a weather station thermometers are placed within a Stevenson screen. This is set on stilts above the ground to ensure that it is air and not ground temperature that is recorded. The box shades the instruments from direct sunlight and the slatted sides allow the free flow of air. The Stevenson screen is painted white to reflect sunlight and is located on open ground away from buildings.

Precipitation

The term **precipitation** includes all types of moisture in the atmosphere from rain to snow and hail to fog.

A **rain gauge** is a cylinder that catches precipitation and funnels it into a measuring flask. It is located in an open area to avoid shelter that trees might provide. Being sunk into the ground avoids excessive evaporation

▲ **Figure 5** Meteorologists are even needed by the army. A soldier watches a helium-filled weather balloon while looking through an instrument that can calculate height and wind speed. Special Forces Combat Weathermen are a little known section of the US army who are responsible for gathering weather information from the battlefield

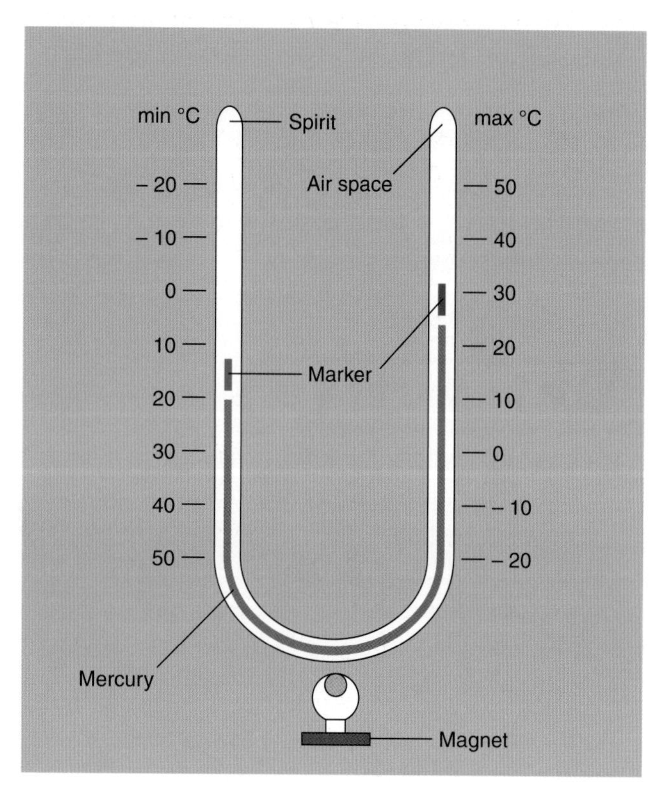

▲ **Figure 6** A maximum–minimum thermometer that is placed inside a Stevenson screen (see Figure 3)

and provides stability in windy conditions. Each day the flask is taken out and the amount of precipitation is recorded in millimetres by transferring the liquid into a small measuring cylinder.

Air pressure

Pressure is the weight of a column of air. The average pressure at sea level is 1012 mb. The **barometer** is used to measure **atmospheric pressure**. There are two main types of barometers: the mercury barometer and the aneroid barometer. The mercury barometer is composed of a glass tube about 1 m tall with one end open and the other end sealed. The tube is filled with mercury. This glass tube sits upside down in a container, called a reservoir, which also contains mercury. The mercury level in the glass tube falls, creating a vacuum at the top. The barometer works by balancing the weight of mercury in the glass tube against the atmospheric pressure. If the weight of mercury is less than the atmospheric pressure, the mercury level in the glass tube rises. If the weight of mercury is more than the atmospheric pressure, the mercury level falls.

Aneroid barometers are commonly found in homes. The aneroid barometer is operated by a metal cell containing only a very small amount of air. Increased air pressure causes the sides of the cell to come closer together. One side is fixed to the base of the instrument while the other is connected by means of a system of levers and pulleys to a rotating pointer that moves over a scale on the face of the instrument. This pointer is usually black and is used to display the atmospheric pressure.

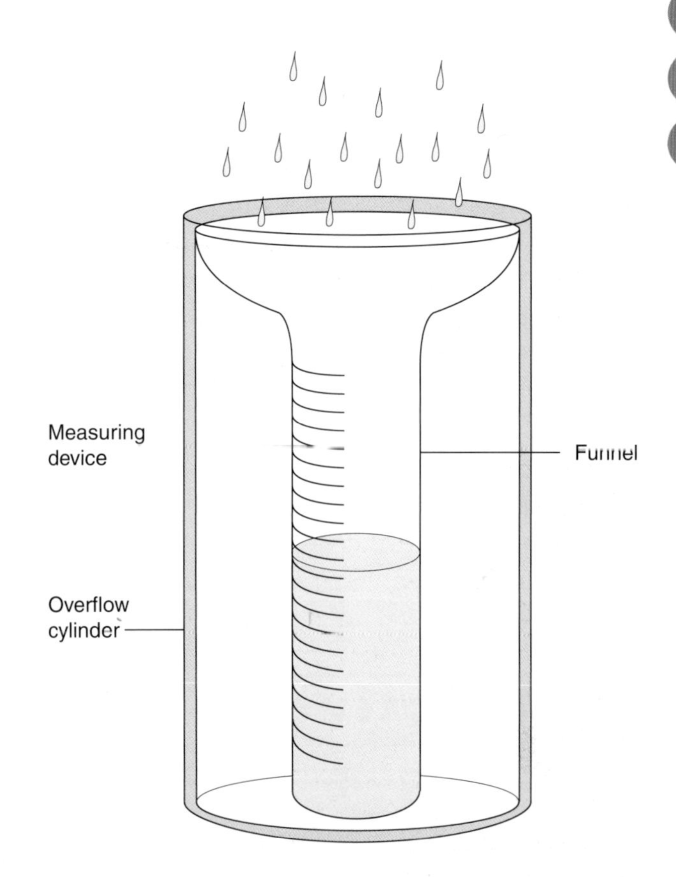

▲ **Figure 7** A rain gauge

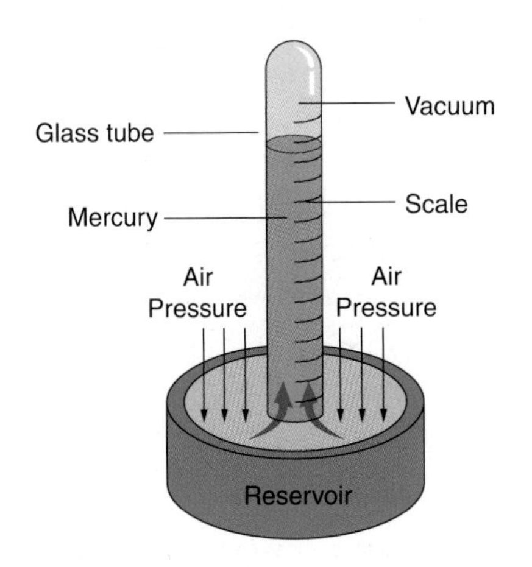

▲ **Figure 8** A mercury barometer

▲ **Figure 9** An aneroid barometer

Wind

Air moves around in the atmosphere, which we feel as **wind**. It is caused by differences in air pressure across the planet's surface. Winds are movements of air from high to low pressure.

The **anemometer** has three cups mounted on a high pole to catch the wind. As the wind blows the cups spin and the **wind speed** is recorded on a dial which can be read a little like the speedometer in a car.

Wind direction is shown by a wind vane. The top section is loose and moves with the wind, the base is fixed and orientated to show the main points of the compass. The arrow points to the direction from which the wind is blowing.

▲ **Figure 10** The world's largest weathervane: it is nearly 15 m high and can be found in Montague, Michigan, USA

Get Active

The Beaufort scale (named after the Northern Ireland man who invented it in 1806) is often used to give wind speed. Find out:

1 How many levels are there to the Beaufort scale and what are they called?
2 What wind speed (in mph or kph) defines each level of the scale?
3 What indicators, such as the movement of smoke or branches, is associated with each force on the scale?
4 Draw a table to record your answers.

Weather forecasting

A weather forecast is made using computers and the records of past weather patterns to predict current weather. Forecasters use data collected from many sources to produce a synoptic chart, which shows the predicted weather conditions.

Weather forecasts are usually accurate for a period of 24 hours and reasonably accurate for up to 5 days ahead. Beyond this they become increasingly unreliable. The chaotic nature of our atmosphere means that it is unlikely that we will ever be able to make accurate long-range weather forecasts.

Get Active

Field work opportunity. Work in groups.

1 Take weather readings every day for a month using the instruments shown in Figure 3.
2 Devise a suitable data collection sheet.
3 Record your measurements and observations.
4 Using ICT, produce appropriate graphs to represent the data you have collected (temperature, precipitation, pressure, wind speed, wind direction, cloud cover, cloud type).
5 Look closely at your table of data and observations and the graphs you have produced:

- Can you identify any relationships between weather variables, e.g. pressure and temperature?
- If so, what are the relationships you have discovered about the climate around your school?
- Did any of your findings surprise you?
- If your school was to set up all the instruments to take weather readings, where would you locate them and why?
- Do you think there are any microclimates around your school? Did you find any evidence to support your view?

What sources of data help meteorologists create a weather forecast?

Weather forecasting began in the late 1700s using only a few unreliable instruments. Today there are more than 10,000 land-based weather stations located in countries all over the world. They collect data on the elements of weather every synoptic hour (that's every 3 hours) every day of the year.

Other sources of weather data include:

- Weather balloons. As they rise up, the balloons gather data on temperature, pressure and wind speeds using a small digital device suspended under the balloon. This device transmits the data back to a computer on the ground.
- Weather buoys are stationed in mid-ocean locations. They transmit weather data via satellite to weather centres for use in forecasting and climate study. Both moored buoys and drifting buoys (drifting in the open ocean currents) are used.
- Most ships have a weather station attached to them. These weather ships record and send data in the same way as the buoys. Mariners need to know future weather hazards.
- Satellites are small spacecraft that carry specific weather instruments. They are launched into space and orbit the Earth recording its weather data. The radiometer provides colour images of clouds. The scatterometer uses microwaves to detect the speed and direction of winds.

If a satellite is positioned over one place and moves at the same speed as the Earth, it is called a geostationary satellite. It only provides data for that one place. Polar satellites offer the advantage of daily global coverage, by making nearly polar orbits roughly 14.1 times daily. Currently in orbit we have morning and afternoon satellites, which provide worldwide coverage four times daily. These satellites are able to collect global data from different places on a daily basis. The ocean temperature information they are gathering is an important source of evidence to support global warming.

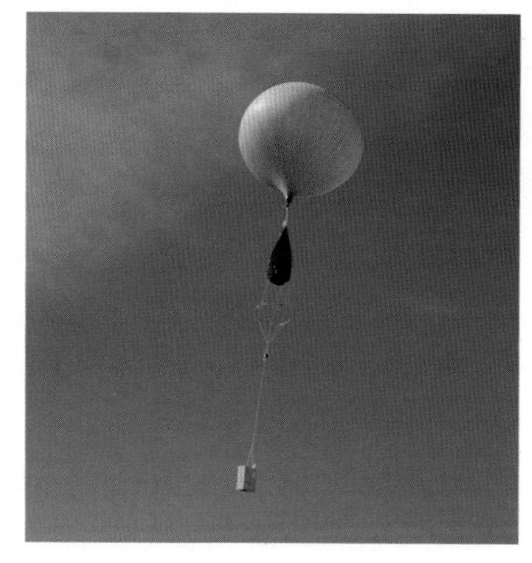

▲ **Figure 11** A weather balloon with its radio sender

▲ **Figure 12** A weather buoy

▲ **Figure 13** Weather instruments on a ship

▲ **Figure 14** A weather satellite orbiting the Earth

● weblinks

www.naturalhistoryonthenet.com/Weather/measuring_weather.htm – Great pictures of weather instruments.

www.bbc.co.uk/weather/weatherwise/activities/weatherstation/wind_measuring.shtml – Information and activites on measuring weather.

www.weatherwizkids.com – A simple, easy site on all things weather.

Weather systems affecting the British Isles

What are air masses?

The British Isles are affected by five main air masses and this makes the weather very changeable. An air mass is a large body of air with similar temperature and moisture characteristics all the way through it.

The characteristics of the air mass depend on where it comes from or the source region:

- A maritime air mass picks up moisture from the sea surface and so brings wet weather to the British Isles.
- A continental air mass is dry because it forms over land surfaces.
- A polar air mass comes from a northerly direction and so brings cold temperatures. Polar continental air masses mainly affect the British Isles during the winter half of the year.
- A tropical air mass comes from a southerly direction and so brings warm temperatures. Tropical continental air is more common in summer than winter, and when it arrives it can create heat-wave conditions.
- An arctic air mass comes from a northerly direction and brings cold, snowy weather in winter and cool, damp weather in summer. It is rarely experienced outside the winter months.

Where air masses meet, a **front** is formed. A front separates warm and cold air masses. The tropical maritime air mass is usually found between the warm and cold fronts (in the warm sector) of depressions.

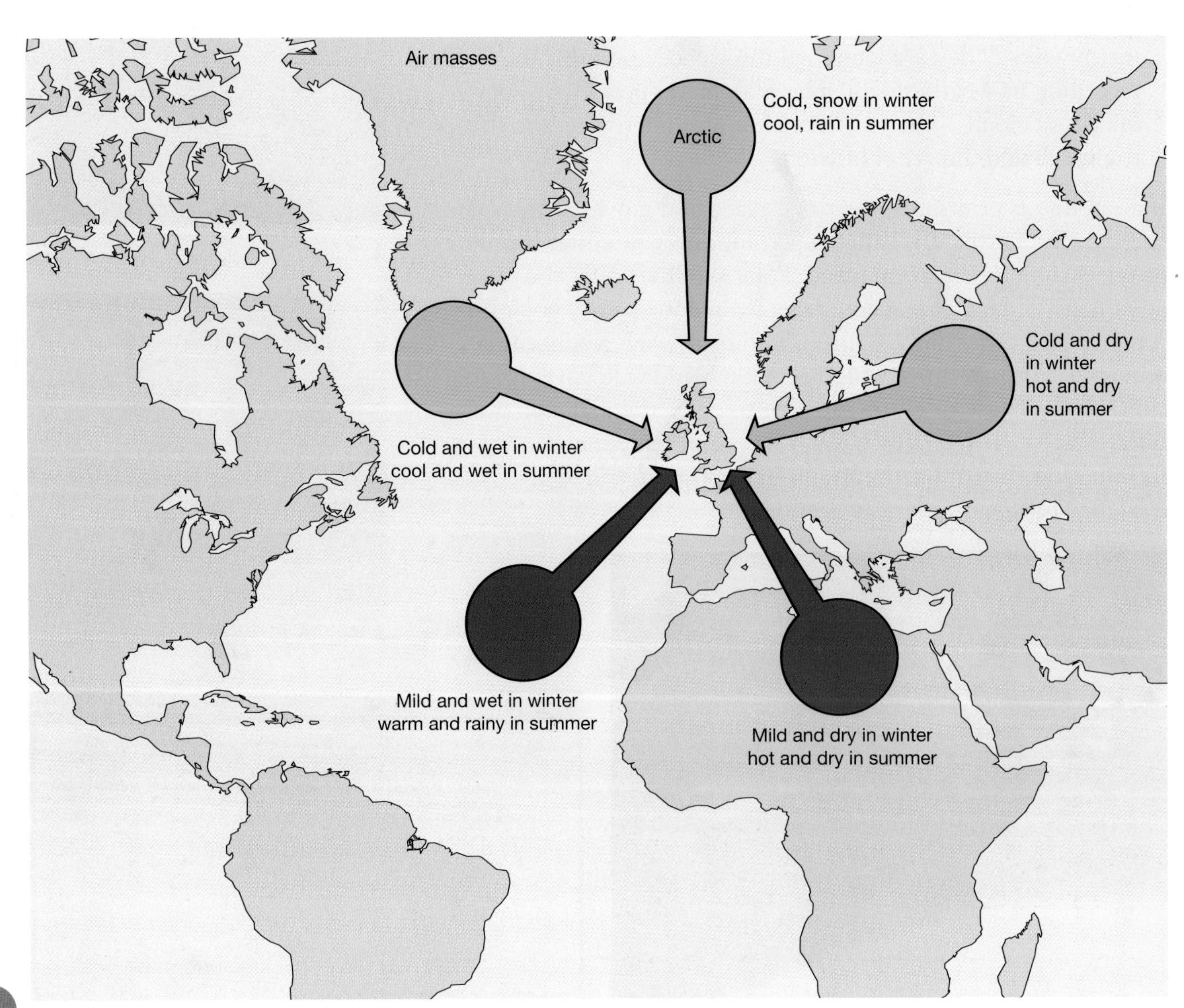

▲ **Figure 15** Map of the British Isles showing the directions of the main air masses

What causes our weather patterns?

There are two main types of weather system that cause our weather patterns: depressions and anticyclones.

Depressions

Depressions are systems of low pressure; they are like whirlpools of air that develop in the main stream of air movement that comes towards the British Isles from the west. They are areas of low pressure, which generally move towards the east. The winds blow anticlockwise and into the centre of the low. The air rises in the centre.

On weather maps (**synoptic charts**) a depression has a circular pattern of isobars with the lowest pressure in the centre and the winds blowing into the centre. Depressions can be hundreds of kilometres wide. Depressions have fronts because they form when a warm tropical air mass meets a cold polar air mass. A front divides the two air masses. The **warm front** and the **cold front** are separated by a wedge of warm tropical air called the warm sector.

Get Active

The idea that northerly winds (winds from the north) are cold, and southerly winds (those from the south) are warm (at least in the northern hemisphere) is quite common. Similarly, air that has travelled over the sea picks up moisture, while air travelling over the land is relatively dry. These simple concepts help in the understanding of air masses. However, as may be expected, there are variations on this theme.

1 Check out this website: www.metoffice.gov.uk/education/curriculum/lesson_plans/weathersystems/partb.html.
2 In your own words define an air mass.
3 Work in groups:
- Individually, make detailed notes on one of the air masses affecting the British Isles.
- Use your notes to explain this air mass to the other members of your group.
- Answer any questions posed by the other group members.
- The group members make their own notes on the air mass you have just explained.

Get Active

Your answers to the following questions should be illustrated with simple sketches/diagrams.

1 What is a front?
2 What is a warm front and how is it shown on a weather map?
3 What is a cold front and how is it shown on a weather map?
4 What is an occluded front and how is it shown on a weather map?

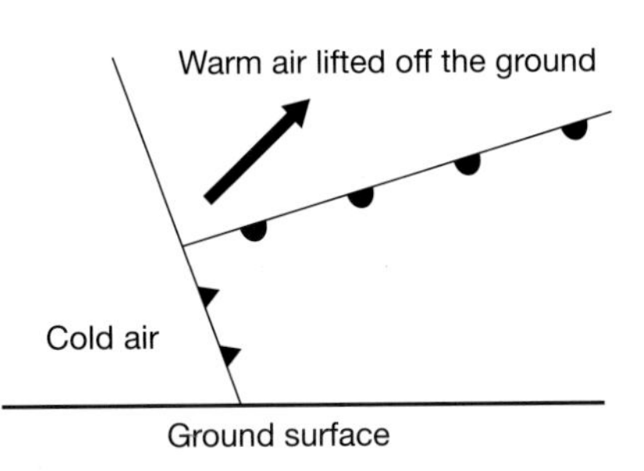

▲ **Figure 16** An occluded front

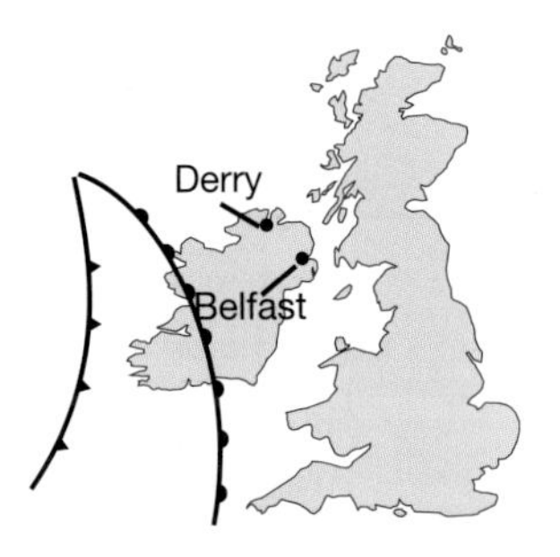

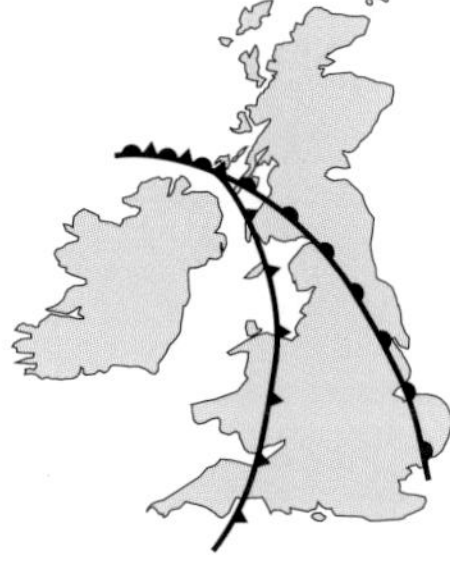

1. A warm front approaches. Skies change from clear, to having high wispy clouds, to developing thicker, lower clouds. Eventually it starts to drizzle.

2. The warm front passes over. Drizzle is replaced by steady rain.
The temperature rises in the warm sector. The sky remains grey and overcast. Rain or drizzle continues. The wind blows from the south-west.

3. The cold front has passed over Northern Ireland resulting in heavy rain and gusty conditions. Temperatures drop as the front passes over. The wind swings around to the north-west. Behind the cold front, the sky clears. The weather now brings sunny intervals with heavy showers.

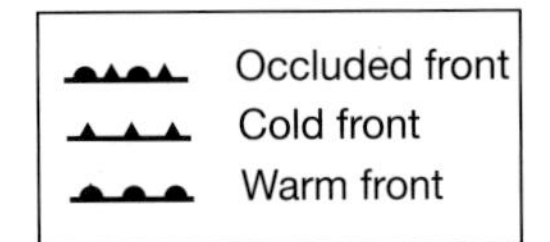

▲ **Figure 17** The sequence of weather as a depression passes

The sequence of a depression from an observer's point of view

- *Ahead of the warm front.* As a depression approaches, a person at ground level will first see cirrus cloud, high up in the sky. There is no rain yet but temperatures are cool and winds may be strong and from the east or south. As the warm front approaches, the cloud thickens and close to the warm front there will be rain and drizzle as warm air is being forced to rise. Pressure is high but decreases towards the centre of the low pressure.
- *In the warm sector.* Here, temperatures increase in the warm tropical air. There is low stratus cloud but it is mainly dry; this is because water vapour can easily be held in the warm, tropical air without condensation taking place. Wind direction becomes more south-westerly and wind speed usually increases. Pressure values are lowest in this central part of the depression.
- *Behind the cold front.* As the cold front passes, the temperatures fall and the winds will change direction and blow from the north-west. The observer will see towering high cumulonimbus clouds at the cold front and there will be heavy rain. This is because the warm air is rising quickly at the steeply sloping cold front. Pressure starts to rise after the cold front as the depression passes. Further behind the cold front are scattered showers from some isolated cumulus clouds; the wind speeds become lighter.

A depression ends when all the warm tropical air in the warm sector is lifted off the ground. This is shown on a weather map by an occluded front. This can happen when the cold front moves eastwards faster than the warm front and so cold air pushes the warm front off the ground. An occluded front brings similar weather to a warm front.

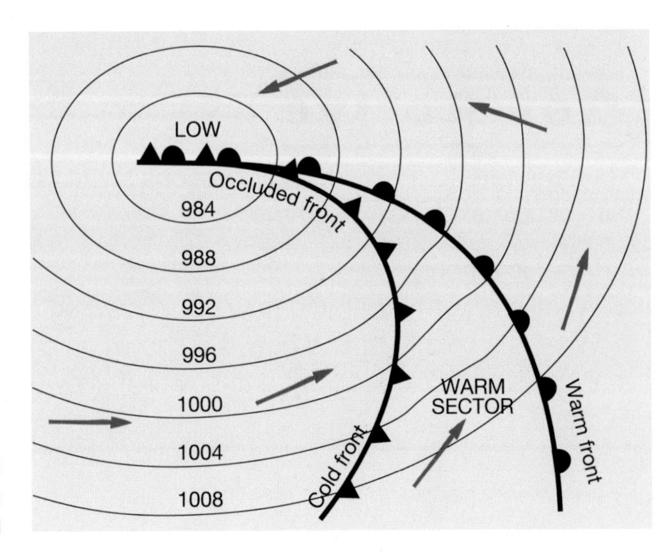

► **Figure 18** Plan view of a depression. The isobars bend abruptly at the fronts; the winds blow anticlockwise and into the centre of low pressure. The air in the warm sector is rising

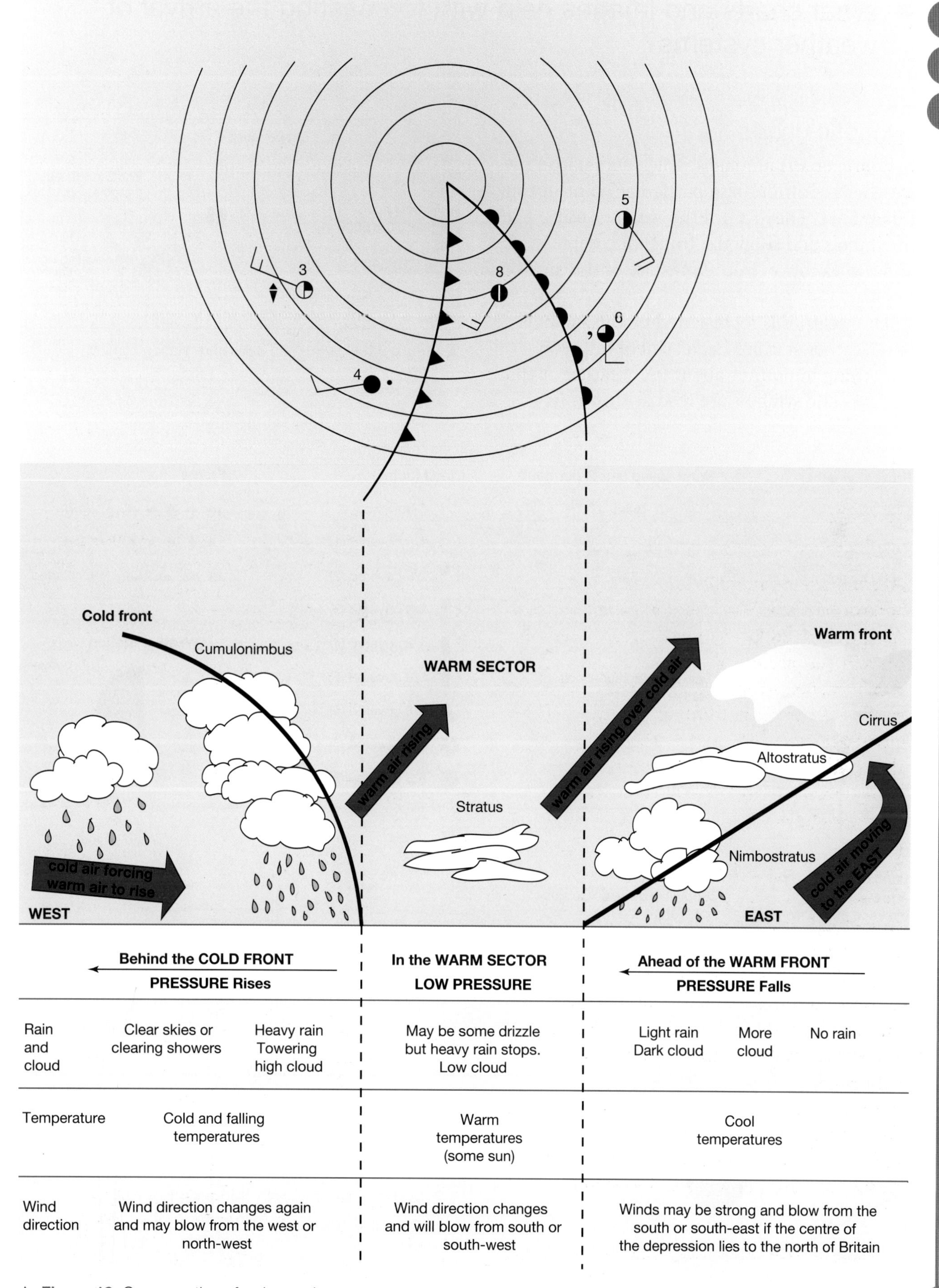

	Behind the COLD FRONT ← PRESSURE Rises		In the WARM SECTOR LOW PRESSURE	Ahead of the WARM FRONT ← PRESSURE Falls		
Rain and cloud	Clear skies or clearing showers	Heavy rain Towering high cloud	May be some drizzle but heavy rain stops. Low cloud	Light rain Dark cloud	More cloud	No rain
Temperature	Cold and falling temperatures		Warm temperatures (some sun)	Cool temperatures		
Wind direction	Wind direction changes again and may blow from the west or north-west		Wind direction changes and will blow from south or south-west	Winds may be strong and blow from the south or south-east if the centre of the depression lies to the north of Britain		

▲ **Figure 19** Cross-section of a depression

What charts and images help with forecasting the arrival of weather systems?

Synoptic charts

Synoptic charts are maps which summarise the weather conditions at a particular point in time for an area. They record the weather using a set of symbols and show the fronts of a depression and the variation in the pressure of the air using isobars.

The weather is represented by the symbols at a weather station. Each symbol tells you something important about the weather at that station. The symbols are read as shown in Figure 21.

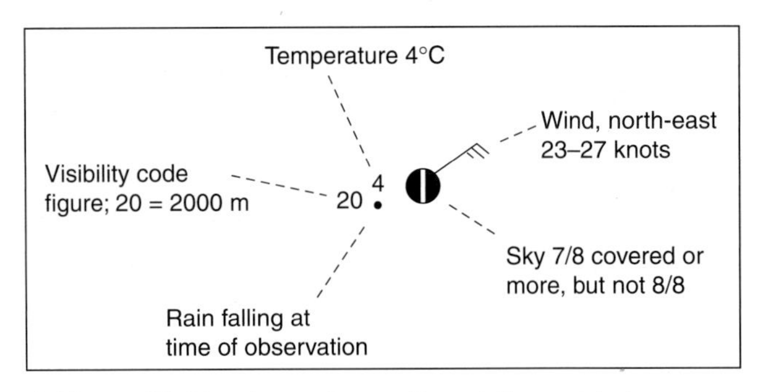

▲ **Figure 21** How to read a weather station symbol

Present weather

- Mist
- Fog
- Drizzle
- Rain and drizzle
- Rain
- Snow
- Rain shower
- Snow shower
- Hail shower
- Thunderstorm

Wind speed (knots per hour)

- Calm
- 1 – 2
- 3 – 7
- 8 – 12
- 13 – 17

For each additional half feather, add 5 knots

- 48 – 52

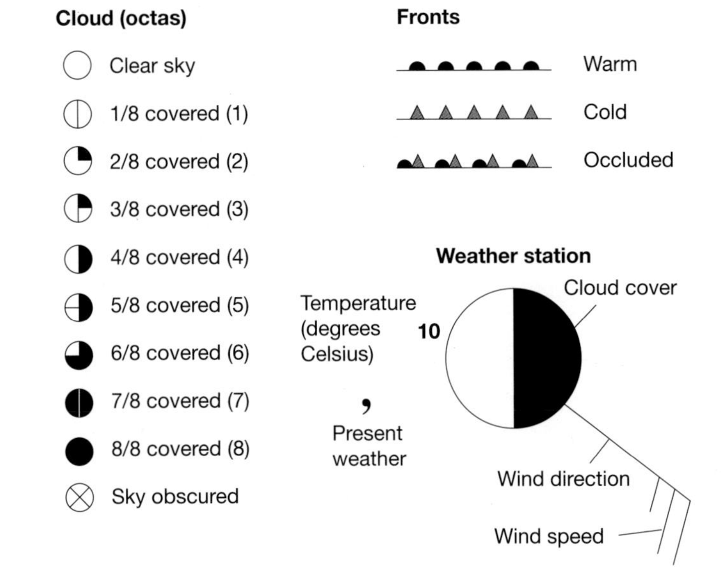

Wind direction
Arrow showing direction from which wind is blowing
i.e. ——► west

Temperature
Shown in degrees Celsius
i.e. 15°C

▲ **Figure 20** Weather symbols used on weather maps

Get Active

1 What is the weather like at this weather station?

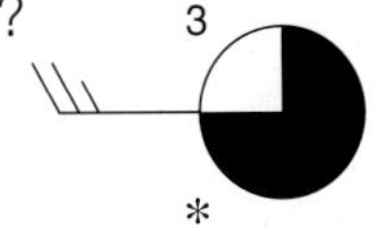

Give precise details of:

- temperature (in °C)
- wind speed (in knots)
- wind direction
- type of precipitation
- amount of cloud cover (in oktas).

2 What is wrong with this weather? Why couldn't this happen?

30

Get Active

The synoptic charts and satellite images below show the development of a depression.

Stage 1: origin and infancy

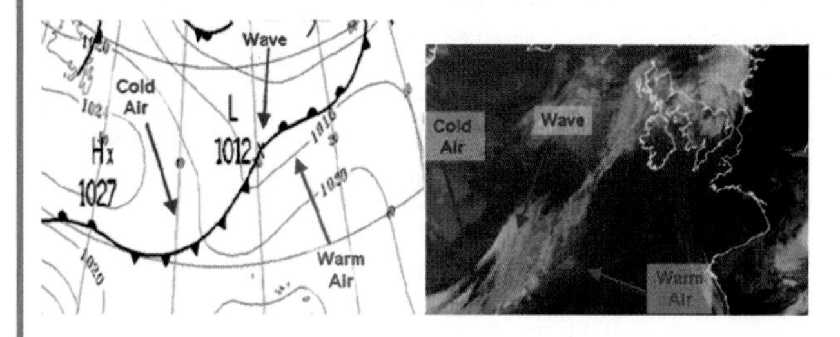

Stage 3: occlusion

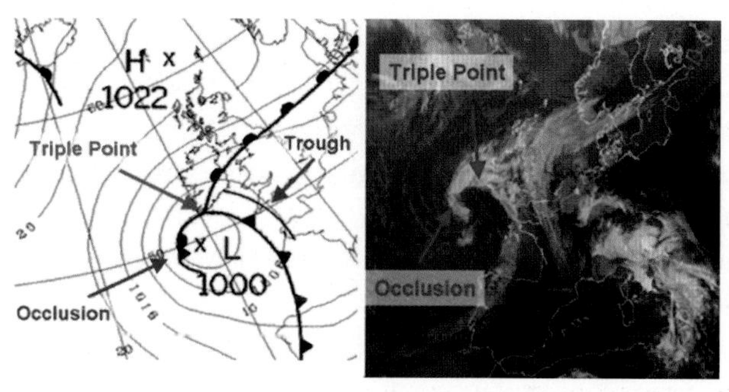

Stage 2: maturity

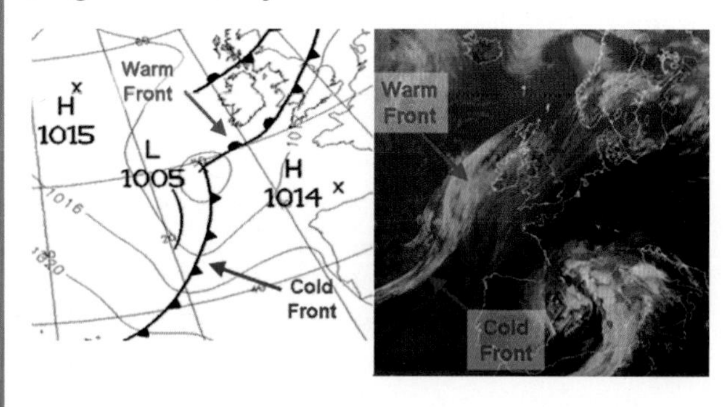

Stage 4: death

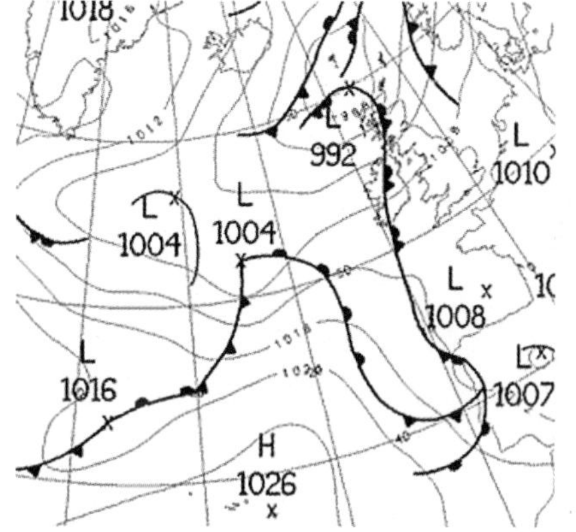

Source: Met Office.

1 Describe what is happening at each of the four stages in the development of a depression. To get some help you might look at: www.metoffice.gov.uk/education/curriculum/lesson_plans/weathersystems/partc.html.

2 a Using Figure 17 describe how the temperatures change at Belfast through the day.
  b Explain why temperatures change as the depression passes.
  c Describe how the wind direction changes at Derry through the day.
  d Explain why the rainfall amount changes during the day.

3 Describe how the changing weather throughout the day would affect each of the following groups of people:
- tourists in Newcastle, Co. Down
- hill walkers in the Sperrin Mountains
- travellers taking the Larne to Cairnryan ferry.

4 Describe the weather associated with the passage of a depression?

Weather associated with the passage of a classic depression

	Ahead of the warm front	Passage of the warm front	Warm sector	Passage of the cold front	Cold sector
Pressure	Starts to fall steadily	Continues to fall	Steadies	Starts to rise	Continues to rise
Temperature	Quite cold, starts to rise	Continues to rise	Quite mild	Sudden drop	Remains cold
Cloud cover	Cloud base drops and thickens (cirrus and altostratus)	Cloud base is low and thick (nimbostratus)	Cloud may thin and break	Clouds thicken (sometimes with large cumulonimbus)	Clouds thin with some cumulus
Wind speed and direction	Speeds increase and direction backs	Veers and becomes blustery with strong gusts	Remains steady, backs slightly	Speeds increase, sometimes to gale force, sharp veer	Winds are squally
Precipitation	None at first, rain closer to front, sometimes snow on leading edge	Continues, and sometimes heavy rainfall	Rain turns to drizzle or stops	Heavy rain, sometimes with hail, thunder or sleet	Showers

Source: Met Office.

Anticyclones

Anticyclones are systems of high pressure. In the centre the air is sinking slowly from great heights; as the air sinks it swirls in a clockwise direction and spreads out at the surface. The sinking air is compressed and warms up as it nears the ground; this means the air can hold more water vapour without condensation taking place and so clouds do not form and it is less likely to rain. This means anticyclones are associated with dry, bright weather.

In an anticyclone, the isobars are spaced well apart and so the pressure gradient is gentle; this means the wind speeds are low and there may even be calm conditions with no wind in the centre of the high pressure. An anticyclone has no fronts and moves very slowly so the weather conditions may not change very much as this system passes across the British Isles.

A summer anticyclone brings cloudless skies and bright sunshine and high temperatures during the day. At night temperatures can fall due to rapid cooling caused by heat escaping through radiation into the atmosphere when there are no clouds. This mist is usually easily evaporated by the strong sunshine in summer.

A winter anticyclone often brings fog or mist; these form at night when rapid cooling occurs and heat is lost by radiation due to the lack of cloud cover. Water vapour in the cold layer of air near the ground condenses and the water droplets are suspended in the air as mist or fog. In winter the low angle of the sun means that the rays cannot disperse the fog or mist and it may persist all day.

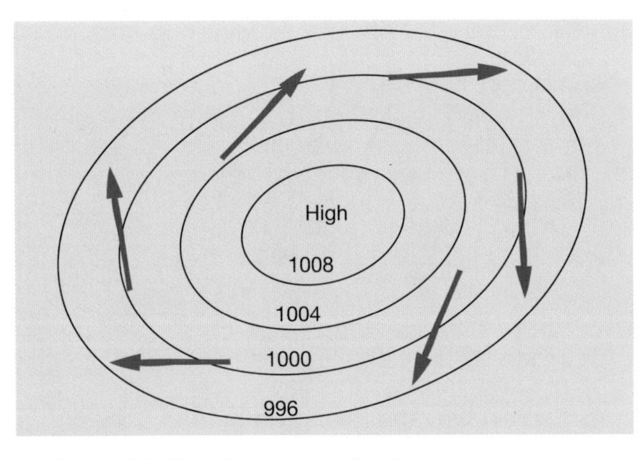

▲ **Figure 22** Plan view of an anticyclone

Get Active

1. Describe the weather conditions shown in the two photographs in Figure 23.
2. Explain why anticyclones bring sunny daytime weather but cold weather at night in winter.
3. Draw a diagram which shows the movement of air in an anticyclone. Use the information provided in the description of this system.

▲ **Figure 23** The weather in a summer anticyclone and a winter anticyclone

Get Active

The synoptic charts below show two anticyclones affecting the UK at different times of year (winter and summer).

Synoptic chart for 10 January 2003

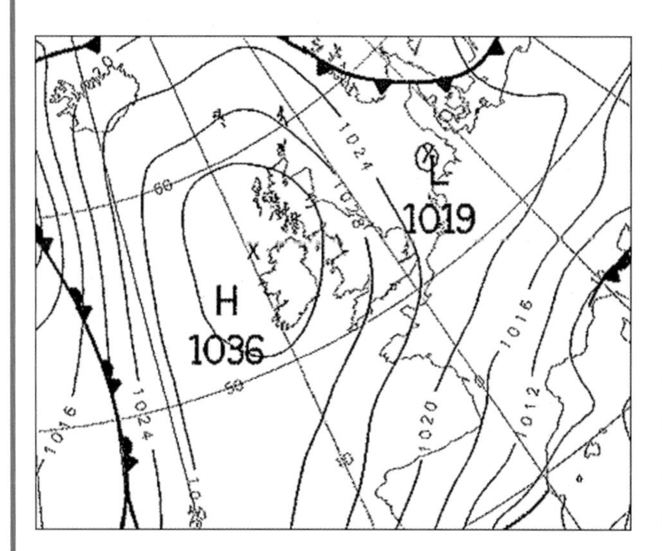

Synoptic chart for 3 September 2003

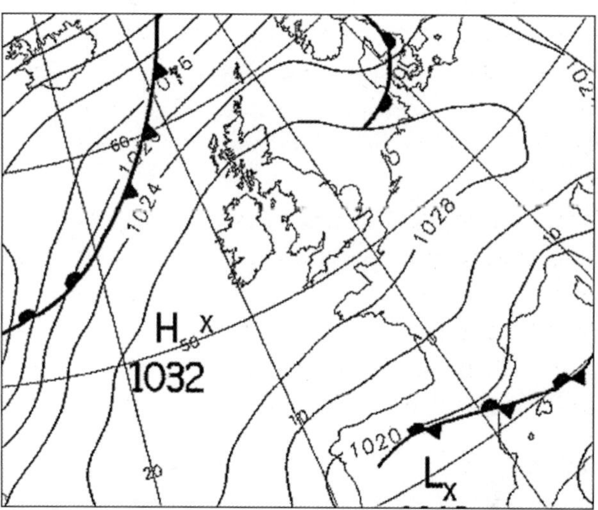

Source: Met Office.

1 Describe the weather conditions that will be experienced in Belfast on the two charts. Make sure you include temperature, general weather conditions and cloud cover.
2 Explain why these differences might occur.

● weblinks

www.metoffice.gov.uk/
www.met.ie/
www.accuweather.com/ukie/index.asp?
www.bbc.co.uk/northernireland/learning/
www.weather.gov/

Get Active

Watch the regional weather forecast on a local television station.

- Note the key points.
- Reflect on the accuracy of the weather forecast 24 hours later.
- How accurate was the weather forecast? How do you explain this?

Satellite images

A **satellite image** is a photograph taken from space and sent back to Earth; it can show the cloud formations and the pattern of clouds at fronts in depressions or the clear skies associated with high-pressure areas.

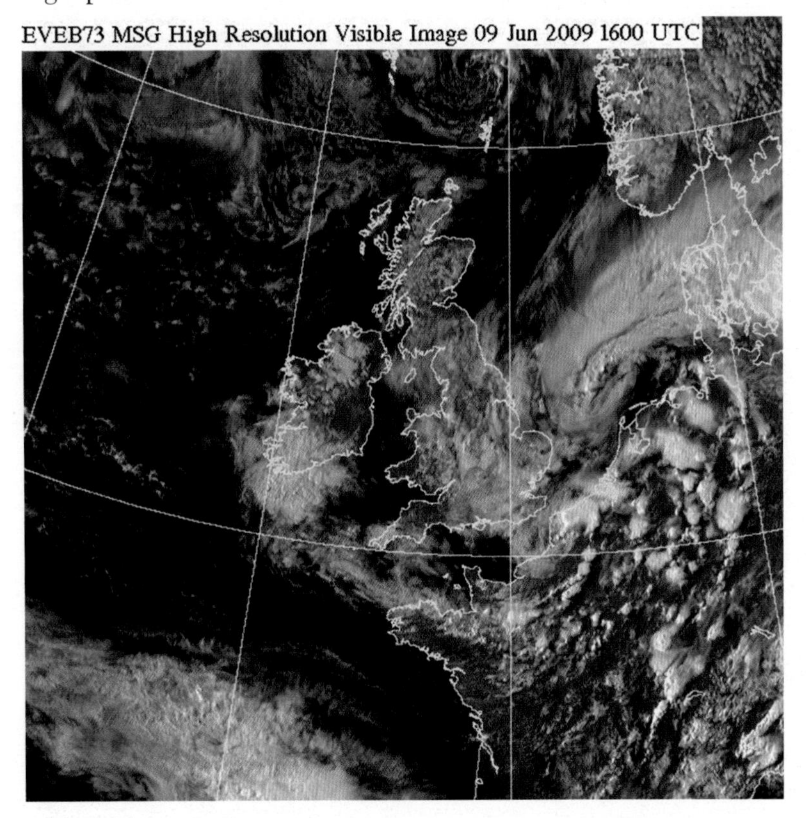

▲ **Figure 24** Satellite image from the Met Office, 9 June 2009

Get Active

- Study the satellite image in Figure 24. How would you describe the weather being experienced by the UK and Ireland at this time?
- On a copy of the satellite image mark on fronts (warm, cold or occluded) and the centres of areas of high or low pressure.
- Add a suitable key to your satellite image.
- Using the evidence from the satellite image, explain the spatial variation, or lack of spatial variation, in the weather over the UK on this day.

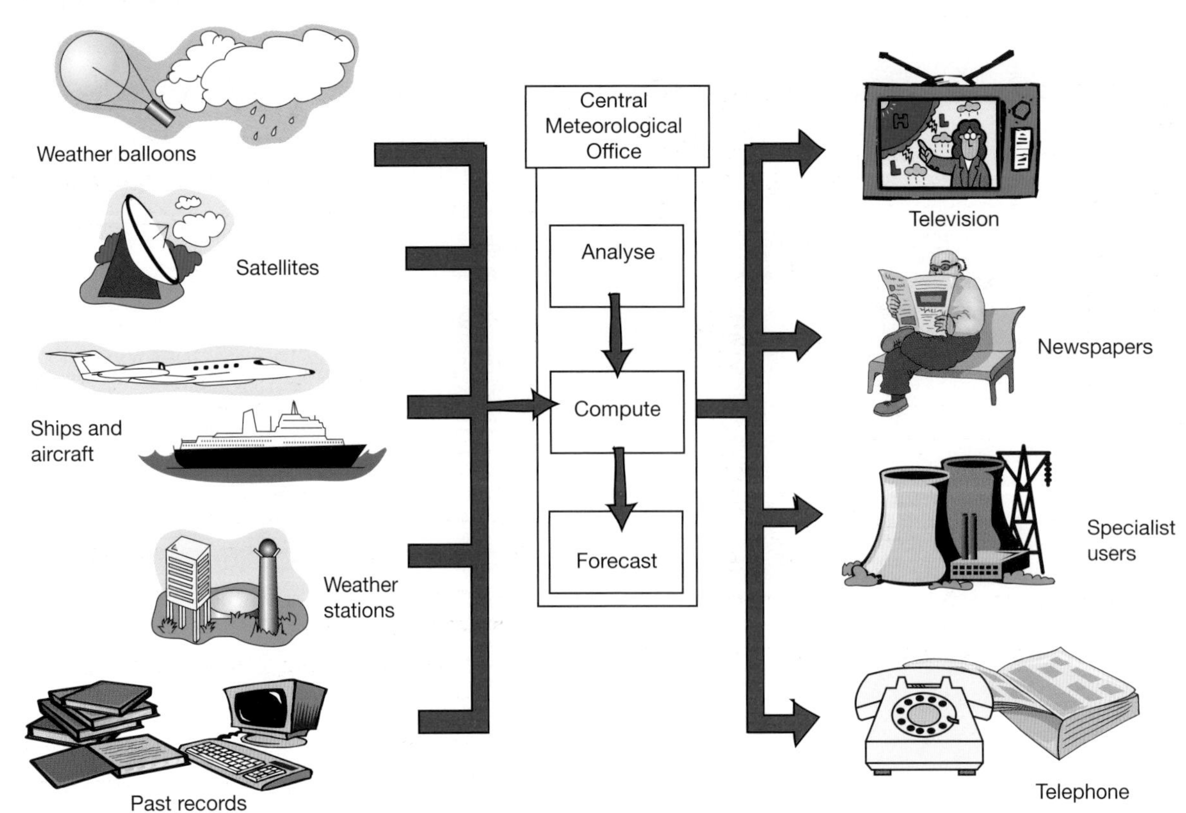

▲ **Figure 25** Inputs and outputs of weather data

What are the effects of weather systems here?

Thankfully we have few extremes of climate in the British Isles. Unlike Bangladesh, we have no monsoon rain to create annual flooding nor is it dry for months on end as in the desert regions of the world. However, our weather systems do affect both people and the economy.

Weather system	Effects on people	Effects on economy
Depression	If a cold front stabilises over one region, the prolonged heavy rainfall can lead to flooding. Frontal rain in the summer can naturally water gardens and fill water butts so people don't have to use their hose-pipes so often.	The rainfall associated with depressions helps crops like wheat and potatoes grow without the need for costly irrigation. Strong winds can mean ferry crossings over the Irish Sea and English Channel are cancelled, so some goods may not be delivered to shops.
Winter anticyclone	People with asthma suffer more from difficulty breathing in cold, frosty weather. Freezing temperatures can kill harmful bacteria which might cause illnesses.	Freezing fog can delay the transport of goods and so reduce potential profit. Frost can break up the soil aiding farmers during spring ploughing.
Summer anticyclone	Elderly people and very young children can become dehydrated in long periods of extreme heat. Warm sunny weather means people can relax and enjoy days out and trips to the beach.	Drought in summer may mean crops die and farmers lose profit. Business like ice-cream vans make more profit.

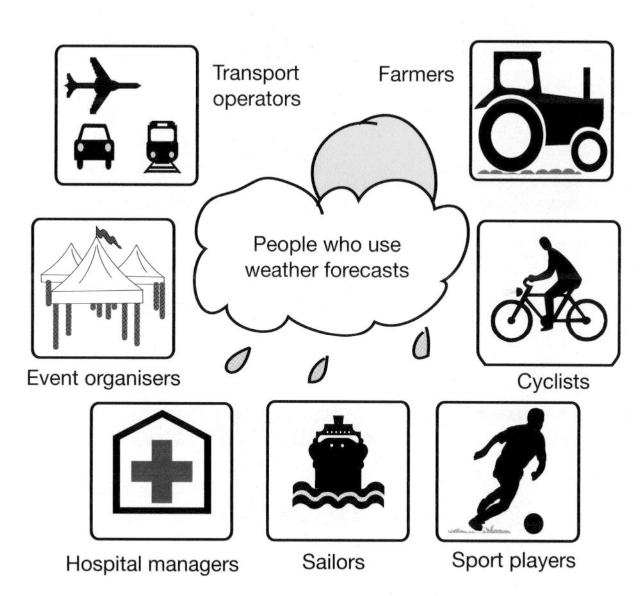

▲ **Figure 26** Groups of people who rely heavily on weather forecasts

● weblinks

www.metoffice.gov.uk/services/business.html – Weather forecasts for those businesses that are affected by the weather.

www.metoffice.gov.uk/weather/uk/ni/ni_forecast_weather.html – Forecasts for Northern Ireland.

Get Active

- Prepare a weather forecast for the next 12 hours for your local area; predict the temperature, wind speed and direction, cloud cover and precipitation, and the pressure.
- Choose two of the groups in Figure 26 and suggest why they might require a weather forecast.

a) **Dublin 5 day forecast**

Tuesday 18th February		Wednesday 19th February		Thursday 20th February		Friday 21st February		Saturday 22nd February
Day Max	Night Min	Day Max	Night Min	Day Max	Night Min	Day Max	Night Min	Day Max
6°C	−1°C	6°C	−2°C	8°C	1°C	7°C	3°C	8°C

b)

Tuesday 18th February		Wednesday 19th February		Thursday 20th February		Friday 21st February		Saturday 22nd February
Day Max	Night Min	Day Max	Night Min	Day Max	Night Min	Day Max	Night Min	Day Max
−4°C	−12°C	−3°C	−12°C	−3°C	−16°C	−4°C	−10°C	−4°C

c)

Tuesday 18th February		Wednesday 19th February		Thursday 20th February		Friday 21st February		Saturday 22nd February
Day Max	Night Min	Day Max	Night Min	Day Max	Night Min	Day Max	Night Min	Day Max
13°C	7°C	14°C	7°C	17°C	6°C	16°C	9°C	16°C

d)

Tuesday 18th February		Wednesday 19th February		Thursday 20th February		Friday 21st February		Saturday 22nd February
Day Max	Night Min	Day Max	Night Min	Day Max	Night Min	Day Max	Night Min	Day Max
11°C	−1°C	11°C	1°C	13°C	3°C	12°C	1°C	13°C

▲ **Figure 27** Tables (a–d) showing weather forecasts for four cities in Europe

Alicante (A), Dublin (D), Oslo (O) and Rome (R)

▲ **Figure 28** Synoptic chart of an anticyclone and its satellite image

Get Active

1 In Figure 27, table a) is for Dublin. Using both the satellite image and the synoptic chart in Figure 28, explain why this weather forecast accurately describes the conditions in Dublin.

2 a Using Figure 28, match the weather forecast in the other tables (b, c and d) to the cities of Oslo, Alicante and Rome.

b Justify your choice in each case, using both the satellite image and the synoptic chart.

● weblinks

www.metoffice.gov.uk/satpics/latest_VIS.html – Visible satellite animation for Europe.

www.eumetsat.int – An international organisation monitoring weather and climate from space.

Get Active

1 Complete the *Odd One Out* activity.

1. rising air
2. rain
3. isobars
4. hot weather
5. increasing winds
6. rain gauge
7. drizzle
8. depression
9. sinking air
10. fronts
11. pressure rising
12. anticyclone
13. warm front
14. pressure
15. hail
16. barometer
17. cold front
18. snow
19. temperature rising
20. warm sector
21. stratus clouds
22. calm winds
23. anticlockwise winds
24. cold air
25. clouds
26. frost
27. clockwise winds
28. clear skies
29. precipitation
30. high temperatures
31. temperature falling
32. relief rain

Task 1
Each of the numbers in the sets of four relates to the topic weather. Can you work out with your partner which is the *Odd One Out* and what connects the other three?

Set A	30	22	2	28
Set B	13	25	9	5
Set C	3	14	16	6
Set D	25	2	15	18
Set E	11	17	31	1
Set F	20	21	7	24
Set G	23	32	8	10
Set H	12	29	27	22

Task 2
Still with your partner, can you find *one more* from the list to add to each of the sets above so that *four* items have things in common, but the *Odd One Out* remains the same? Think about why you have chosen each one.

Task 3
Now it's your turn to design some sets to try out on your partner! Choose three numbers that you think have something in common with each other and one that you think has nothing to do with the other two. Get your partner to find the *Odd One Out*, then do one of theirs. Try a few each, but remember to be reasonable.

Task 4
Can you organise all the words into groups? You are allowed to create between three and six groups, and each group must be given a descriptive heading that unites the words in the group. Try not to have any left over. Be prepared to rethink as you go along.

Source: *Thinking Through Geography Material*, N.I. Education Boards (Nov. 1999)

2 Look at the data on a typical October depression.

Passage of a depression

Date	Time	Rainfall (mm)	Temp. (°C)
29/10/00	10.00	0.0	10.0
29/10/00	11.00	0.0	10.8
29/10/00	12.00	0.0	11.6
29/10/00	13.00	0.0	11.6
29/10/00	14.00	0.0	11.8
29/10/00	15.00	0.0	11.6
29/10/00	16.00	0.0	10.5
29/10/00	17.00	0.2	10.8
29/10/00	18.00	1.6	11.4
29/10/00	19.00	2.0	12.1
29/10/00	20.00	2.4	11.7
29/10/00	21.00	2.4	11.7
29/10/00	22.00	1.6	13.2
29/10/00	23.00	0.8	11.4
30/10/00	00.00	5.4	13.1
30/10/00	01.00	2.4	13.3
30/10/00	02.00	2.4	13.2
30/10/00	03.00	1.6	13.1
30/10/00	04.00	1.6	13.0
30/10/00	05.00	2.0	13.1
30/10/00	06.00	1.4	12.8
30/10/00	07.00	2.8	9.8
30/10/00	08.00	5.0	10.2
30/10/00	09.00	1.0	8.9
30/10/00	10.00	0.0	8.4
30/10/00	11.00	0.0	6.6
30/10/00	12.00	0.2	7.6
30/10/00	13.00	0.4	9.9
30/10/00	14.00	0.2	10.8
30/10/00	15.00	0.0	11.3
30/10/00	16.00	0.0	11.0
30/10/00	17.00	0.0	10.5

Source: *Cut, Paste & Surf* by Philip Webster (Nelson Thornes, 2002)

1 Use the data in the table to create a spreadsheet.

2 Draw appropriate graphs to show how rainfall and temperature change as a depression passes.

3 Add suitable titles and axes labels to each graph.

4 Write a paragraph to describe how the weather changes as a depression passes.

5 Using your knowledge of depressions explain why these changes occurred.

The causes and consequences of climate change

What's the difference between global warming and the greenhouse effect?

The 1990s was the hottest decade on record and 2007 was the wettest year on record in England and Wales; it brought floods to many areas, destroying people's possessions, and ruining their homes and livelihoods. **Global warming** became front page news as the Deputy Prime Minister of the UK said that the country's power lines, drainage systems and flood defences could no longer cope with the more extreme weather in Britain.

Global warming means the increased heating of the atmosphere caused by human activities. World temperatures are estimated to have risen by 0.5°C in the twentieth century and could rise by up to 5.8°C by the end of the twenty-first century. A 1°C rise in world temperatures could mean significant melting of the polar ice caps, worldwide rises in sea level and serious damage to existing ecosystems.

The mechanism that creates global warming is the **greenhouse effect**.

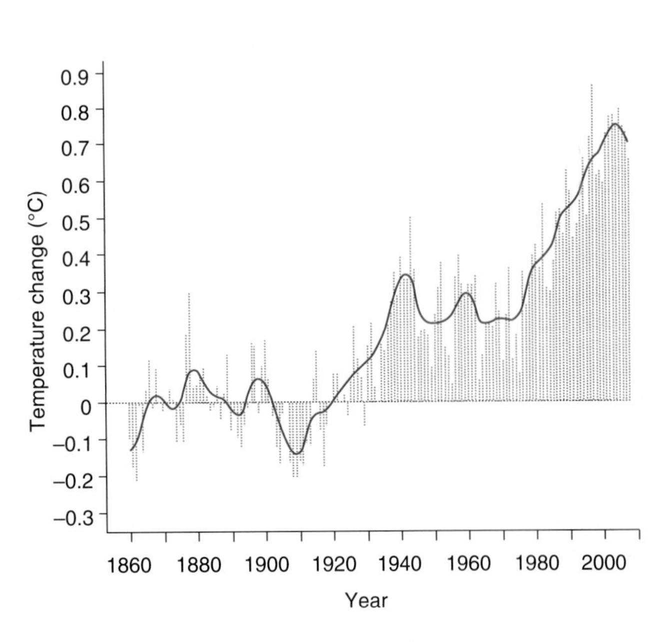

▲ **Figure 29** Graph of temperature change

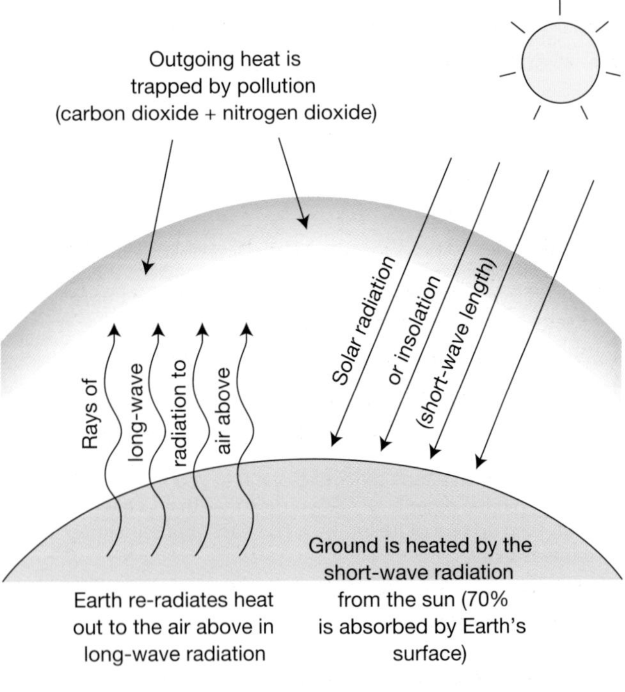

▲ **Figure 30** The greenhouse effect

Get Active

Quoting actual figures and dates from Figure 29 describe how temperatures have increased over time.

Get Active

Use Figure 30 to help you explain how the greenhouse effect contributes to global warming.

What are the causes of climate change?

Natural causes of climate change

Natural climatic cycles

The Earth's orbit changes very slightly between nearly circular and more elongated every 100,000 years. This cycle is evident in the glacial/interglacial cycles of roughly the same period. Sunspots can also affect temperature. The period between 1645 and 1715, a time during which very few sunspots were seen, coincides with a very cold period in Europe known as the little ice age.

Volcanic activity

When a volcano erupts it throws out large volumes of sulphur dioxide, water vapour, dust, and ash into the atmosphere. Although the volcanic activity may last only a few days, the large volumes of gases and ash can influence climatic patterns for years. The gases and dust particles partially block the incoming rays of the sun, leading to cooling. Sulphur dioxide forms small droplets of sulphuric acid in the upper atmosphere which reflect sunlight, and screen the ground from some of the energy that it would ordinarily receive from the sun.

Human causes of climate change

Global warming

Global warming is caused by an increase in the amount of greenhouse gases which trap heat in the atmosphere; the main greenhouse gases are carbon dioxide, nitrogen dioxide and methane. Carbon dioxide is responsible for 50% of global warming. It is feared that as rainfall belts shift, areas now covered by tropical rainforest could change into grassland or even desert. These would accelerate the rates of warming as fewer trees means an increase in the amount of carbon dioxide in the atmosphere. Methane production from large numbers of cattle is increasing very fast and so is nitrogen dioxide given off by fertilisers.

There are two human activities which are major sources of greenhouse gases:

- *Burning fossil fuels*. In the past 200 years the need for more energy has grown as industrial development, population growth and prosperity have all increased. Most of this energy has come from burning **fossil fuels**. When coal, oil or gas is burned in power stations to generate electricity, gases such as carbon dioxide are emitted into the atmosphere and form a blanket of pollution.
- *Vehicles*. During the twentieth century more and more vehicles were using the roads, a trend that is continuing into the twenty-first century. The exhausts of cars and lorries emit polluting gases such as nitrogen dioxide which add to the pollution in the atmosphere.

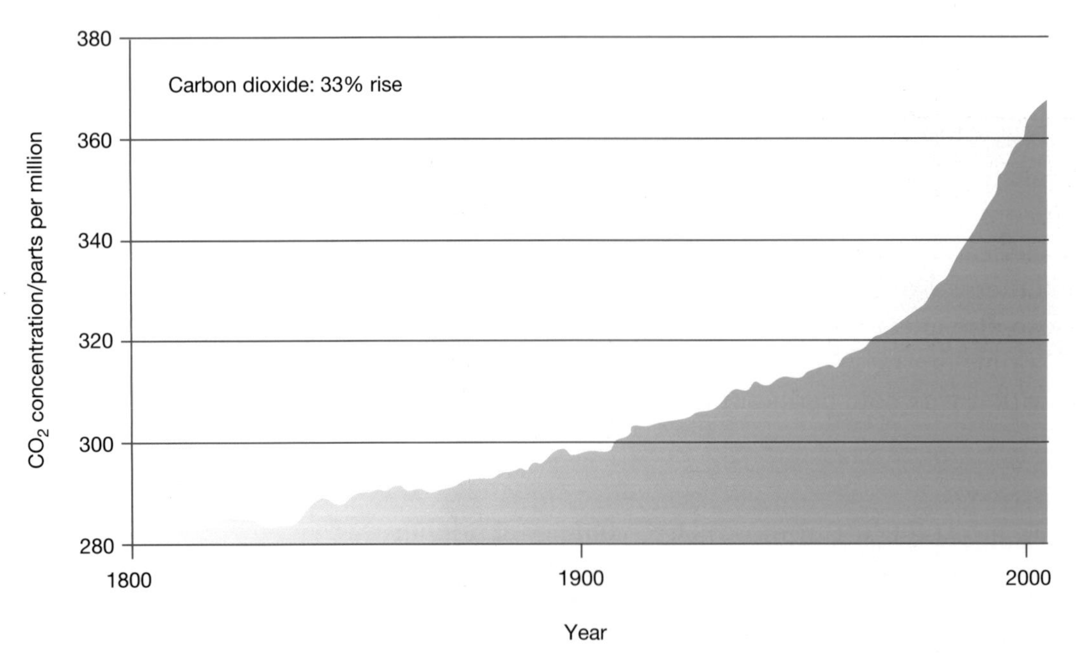

▲ **Figure 31** Increase in carbon dioxide (CO_2) levels since 1800

Get Active

Individually:

- Use Figure 31 to describe how levels of carbon dioxide in the atmosphere change between 1800 and 2000.
- In Figure 33, what message is the cartoonist trying to get across to the public?
- Do you think the cartoon gets across the message?
- Who might this type of approach appeal to and why?
- Do you like this way of drawing people's attention to major issues of the day?
- What other strategies might have been used to get the message across?

In groups:

- List all the strategies those in your group have thought of.
- Rank them according to how useful you think they would be (your 'best' strategy would be ranked number 1).

There have now been 22 years in a row with above average global temperatures. The 10 warmest years on record since 1860 have all occurred since 1983, and eight of the top 10 have occurred since 1990. When we look at the patterns of change, we increasingly believe that a large part of the recent warming is due to fossil fuel burning.

Source: Met Office

▲ **Figure 32** Met Office press release, 19 December 2000

▲ **Figure 33** A cartoonist's view of global warming

How serious are the consequences of climate change?

- *Sea level changes*. Sea levels could rise by up to 1.5 m because the sea expands as it is heated.
- *Climate changes*. Patterns of world precipitation could change and rainfall become more unreliable so that some places will be wetter and others drier.
- *Tourism*. Places such as the Alps could have less snow due to the rising temperatures, so reducing the conditions for skiing; this could have negative effects on employment, economic prospects and income for this region.
- *Agriculture*. The types of crops grown and their yields will be affected by increased temperatures; more extreme climatic conditions may affect how the land is farmed.
- *Health*. The increasingly hot temperatures in northern Europe could put people at greater risk from heatstroke in cities, bringing a rise in deaths.
- *Economy*. More money may need to be spent on expensive flood protection schemes to protect coastal cities, defend low-lying coastal land and safeguard ports and harbours.

Get Active

Draw a series of cartoons or sketches to illustrate the points being made above.

case study

Effects of climate change in an MEDC

Many areas will experience the effects of climate change in the next few decades. LEDCs like Tuvalu in the South Pacific may disappear under the ocean; Bangladesh will have more frequent excessive flooding and semi-arid regions of Africa may become desert. However, MEDCs areas do not escape climate change.

Increases in pests and diseases. More insect pests (e.g. aphids, mites, etc.) could attack crops. Tropical diseases such as malaria could spread to the UK

Growth of trees extends northwards and increases in altitude

Rising temperatures and lower winter snowfall could cause the Scottish skiing industry to disappear, but more people could spend the summer at home in southern England, e.g. during the heatwave of 1995, tourist spending in Kent, Surrey and Sussex reached a record £1.5 billion in July

Higher yield of oats, barley and wheat

Vines grown in northern England

Rising sea levels could flood estuaries and salt marshes, destroying wildlife habitats

–1.8°C

Low-lying areas near sea level (e.g. the Fens, Somerset) could be flooded unless sea defences are strengthened. This could destroy farmland

Plant and animal species living in high mountains (e.g. arctic alpine plants, mountain hares, etc.) could become extinct

Higher yields of potatoes, sugar beet and outdoor tomatoes

2.4°C

2.0°C

Warmer tropical air flows are holding more moisture and so bring more rainfall. The autumn of 2000 was the wettest on record and caused peak river flows for as long as 90 days in some parts of the UK

Higher yields of maize

Southern Britain could become drier causing severe water shortages. Society may have to adapt, e.g. by applying hose-pipe bans

Sunflowers grown as a commercial crop in southern England

Southern England has warmer summers, similar to those in south-west France today. There is a 1 in 40 chance that by 2012 south-east England will experience a heatwave that could kill 3000 people

Effects on environment
Effects on society/people
Effects on economy

▲ **Figure 34** The possible effects of climate change in the UK

Get Active

In groups, examine Figure 34. Discuss the possible effects of climate change in the UK.

1 Sort the effects into different categories:
   - positive and negative
   - long term and short term.
2 Will climate change be positive or negative for the UK? Why?

Extension

Use the internet to research information and develop a case study on the effects of climate change on an LEDC.

How can we deal with climate change?

We are all responsible for our own carbon footprint. As it is a global problem, international co-operation between governments is vital. One of the ground-breaking international treaties was signed in Kyoto in Japan.

The Kyoto Agreement of 1997

Many countries signed up to reduce emissions of greenhouse gases by 5.2% and are taking steps to introduce measures to slow down global warming.

- The USA signed up to the agreement but is still reluctant to make any cuts because it is worried that cuts will damage its economy. This is despite the fact that the USA produced 21% of global carbon dioxide in 1996 but had only 4% of the world's population. By 2002 the USA was the world's largest producer of carbon dioxide both in total and per person; it produced over 15 tonnes of carbon dioxide per person per year in 2002.
- Some LEDCs are trying to develop their economy and feel they need to increase their use of energy to create new jobs and improve their standards of living.
- It was suggested that compensation be paid to countries that lose money if less of their oil is used, and payments be made to LEDCs to help them adapt to climatic change.

Major carbon dioxide polluters (e.g. Japan) are able to buy carbon credits from less-polluting countries (e.g. Australia).

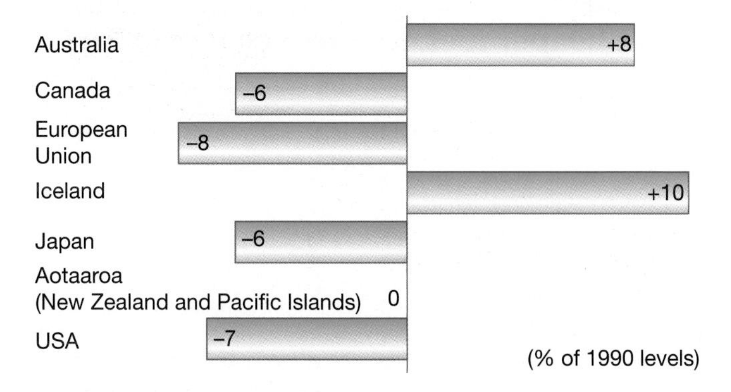

▲ **Figure 35** Greenhouse gas emission targets set at Kyoto, 1997

LEDCs are concerned that their economic development might be restricted if they also have to implement measures to reduce pollution.

The 2007 White Paper 'Meeting the Energy Challenge' sets out the British government's international and domestic energy strategy to address the long-term energy challenges faced by the UK, and to deliver several key policy goals. The main one is to put the UK on a path to cut carbon dioxide emissions by some 60% by about 2050, with real progress by 2020.

Rich Nations Urged to Transfer Green Tech

By Fu Jing

Premier Wen Jiabao on Friday urged rich nations to transfer greenhouse gas emissions-curbing technology to China and other developing countries, and address climate change responsibly by changing their unsustainable lifestyles.

The international community should establish a fund and mechanism for overcoming technology transfer barriers, he said in a two-day international climate change conference's opening speech.

He also said climate change efforts should not lose momentum despite challenges.

'As the global financial crisis spreads, the international community must not waver in its determination to tackle climate change.'

▲ **Figure 36** *China Today* news article, 8 November 2008

Alternative sources of energy

As fossil fuels are very polluting and contribute to climate change we will have to begin using alternative energy sources which are less harmful to the environment. Instead of burning oil or coal for energy, more renewable energy sources will become an increasingly important sector of electricity production.

In 2007 the percentage of primary energy derived from major sources was as follows:

- oil: 38.0%
- natural gas: 37.7%
- coal: 16.7%
- nuclear power: 5.8%
- renewable: 1.8%.

The British government's goal for renewable energy production is to produce 20% of electricity in the UK by the year 2020. The 2002 Energy Review set a target of 10% to be in place by 2010/11. The target was increased to 15% by 2015 and most recently the 2006 Energy Review further set a target of 20% by 2020.

In 2005, the UK's end-use energy percentage was approximately:

- transport: 35%
- space heating: 26%
- industrial: 10%
- water heating: 8%
- lighting/small electrics: 6%
- other: 15%.

Transport accounts for the biggest single cause of energy use in the UK. In order to address this, the government is trying to reduce the use of private cars. Public transport is receiving government investment and actions are being taken such as having priority bus lanes to make this form of transport a faster option than driving to work. Congestion charging has been effective in some cities such as London.

Renewable energy

- *Advantages*. The main advantage associated with using renewable energy is the lack of greenhouse gas emissions and other airborne pollutants. Once renewable energy plants are built the electricity generated is free.
- *Disadvantages*. The main problem with renewable energy sources is that they cannot generally be relied on as a continuous source of energy, for example tidal and solar energy are only available at certain times.

Get Active

Use the internet to help you create a PowerPoint presentation on the benefits of using wind power and solar power as alternative sources of energy.

Cheaper fuel from recycled chip fat

CHEAP fuel in return for a bucket of old chip pan oil is being offered to motorists in Northern Ireland.

Special buckets are being given out by a Tyrone fuel company to collect used cooking oil to be recycled into "biodiesel".

A full bucket of fat collected from the frying pan or chip pan earns – under a special promotion – seven pence per litre off a fill-up at the pumps.

O'Neill's Fuels in Coalisland is believed to be the first company in Ireland to produce and sell biodiesel on a commercial basis – and it costs a lot less than ordinary diesel to buy.

The company has been developing the product for the past two years and has just put it on the market – and motorists can't get enough.

Not only does it cost a lot less, but it appears to provide the odd extra mile to the litre.

Director Tracy O'Neill said she had put it on sale at their own garage but hoped to eventually supply every filling station in Northern Ireland.

Biodiesel is suitable for all cars and is around 20p cheaper than the ordinary stuff.

"The benefits of this fuel are numerous," she said.

"It's low-sulphur fuel, therefore there are lower emissions into the atmosphere. It's also cheaper."

"Most people just dump their used cooking oil so this is a good chance for them to play their part in helping the environment."

▲ **Figure 37** Newspaper article on biodiesel

Get Active

Using ICT, draw an appropriate graph to show what energy was used for in the UK in 2005.

Reduction on private car usage

Get Active

1 Study Figure 38 which gives information about congestion charging for vehicles in London.
   a Explain how congestion charging helps control traffic within the charging zone.
   b Suggest how the congestion charge helps London become a more sustainable city.
   c For a named city in the European Union (EU) (excluding the British Isles) state fully how *one other* control measure has reduced a traffic problem (see page 196).

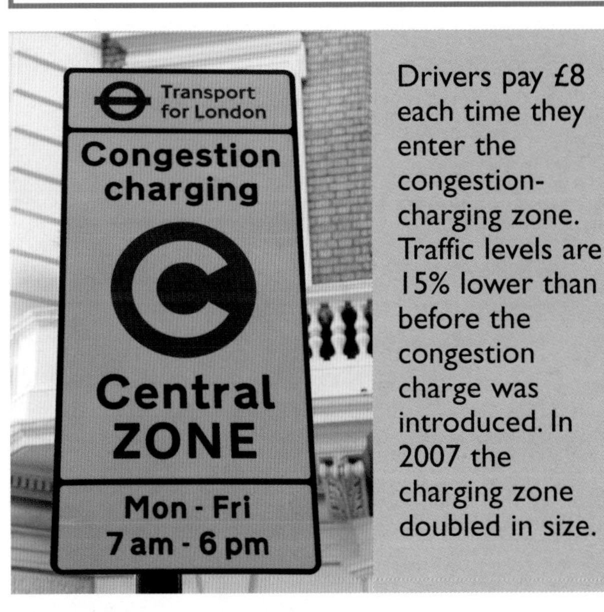

▲ **Figure 38** London's congestion charge

Slowing deforestation

Trees act as stores of carbon and release oxygen into the atmosphere, so the more trees there are in the world the better. In LEDCs attempts are being made to slow down the rate of habitat destruction. The deforestation of tropical rainforests is of particular concern as many of the trees are burned in the process and in so doing release more carbon dioxide into the atmosphere.

In the USA a proposed policy called REDD (Reducing Emissions from Deforestation and Degradation) aims to compensate tropical countries for safeguarding their forests. This is already happening using the money markets. In February 2008 a historic deal was struck between a London-based firm (Canopy Capital) and the government of Guyana. They bought a 371,000 ha reserve in the South American country, and planned to develop the environmental services provided by the forest.

In May 2008 Prince Charles called for rainforest protection to fight climate change. Ending the destruction of tropical rainforests is the simplest step to helping address climate change, said Prince Charles in an interview with the BBC: 'When you think [rainforests] release 20 billion tonnes of water vapour into the air every day, and also absorb carbon on a gigantic scale, they are incredibly valuable, and they provide the rainfall we all depend on.'

'The trouble is the rainforests are home to something like 1.4 billion of the poorest people in the world. In order to survive there has to be an effort to produce things which tends to be at the expense of the rainforest,' he continued. 'What we've got to do is try to ensure that those forests are more valuable alive than dead. At the moment there's more value in them being dead. This is the crazy thing.'

▲ **Figure 39** Transcript from a radio show

● weblinks

www.ciel.org

http://news.mongabay.com

http://environment.nationalgeographic.com/environment/global-warming/quiz-global-warming.html and www.geogonline.org.uk/Global%20Warming%20-%20Quiz.htm – Quizzes on global warming.

http://video.google.com/videoplay?docid=62576642154215189688&hl=en, http://video.google.com/videoplay?docid=2078944470709189270&hl=en and http://video.google.com/videoplay?docid=84534423778781754 40&hl=en – Short video clips to raise discussion on how the issue is viewed.

Get Active

1 Describe in detail two sustainable solutions to the problem of global warming.
2 Explain why a) the USA and b) LEDCs have important parts to play in reducing global warming.
3 To what extent are each of the principles established at the World Summit on Sustainable Development sustainable?
4 Explain why it is so difficult to reach sustainable solutions to global warming.

Many countries are trying to reduce their carbon emissions, but it costs money and means people must also change their attitude about lifestyle. If all the world's people lived the kind of life which we do here in Northern Ireland, we would need the resources of eight planets. A big issue about climate change includes individual choice and responsibility. Are we ready to own less? To travel more by bus or train? Government policies can even seem contradictory, with taxes on the most polluting cars, but yet plans being discussed about adding new runways to airports to allow more planes to fly. There must also be international co-operation because the pollution mostly is being generated by MEDCs who are also rich enough to come up with some solutions to climate change issues, such as better flood defences for cities. Yet the effects of their pollution also affects countries that emit few greenhouse gases.

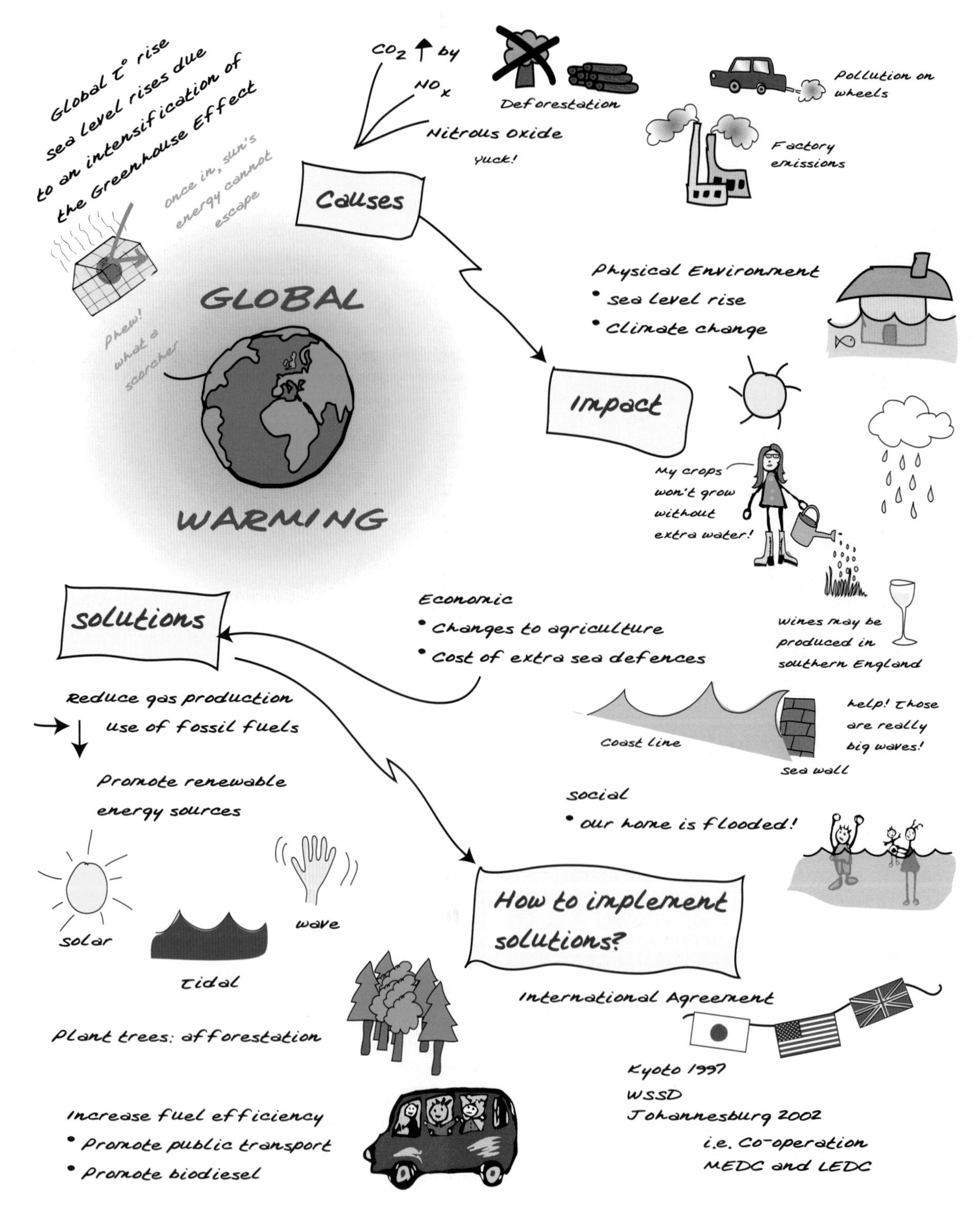

▲ **Figure 40** Spidergram for global warming

Get Active

Extension

The spidergram in Figure 40 shows visually what one person knows and understands about global warming. In groups:

1. Review the spidergram. Does it show the full picture? Are there any gaps or important omissions?
2. Revise the spidergram in the light of all the things you have learned in the course of this unit.

What have I learned?

In groups, look more closely at one of the UK case studies on the Met Office website www.metoffice.gov.uk/education/teens/:

- Boscastle floods (August 2004).
- Bodmin snow (November 2005).
- Strong winds (June 2004).

1. Describe the type of weather experienced.
2. Outline the area affected.
3. Describe the impact on people, the built environment and the natural environment.
4. Relate what happened to what you have learned about weather (theory) in this chapter.

In your groups you must decide on how to present your information to the rest of the class. Remember to include a location map, photographs, satellite images and weather charts. Make sure that each person in the group understands their role and what is expected of them. Present to the rest of the class.

Have a look at today's weather for the UK.

1. Get a chart like the one below at: www.metoffice.gov.uk/weather/uk/surface_pressure.html.

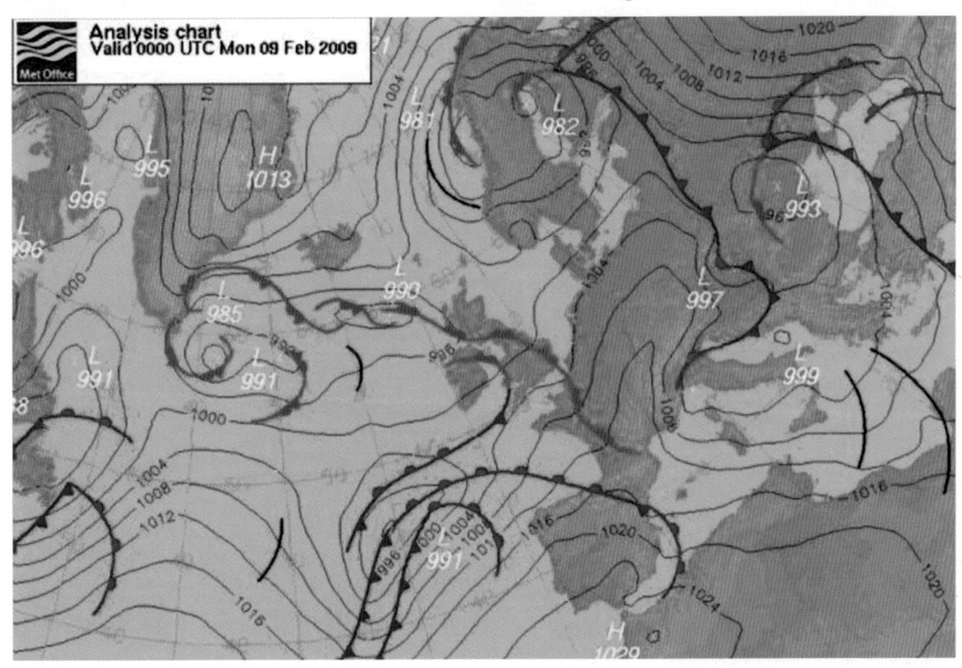

2. Get the latest United Kingdom weather observations at: www.metoffice.gov.uk/education/archive/uk/observation_0.html.
3. Prepare a 1-minute weather forecast for England, Scotland, Wales and Northern Ireland to be read out on a national radio station.

Sample examination questions

1 Measuring the elements of the weather

Foundation Tier

(i) State if the following sentences are true or false. One has been completed for you.

Air pressure is measured in millibars ___True___

Temperature means how hot or cold it is ____________

Wind speed is measured in millimetres ____________

A rain gauge measures rainfall ____________

An anemometer measures temperature ____________ [4]

(ii) Explain why thermometers must be placed in the shade. [3]

(iii) State the meaning of the term weather. [2]

(iv) Explain how satellites can help to create a weather forecast. [3]

Higher Tier

Picture of weather instrument	Name of instrument	Element of weather measured	Unit of measurement
	Wind vane		Compass points
	Maximum–minimum thermometer	Temperature	
			mb

(i) Complete the table. [4]

(ii) Explain the difference between weather and climate. [3]

(iii) Name the instrument used to measure rainfall and explain two factors which must be taken into account when placing this instrument within a land-based weather station. [5]

2 Weather systems affecting the British Isles

Foundation Tier

(i) Underline the type of air mass which brings warm and wet air. Choose your answer from the list below.

Tropical continental Tropical maritime Polar maritime [1]

(ii) Describe the typical weather a summer anticyclone brings to the British Isles. [3]

(iii) Explain why depressions can cause problems for people. [4]

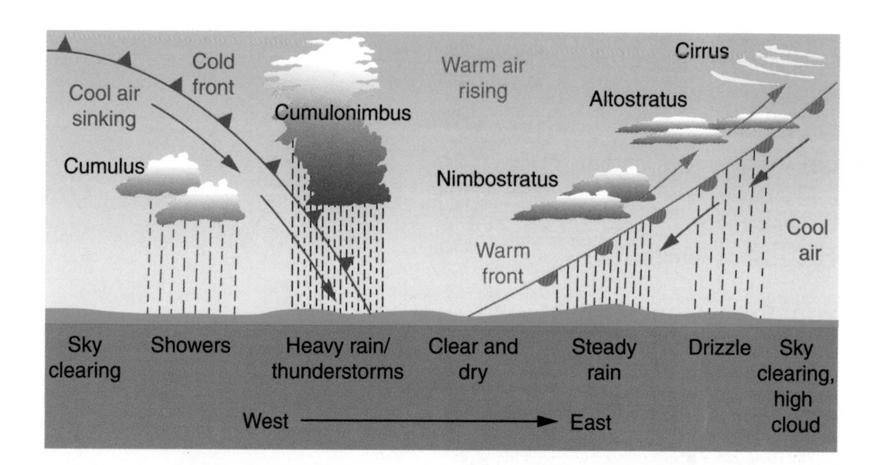

(iv) Using the diagram above, state the sequence of cloud types an area experiences as a depression passes. [4]

Higher Tier

(i) Name the air mass which brings warm and moist air to the British Isles. [2]

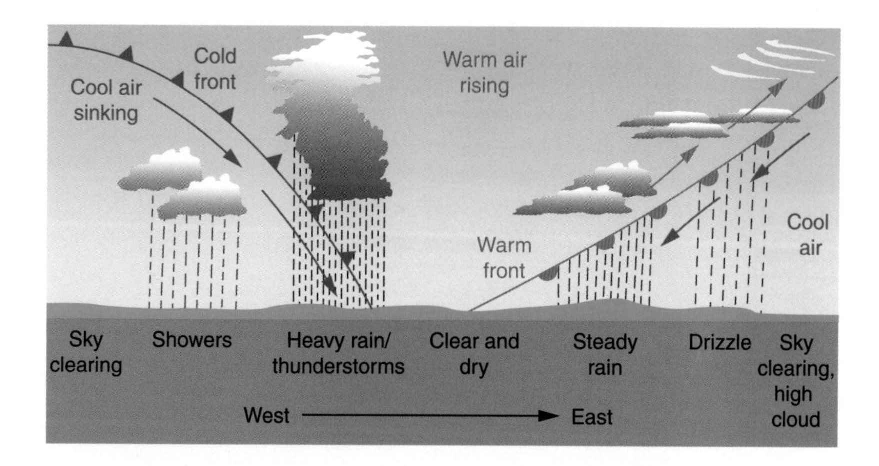

(ii) Using the diagram above, describe the sequence of weather experienced in a place a depression passes. Name cloud types in your answer. [5]

(iii) Compare the negative effects depressions and anticyclones have on the economy of an area. [6]

3 The causes and consequences of climate change

Foundation Tier

(i) State the meaning of the term greenhouse effect. [2]

Study the information below on how polar bears are threatened by global warming. Answer the questions which follow.

Global warming blamed for the death of polar bears

Since 1979 over 20% of the polar ice cap has melted due to global warming. A growing number of polar bears are drowning as they are forced to swim more often, and for longer distances, in search of food.

(ii) State one way in which global warming is causing the death of polar bears. [2]

(iii) State the meaning of the term global warming. [2]

(iv) Explain how global warming might be caused by human activities. [4]

(v) Name one country which is being affected by climate change and describe how climate change is impacting upon its environment. [4]

Higher Tier

(i) Explain how the greenhouse effect works. [4]

(ii) Describe and explain one cause of climate change. [4]

(iii) Evaluate the effects of climate change on the environment of a country which you have studied. [6]

(iv) Evaluate at least two strategies which you have studied which deal with climate change and explain why it is hard to secure international agreement on climate change. [9]

UNIT ONE

Understanding Our Natural World

The Restless Earth

Learning outcomes

In this theme you will learn:

- to recognise rock types and explain how they were formed
- to describe the structure of the Earth
- what the theory of plate tectonics is and what the processes and landforms associated with plate margins are
- what the landscape features associated with tectonic activity are
- why earthquakes occur in the UK and what their impacts are
- to interpret global earthquake patterns and understand how they link to plate tectonics
- about the outcomes of earthquakes
- what the cause, impacts and response are of two earthquakes: one in an MEDC and one in an LEDC.

The Restless Earth

Basic rock types

How are rocks formed?

Rocks are classified by the manner in which they were made, how they have been changed and what they are made from. There are three basic **rock types**.

Igneous rocks

These are formed when molten lava or magma cools and hardens. If the lava has been exposed on the surface, it may cool quite quickly, producing few if any crystals within its structure. The Giant's Causeway in County Antrim is made of one such stone – basalt. If the igneous rock is made from magma that cooled slowly underground, then large mineral crystals form, and speckled igneous rocks form. The granite that is found in the Mourne Mountains in Co. Down was created this way.

Sedimentary rocks

Weathering and erosion of rocks produce sediments, small fragments or particles, which accumulate on land, coasts and marine environments. Over time, layers of these fragments form on top of one another, causing the air and moisture to be squeezed out, and a solid rock to be created. These are sedimentary rocks. The line between layers of sediment is a line of weakness called a bedding plane.

As well as being made from fragments of rocks, sedimentary rocks can be made from the chemicals left after the evaporation of water, or from layers of plant and animal remains. Occasionally, plant and animal remains do not get crushed by the process and remain trapped in the rock as a fossil.

Metamorphic rocks

The final group of rocks is the metamorphic rocks. These are rocks that have been altered or changed by extreme heat or pressure. They were once either igneous or sedimentary rocks. Sometimes the pressure and heat have changed the rock so much that it can be very hard to tell what it originally was.

We can do simple experiments to investigate the origin of metamorphic rocks. Marble is a

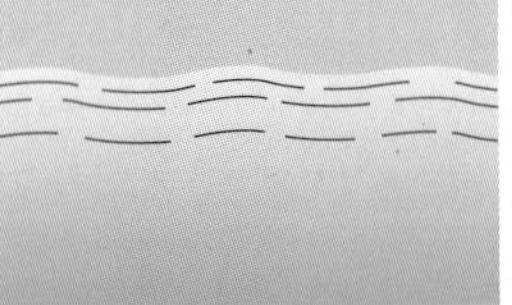
Over 300 million years ago the land that became the UK was under the sea

Fish and other creatures were the only inhabitants

When these creatures died the skeletons and shells became sediment

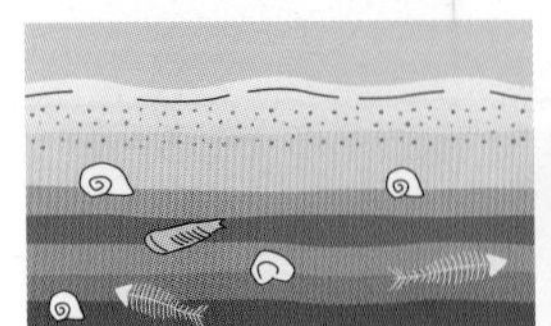
Over the millennia, the sediment grew thicker and heavier

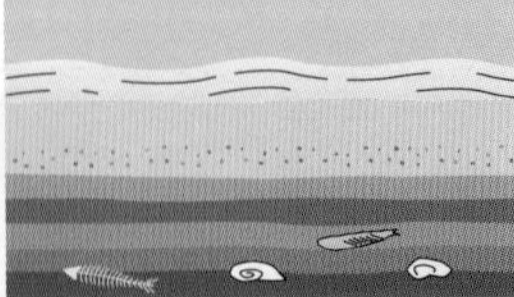
The sediment was compressed and it became limestone

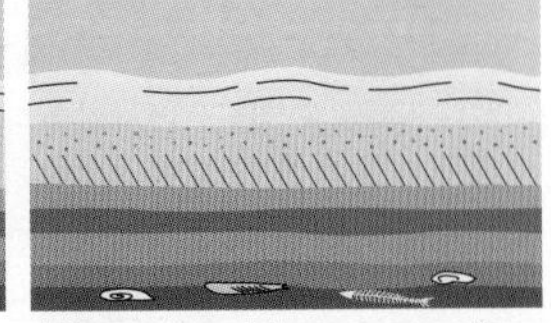
Rivers would carry sand and grit to the sea, when these fell as sediment they eventually became sandstone and gritstone

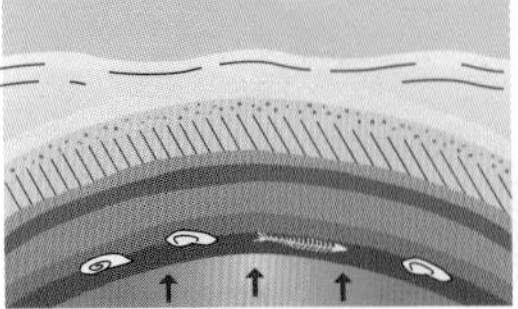
Strong forces in the Earth's crust began to push the seabed upwards

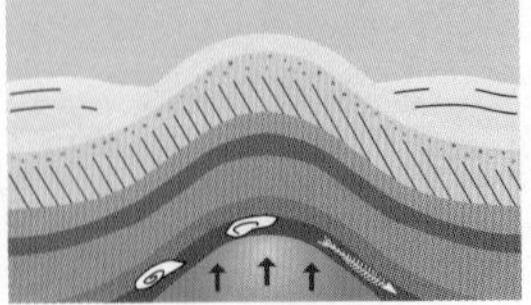
As the sea drained away, the rock that was on the seabed became dry land

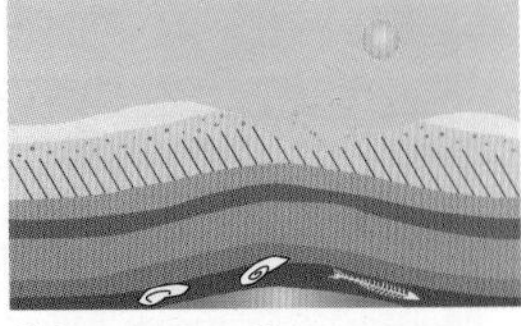
We can see the sedimentary rocks, e.g. limestone and sandstone that are formed in this way.

▲ **Figure 1** How sedimentary rock is formed

metamorphic rock that fizzes when acid is poured on to it, just like limestone fizzes under the same experimental conditions. Further chemical analysis of the two types of rock shows that they are both mostly made from calcium carbonate. The fragments of shell that created the limestone have been crystallised by heat to make marble.

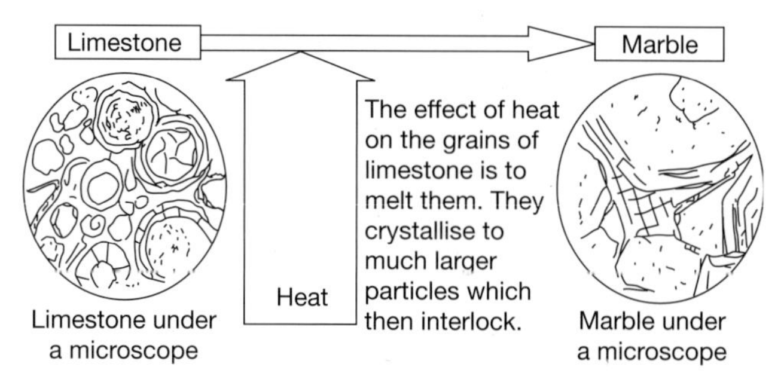

▲ **Figure 2** The metamorphosis of limestone into marble

● Rock-spotter's guide

There are hundreds of different kinds of rocks, but every rock is either sedimentary, igneous or metamorphic. All these rocks are made from pure minerals, but their method of creation is very different.

Figure 3 shows some of the most common rocks and crystals.

Igneous rocks	Sedimentary rocks	Metamorphic rocks
Granite	*Limestone*	*Slate*
Rough texture and speckled colour, often pink or grey. Glittery crystals can be seen. Hard and non-porous rock.	Grey, white or yellow rock. May be hard. You see fossils and layers. Porous.	A dark grey rock with layers which are easily split apart. The surface of each layer is smooth. Impermeable on the flat surface.
Basalt	*Sandstone*	*Marble*
Very hard, dark grey rock. Often feels rough and heavy. Small glittery speckles may be visible.	Rock made from grains of sand. No crystals. Feels rough to touch and is quite hard. Sand will rub off it.	May be pure white or have swirly bands of colour running through it. Unpolished, it feels rough and grainy.

▲ **Figure 3** Rock-spotter's guide

Get Active

- What is the difference between basalt and granite? How would you know which one you had in your hand if someone gave you either to examine and describe?
- Limestone is an example of a sedimentary rock. In your own words, explain how it was formed. Find out (perhaps by completing an internet search) some areas in Northern Ireland, Ireland and Britain where limestone can be found.
- Look for a geology map of Ireland (you could find one on the internet). Name some metamorphic rocks found in Ireland and the UK and name the areas where they are found. Present your findings in a simple table.

Plate tectonics theory

What is the Earth like inside?

The Earth is made up of a series of layers.

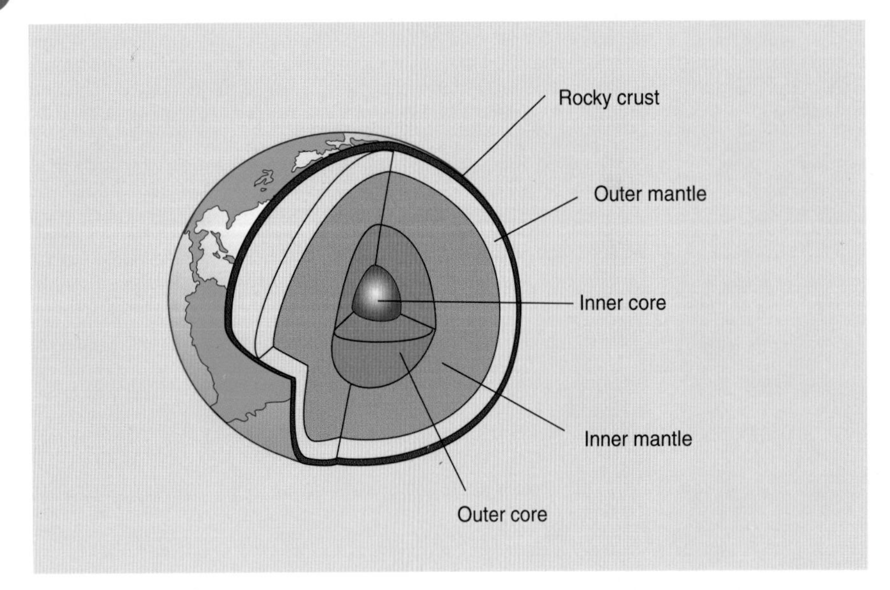

▲ **Figure 4** Layers of the Earth. Did you know you are moving even though you think you are sitting still on your chair in a classroom? The bit of the Earth you are sitting on is moving at 70 mm per year. The Earth is revolving round the Sun at 30 km per second. Our solar system is revolving around the centre of the galaxy at 300 km per second and even our galaxy is moving through the universe at 600 km per second! Astonishing speeds!

Is the Earth's crust solid?

Plate tectonics theory proposes that the Earth's **crust** is split into sections called **plates**. These plates are constantly moving around on top of the **mantle**, at an average speed of 70 mm per year. The places where plates meet, called **plate margins**, are related to seismic (**earthquake**) and volcanic activity.

The consequences of such movements of landmasses and having new oceans and seas opened are far reaching. It has influenced climate change and even the spread of plants and animals.

What causes plate movement?

In a more detailed cross-section of the Earth (Figure 5) it can be seen that the crust on which we live acts as though it is floating on a layer of molten material, called the mantle. Inside the Earth there are **convection currents** within the mantle, moving heated molten material upwards from the **core**, up towards the crust. Here it cools and sinks back down to the core, so that the cycle can start again. It is these convection currents that cause the crust above them to move.

Where currents descend (go downwards) they drag crust into the mantle, creating a destructive plate margin. Here crust is destroyed as it descends down into the hot mantle, where it melts.

Where currents ascend (rise up) they pull the crust apart, creating a constructive plate margin. Molten material from the mantle rises to plug the gap in the crust, creating new crust.

It was these same convection currents that first broke up the crust, creating plates. The theory that explains this process and the related landforms and hazards is plate tectonics theory.

All this moving of plates has affected the **geology** of Ireland, as we have not always been located between 50 and 60° north of the equator. Indeed 500 million years ago Ireland was not a single island and we were in the southern hemisphere!

The tropical ocean location we had about 300 million years ago allowed deep layers of marine clays and limestone to be laid down. This limestone creates the bedrock of almost half of Ireland.

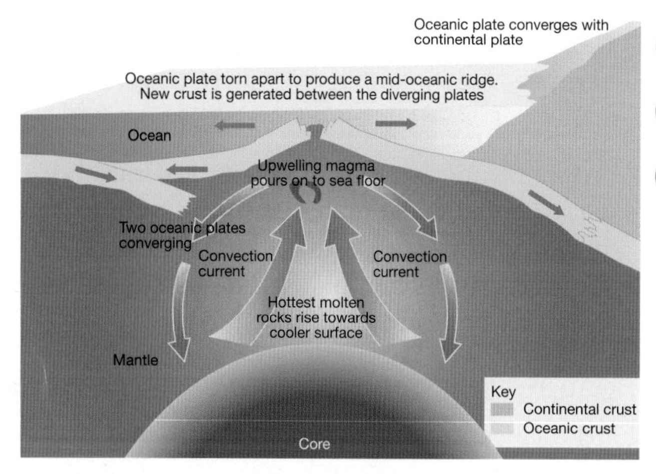

▲ **Figure 5** Convection currents in the mantle

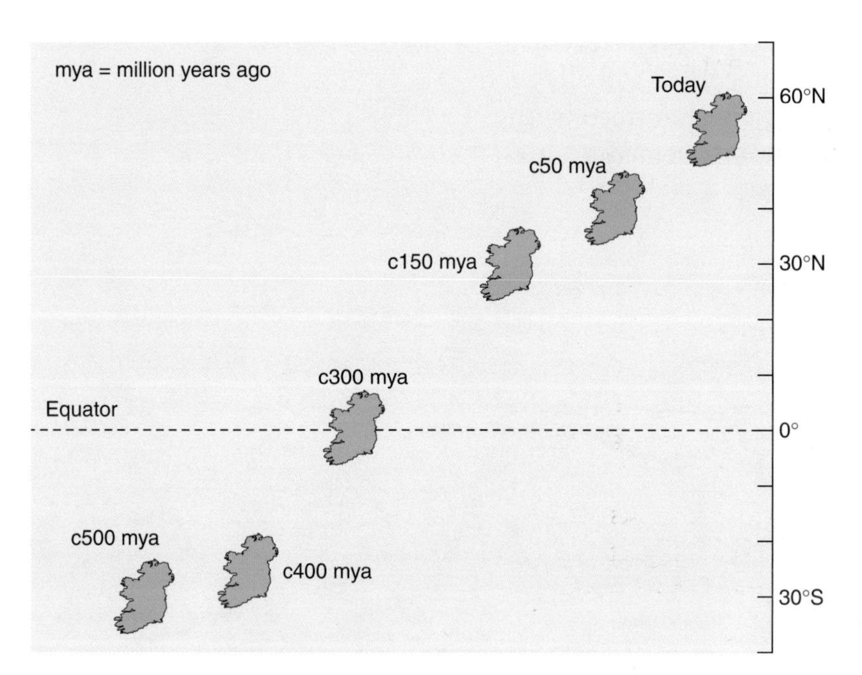

▲ **Figure 6** The changing position of Ireland over the past 500 million years caused by plate movement

Get Active

Quoting actual information from Figure 6, in terms of latitude explain how the location of Ireland has changed in the past 500 million years. As well as quoting historical references, remember to give directional movements.

Types of plate margin

There are three main types of plate margin:

- Constructive: when plates are pushed apart, so they move away from one another and new crust is created.
- Destructive: when plates crash into one another and crust is destroyed.
- Conservative: when plates slide past each other. Crust is neither created nor destroyed.

Features of plate margins: earthquakes and volcanoes

Earthquakes are the shaking of the ground surface caused by a sudden movement of the Earth's crust. Earthquakes can happen anywhere but, as Figure 7 shows, they are mostly found along three main belts:

- encircling the Pacific Ocean
- along the coast of the Mediterranean Sea and through southern Asia, towards the Pacific Ocean
- through the middle of the Atlantic, Southern and Indian oceans.

Figure 7 also shows the location of some of the most recent earthquakes. Remember, earthquakes are very frequent events. There are more than 150,000 earthquakes recorded globally each year. The world's main fold mountains have been formed by the buckling of the Earth's surface during crustal movements felt as earthquakes.

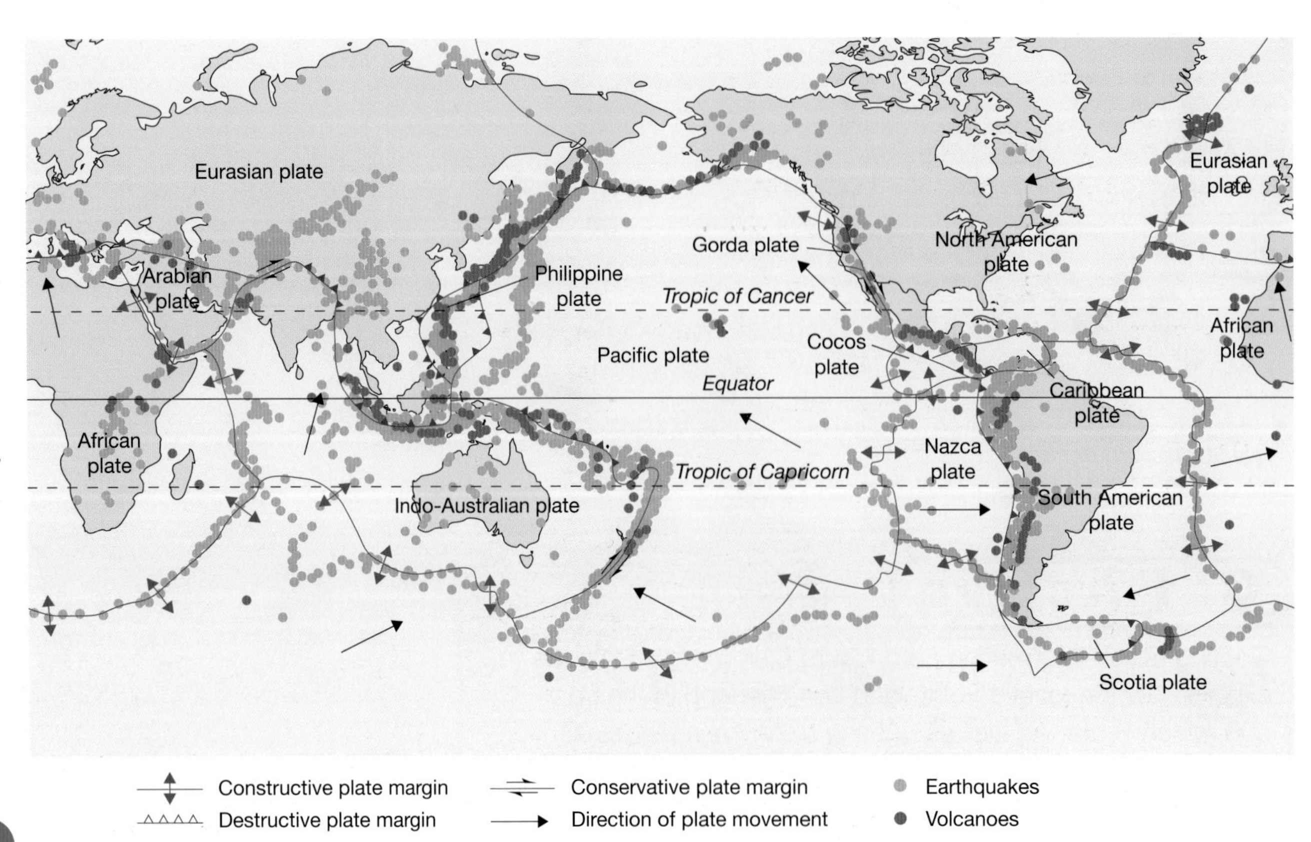

▲ **Figure 7** Global map showing earthquake activity, volcanic activity and plate margins

Volcanoes are mountains, often cone-shaped, formed by surface eruptions of magma from inside the Earth. During eruptions, lava, ash, rock and gases may be ejected from the volcano. Figure 7 shows the location of areas that experience volcanic activity. They also form three main belts:

- around the edge of the Pacific Ocean – known as the 'ring of fire' because there are so many active volcanoes
- through the Mediterranean Sea, and down the east coast of Africa
- down the middle of the Atlantic Ocean.

Volcanoes are also found in isolated clusters, such as the Hawaiian Islands in the middle of the Pacific Ocean, and Réunion in the Indian Ocean.

When we look at the locations of areas that have both earthquakes and volcanoes (zones of activity) we see a definite pattern which corresponds to plate margins.

Get Active

Examine Figure 7. To complete this activity you will need to have an atlas.

1 Name three countries that experience both volcanoes and earthquakes.
2 Name the main countries that make up the 'ring of fire'.
3 What type of plate margin is found:
   - south-east of Australia?
   - south-west of Australia?
   - west of South America?
4 In which direction are the following plates moving:
   - the Nazca plate west of Chile?
   - the Indo-Australian plate south of India?
   - the North American plate east of USA?

Features and characteristics of each plate margin

The features and hazards of each plate margin depend on the type of margin (constructive, destructive or conservative) and the type of crust involved (oceanic or continental).

The table in Figure 8 summarises the characteristics of the two different types of crust.

Oceanic crust	Very dense (heavy). Mean density is 3000 kg m^{-3}.	Thin: 5–10 km	Can sink into the mantle	Easily destroyed	Young crustal material
Continental crust	Less dense (light). Mean density is 2700 kg m^{-3}.	Thick: 30–70 km	Does not sink easily into the mantle	Hard to destroy	Old crustal material

▲ **Figure 8** The characteristics of oceanic and continental crusts

Get Active

In your own words, describe oceanic and continental crusts. How do they differ?

Constructive margin

One constructive margin is found in the middle of the Atlantic Ocean. Here the Eurasian and North American plates are being pulled apart, moving away from one another. This means the Atlantic Ocean is getting wider by about 3 cm a year. This movement causes regular, but weak earthquake activity. Magma wells up from the mantle to plug the gap, so there is often frequent, gentle volcanic activity even here under the ocean. This rising of material causes the crust to rise slightly at either side of the plate margin creating a **mid-oceanic ridge**. The volcanoes found along the ridge are called smokers. This chain of volcanic mountains is the longest in the world and means that the middle of the Atlantic is relatively shallow. The hardened lava erupted from volcanoes forms new crust.

Constructive margins are also found where continental crust is splitting apart.

Rift valleys are seen at constructive margins on continental crust. One example is the Great Rift Valley in eastern Africa.

Plan view

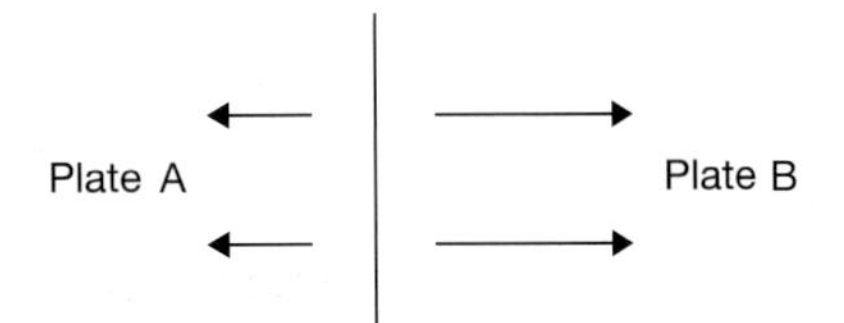

Cross-sectional view

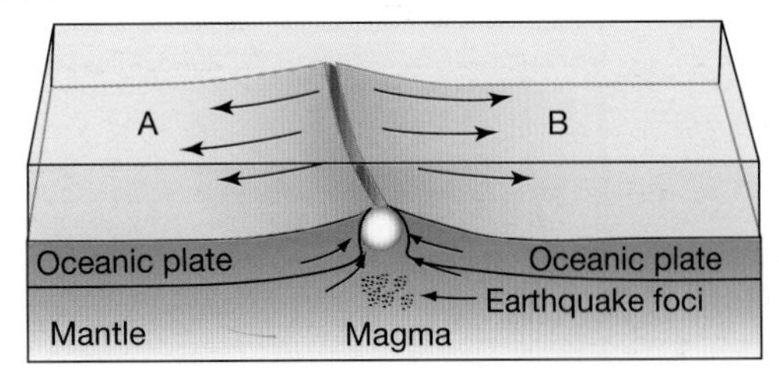

▲ **Figure 9** Constructive (spreading) margin

Get Active

- How is an oceanic ridge formed?
- What is meant by the term 'smoker'?
- Do an internet search on the Great Rift Valley in eastern Africa. Explain how it was formed and describe what it looks like today. Illustrate your answer with an annotated photograph or labelled sketch or diagram.

Destructive margin

Destructive margins have a zone of **subduction**. Here crustal material is being pulled into the mantle, where it melts and is destroyed.

This type of margin falls into three types:

1. Oceanic crust crashing into continental crust.
2. Oceanic crust crashing into oceanic crust.
3. Continental crust crashing into continental crust. (Collision zone.)

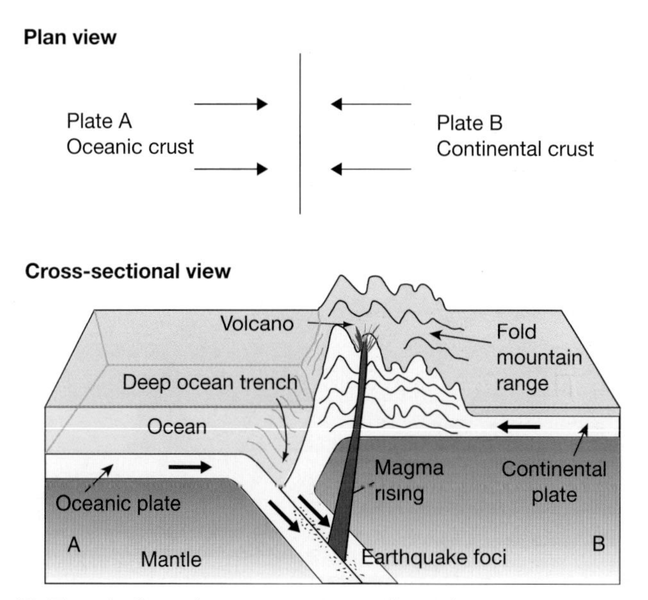

▲ **Figure 10** Type 1: Oceanic crust meets continental crust

Oceanic crust–continental crust margin

An example of where oceanic crust is crashing into continental crust can be found on the western coast of South America. Here the Nazca plate, made of oceanic crust, is disappearing below the South American plate. At the plate margin, the heavy oceanic crust is being pushed downwards into the mantle. It is dense (heavy), and so it falls below its normal level as it sinks into the mantle, creating a deep **ocean trench** called the Peru–Chile trench. This linear trench follows the line of the western coast, and is very deep in places. It is up to 8050 m deep!

The movement of the Nazca plate against the South American plate is not smooth, because of the friction between the rough surfaces. The plates may become stuck for years, until the pressure for the plates to move is greater than the friction preventing them from moving. The pressure is released suddenly and the two plates will jolt many centimetres at once. This sudden movement is felt on the Earth's surface as an earthquake. The further inland the earthquake occurs, the deeper its focus will be (the point of origin of an earthquake below the Earth's surface) and the weaker the shockwaves are when they reach the surface – meaning a less destructive earthquake.

As the Nazca plate is subducted (disappears down) into the mantle, it begins to melt due to intense heat. Because it was once oceanic crust, it is saturated with water. The magma created is therefore chemically different from any naturally found in the mantle – it is full of gas bubbles, created by the evaporating water. Together these mean that this melted oceanic crust is less dense (lighter) than the surrounding mantle, so it rises upwards as an explosive type of magma. If it breaks through the surface, it creates a volcano (e.g. Cotopaxi and Chimborazo in Ecuador). The continental crust that makes up the South American plate is not dense like oceanic crust, so it is not subducted easily. Instead it folds and buckles upwards to create a linear fold mountain range, such as the Andes.

Get Active

Find the names of any mountains that rise to 8050 m.

Get Active

Create volcano fact files on Cotopaxi and Chimborazo.

As a class, decide on the information that must be included in the volcano fact file. Think about textual information (e.g. facts and figures, etc.) and visual information (e.g. location maps, photographs, explanatory diagrams or sketches).

Work in pairs to prepare the volcano fact files.

Oceanic crust–oceanic crust margin

An oceanic crust margin, where oceanic crust and oceanic crust meet, has many similar features to the first type of destructive margin. An arc of volcanic islands and a deep ocean trench are located at this margin. In fact, the oceanic trench can be even deeper; for example, the deepest part of the Mariana Ocean trench, in the Pacific, is 11,022 m. This could easily swallow Mount Everest, the tallest mountain on the surface, which is 8848 m in height. There are no fold mountains as there is no continental crust to buckle upwards.

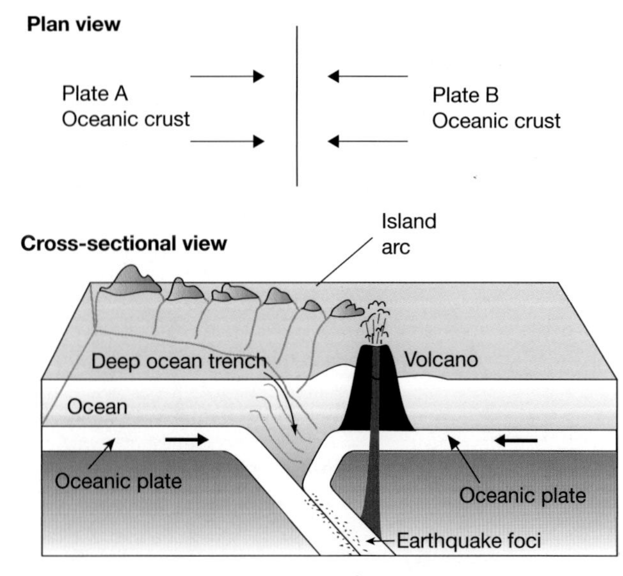

▲ **Figure 11** Oceanic crust meets oceanic crust

Get Active

Look back at Figure 7. Where can an arc of volcanic islands be found?

Continental crust–continental crust margin

Where two continental plates meet is a collision zone, the crusts of both plates buckle and fold upwards. The two sets of fold mountains overthrust one another, creating a large range of high mountains. There is little material melting, and that which does cannot make it through the high mountains to create a volcano. Instead the magma forms large intrusions into the mountain range, called batholiths. The magma cools slowly to form granite cores to the mountains. Good examples of mountains formed at this type of margin include the Himalayas and the Zagros ranges.

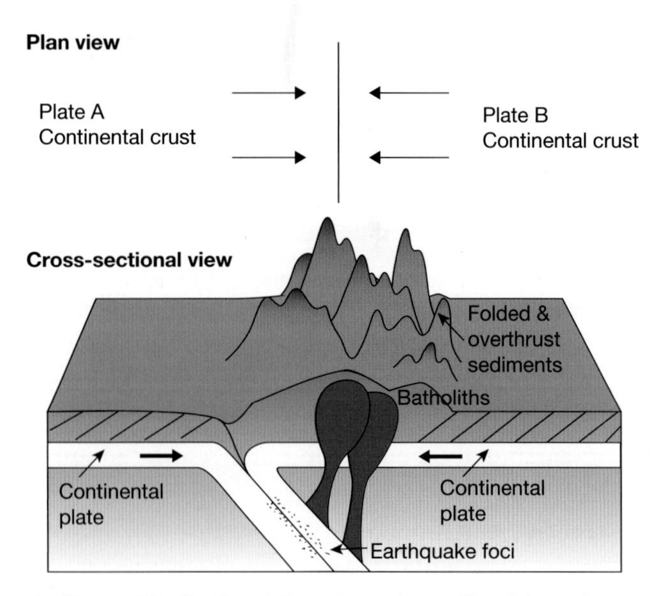

▲ **Figure 12** Continental crust meets continental crust

Get Active

Describe in your own words how the Himalayan mountains were formed.

Conservative margin

At conservative margins, such as the San Andreas **fault line** in California, two plates try to slide past one another. When friction causes the two plates to stick, pressure to move builds up. This pressure is eventually released as an earthquake when the plates move suddenly. As crust is neither created nor destroyed at conservative margins, there are no volcanic eruptions. Over 20 million people live along the San Andreas fault. The movement along this conservative margin can be seen in offset streams and orchards.

● weblinks

http://geology.com/plate-tectonics.shtml – An interactive map of some tectonic landforms.

www.geography-site.co.uk/pages/physical/earth/tect.html – History and rules of plate tectonics.

www.weatherwizkids.com/volcano1.htm – A simple intro and good animation.

www.enchantedlearning.com/subjects/astronomy/planets/earth/Continents.shtml – Lots of facts and interactive quizzes.

Get Active

Find out about the San Andreas fault (you could carry out a Google search). Read a number of the key articles. Try Google Images to see if you can find any relevant and interesting photographs.

Your task is to produce an A3 poster on the San Andreas fault. It should include:

- a location map
- a photograph
- explanatory text
- anything of interest that you find out.

Tectonic activity in the British Isles

Evidence for tectonic activity is all around us in the British Isles. We may not have active volcanoes today, but evidence of the most recent eruptions (almost 50 million years ago) is now one of the most famous tourist sites: the Giant's Causeway, Co. Antrim, Northern Ireland.

Basaltic columns

The basalt which poured out along the causeway cooled down very slowly in a large hollow. The contraction which happened on cooling created almost perfect hexagonal and pentangular columns. These were later exposed following coastal erosion. The Giant's Causeway is so important it was made Ireland's only world heritage site.

▲ **Figure 13** The Giant's Causeway

Get Active

1. Complete an internet photograph search for the Giant's Causeway.
2. Save the photographs you like best.
3. Print out these photographs.
4. Create a photograph collage on the Giant's Causeway.
5. Choose your favourite photograph of the Giant's Causeway.
6. Explain why you like this particular photograph. What sets it apart from the others?

Lava plateau

During the Tertiary era outpourings of lava created the large expanse of the Antrim plateau. This is an extrusive feature which covers an area over 3900 km^2 in the north-east of Northern Ireland. Rather then erupting through a mountainous volcano, these basalts rose to the surface through long fissures (cracks in the crust through which lava erupts). From Cave Hill along to Divis mountain is the visible edge of the **lava plateau** where it stopped just short of Belfast. Today this geographical feature is constricting the growth of Belfast in a northerly direction.

▲ **Figure 14** The edge of the basaltic plateau at Cave Hill, Belfast

Get Active

1. On an outline map of Northern Ireland mark on the location of the Antrim plateau.
2. Using an atlas, find out the altitude of the highest point on the Antrim plateau. Name this particular location.
3. Find out about the character of the landscape on the Antrim plateau. How would you describe it? What does it look like?
4. What do you think most of the land on the Antrim plateau is used for? Outline the reasons for your answer.

Volcanic plug

A **volcanic plug** is an intrusive feature formed when magma hardens inside the vent of a volcano. The resulting rock called dolerite is more resistant to erosion than the flanks of the volcano, so can be exposed following erosion of the surrounding rock, producing a distinctive landform called a plug.

One example of a plug is Slemish Mountain in Co. Antrim. It is about 450 m above sea level.

▲ **Figure 15** Slemish Mountain, Co. Antrim

Get Active

How was Slemish Mountain as we see it today formed? Draw a labelled diagram to illustrate your answer.

Do we have earthquakes in the British Isles?

Although we don't have frequent or devastating earthquakes in the British Isles, we do experience this hazard.

Most of the world's earthquakes occur at plate margins. However, the British Isles sits in the middle of the Eurasian plate and although we are far from any plate margin some of this stress is transmitted into the middle of the plate and can result in 'intraplate' earthquakes.

case study

The causes and impact of an earthquake in the British Isles

In February 2008 Market Rasen in Lincolnshire, England experienced the UK's largest earthquake in 25 years. It was a magnitude 5.2 earthquake. This quake was caused by the sudden release of stress along a nearby strike slip fault line. Many of the impacts were recorded by the BBC.

▲ **Figure 16** Diagram of a strike slip fault

▲ **Figure 17** Experiences of the earthquake

Get Active

1 Find out more about the earthquake in Market Rasen. Begin by looking at: www.marketrasenmail.co.uk/news/Massive-earthquake-hits-Rasen.3818704.jp.

- Do an internet search on the earthquake in Market Rasen. Get all the details, including the testimony of eye witnesses (try websites of news outlets such as the BBC, CNN or Sky News).
- Make detailed notes.
- Save photos and any relevant maps and explanatory sketches or diagrams.
- Use all the information you have collected to write your own front-page newspaper report on the event. (You could use Microsoft Publisher or any other software package that allows you to create a newspaper report including both text and visuals.)

2 When were the most recent earthquakes in the UK? When and where did they happen and how severe were they? To find out visit: www.earthquakes.bgs.ac.uk.

- Make a copy of the table like the one below to record your findings:

Recent earthquakes in the UK		
Date	**Location**	**Magnitude**

Earthquakes: can they be managed?

Earthquakes are a natural hazard. Major earthquakes can release the same amount of energy as a large nuclear explosion. The destructive power of an earthquake is measured by the amount of energy it releases. Earthquakes are recorded using **seismographs**.

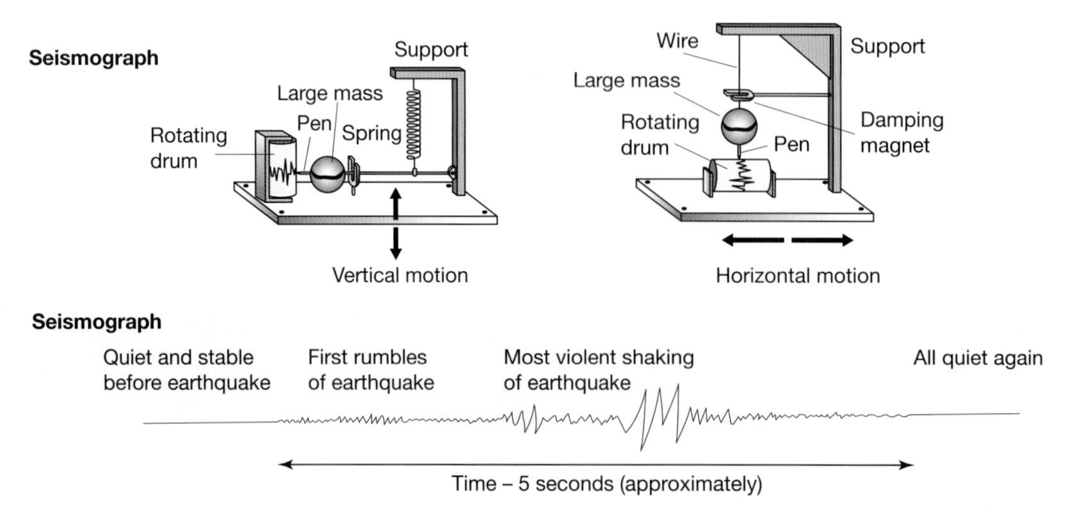

▲ **Figure 18** A seismograph diagram

The paper tracing of the seismic waves (seismogram) is then converted to a level on the **Richter scale**. The Richter scale ranges from 0 to 9, with each point on the scale representing an earthquake 10 times the magnitude and which releases 30 times more energy than the point before. Figure 19 shows the whole Richter scale.

Earthquake size (magnitude measured by seismograph)

Possible effects

Scale	Possible effects
0	
1	
2	Normally only detected by instruments
3	
4	Faint tremor, little damage
5	Structural damage to chimney-pots
6	Distinct shaking, poorly built houses collapse
7	Major earthquake, large concrete buildings destroyed
8	
9	Ground seen to shake, fissures open up

Earthquake	Magnitude
Assisi 1997	5.7
Iran 2003	6.3
India 1993	6.4
San Francisco 1989	6.9
Kobe 1995	7.2
El Salvador 2001	7.6
India 2001	7.9
San Francisco 1906	8.2
Lisbon 1755 (largest estimated modern earthquake)	8.8

▲ **Figure 19** The Richter scale measures the size of the seismic waves during an earthquake

The main features of an earthquake are shown in Figure 20. The place where an earthquake starts is termed its **focus**. Shock waves spread from this point, like ripples on a pool after a stone is dropped in. The most deaths and maximum destruction are normally seen right at the **epicentre**, the point directly above the focus, where shock waves are first felt on the surface. The amount of damage decreases as distance increases from the epicentre. This is described as a negative relationship.

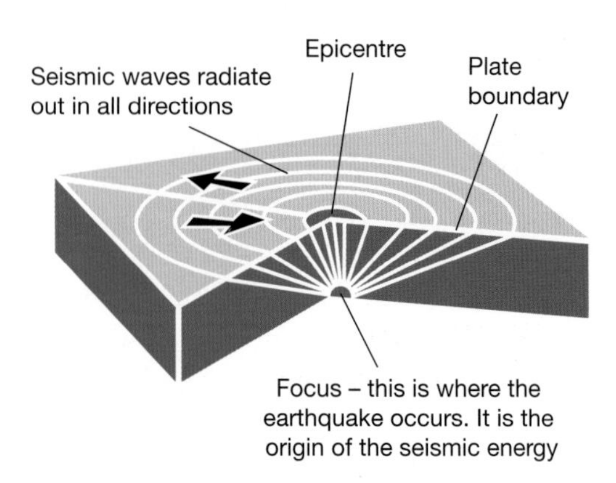

▲ **Figure 20** Features of an earthquake

The global distribution of earthquakes

The global distribution of earthquakes shows a **linear pattern** and is closely related to plate margins.

The main belts/lines of earthquakes are:

- around the Pacific Ocean (the ring of fire)
- down the middle of the Atlantic Ocean
- in a line linking the Atlantic and Pacific Oceans going through southern Europe and Asia.

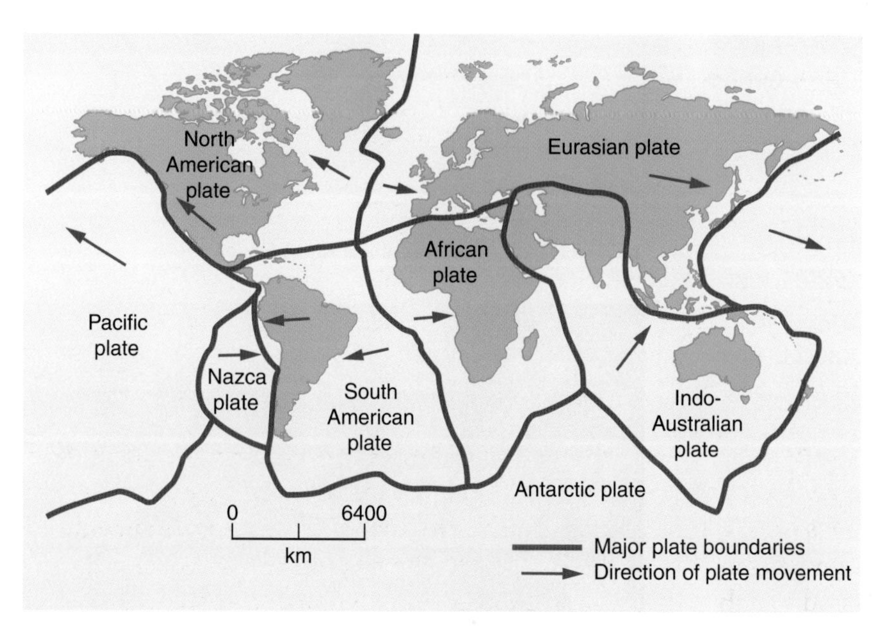

▲ **Figure 21** Main global plates

Get Active

What is the connection between what is shown in Figures 7 and 21?

Earthquakes can have physical impacts on the place they happen. Two of the main ones are **liquefaction** and **tsunamis**.

Liquefaction happens when an earthquake shakes wet soil. The water rises to the surface and turns solid soil into liquid mud. Buildings can sink into this mud.

A tsunami is a large wave of seawater that can travel for thousands of miles and is triggered by an underwater earthquake. Every time you slide around in the bath and make the water create waves that slap over the edge of the bath you have created your own mini-tsunami.

These physical impacts are discussed in more detail by using case studies.

Get Active

1 Check out the following website: www.ce.washington.edu/~liquefaction/html/what/what1.html.
   - Explain liquefaction in your own words.
2 Check out the following website: www.ess.washington.edu/tsunami/index.html.
   - Describe how tsunamis form.

case study

An earthquake event in an MEDC: Kobe, Japan

The Kobe earthquake occurred at 5.46 a.m. on 17January 1995. During the quake the ground moved up to 1.2 m vertically and 2.1 m horizontally. It measured 7.2 on the Richter scale and lasted only 20 seconds. The damage was so great because it was a very shallow earthquake; the focus was near to the surface. The epicentre was 20 km south-west of central Kobe, making it very close to the second most densely populated area of Japan.

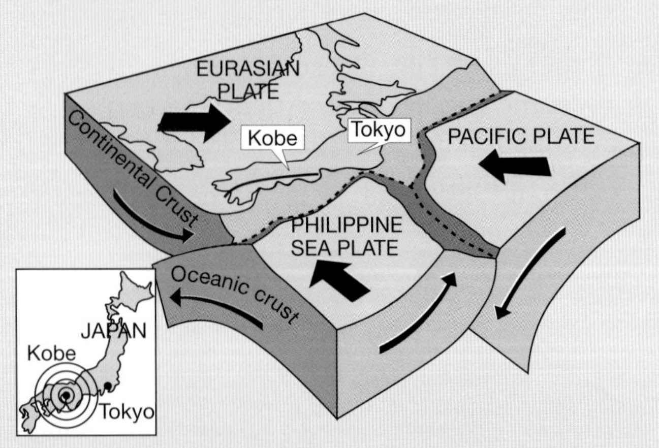

▲ **Figure 22** Plate margin of Kobe Bay

Causes

Japan is next to a destructive plate margin, where three plates meet (see Figure 22). Just off the Kobe coastline a dense oceanic plate, the Philippine plate, is being subducted under the lighter continental Eurasian plate at a rate of approximately 10 cm per year. The movement of one plate against the other has led to many earthquakes in this region of Japan.

Key
RED = IMPACT ON PEOPLE
GREEN = IMPACT ON ENVIRONMENT

Short-term impacts

Over 40,000 were injured as buildings, roads and bridges collapsed.

Over 200,000 buildings collapsed. Many of these were the two-storey wooden houses built just after the Second World War. They only had thin walls, but a heavy roof made of tiles. During the quake the roofs tended to fall in, collapsing the walls as they did so.

Transport routes were disrupted. A 1-km stretch of the Hanshin Expressway collapsed and the track of the Shinkansen bullet train snapped in eight places. The roads became grid locked, delaying ambulances and fire engines.

The wetter ground here suffered liquefaction, that is when shaking brings underground water to the surface, turning what was solid ground into mud. Industry in the area, including major firms such as Mitsubishi and Panasonic, was forced to close. More than 90% of the port's berths were destroyed by liquefaction.

▲ **Figure 23** Kobe Bay – after the earthquake

More than 150 fires, started by the broken gas mains and sparks from cut-off electrical cables, raged for days in the city, destroying an estimated 7500 homes. These fires released acrid (foul-smelling) smoke into the air, creating a smog so thick that it obscured the Rokko Mountains behind the city.

It is worth noting that all of the initial impacts happened in about 20 seconds!

Long-term impacts

Over 5500 people died. Some died as buildings, roads and bridges collapsed, but more died in the fires that broke out all over the city.

It took until July before water, electricity, gas and telephone services were fully operational, and until August for rail services to get back to normal.

One year later the port of Kobe was 80% functional, but the Hanshin Expressway remained closed.

It took a long time to rebuild the houses and repair buildings. Even in January 1999 some people were still living in temporary accommodation.

Right-lateral surface faulting was observed for 9 km with horizontal displacement of 1.2–1.5 m in the northern part of Awaji Island. Also on Awaji Island a **landslide** changed the shape of the fields.

▲ **Figure 24** A fault line in a field on Awaji Island as a result of the 1995 earthquake

What was the management response?

The Japanese have always had to live with the threat of earthquakes. Once they attributed the Earth **tremors** to the thrashing of a giant catfish called Namazu. Today, the Japanese have put their faith in science and research to help them predict earthquakes, engineer earthquake-proof buildings and co-ordinate the most efficient quake relief.

Before the earthquake: prediction and precautions

The Japanese are perhaps the world leaders in designing buildings to withstand earthquakes, using springs or rubber pads to absorb the shock of the tremors. However, the Kobe earthquake was the worst to hit Japan since 1948. A section of the elevated Hanshin Expressway collapsed. Although the Expressway had been designed to withstand earthquakes, it had not been strengthened to current standards.

Minor tremors are felt in Japan nearly every day. As a result, millions of pounds are spent strengthening buildings by adding things like cross-beams that will spread any shockwaves more evenly across a building or by using specially reinforced concrete in construction. Buildings are stronger than in California and some of the more modern buildings survived the earthquake. The Kansai International Airport and Akashi Bridge, which were newly opened in 1995, were both undamaged, presumably due to their high-tech construction.

Japan has a public education programme, producing pamphlets, broadcasts and lectures about earthquake survival. On the anniversary of the Great Quake of 1923, each 1 September, there is a public holiday to practise earthquake drills.

Tokyo Metropolitan government
What to do if a big earthquake hits

The worst shake is over in about a minute, so keep calm and quickly do the following:

- Turn off all stoves and heaters. Put out fires that may break out. Do not become flustered by the sight of flames, and act quickly to put out the fire.
- Get under a table or desk to protect yourself.
- Open the door for an emergency exit. Door frames are liable to spring in a big quake and hold the door so tight they cannot be opened.
- Keep away from narrow alleys, concrete block walls and embankments, and take temporary refuge in an open area.
- For evacuation from department stores or theatres, do not panic and do as directed by the attendant in charge.
- When driving in the streets, move the car to the left and stop. Driving will be banned in restricted areas.
- Evacuate to a designated safety evacuation area when a big fire or other danger approaches.
- Walk to an emergency evacuation area. Take the minimum of personal belongings.
- Do not be moved by rumours. Listen for the latest news over the radio.

Households are encouraged to keep earthquake kits, containing bottled water, rice, a battery powered radio, a fire extinguisher and blankets.

A 10-day supply of water is stored in underground cisterns and quakeproof warehouses.

Get Active

How do you explain why the Hanshin Expressway collapsed while the Akashi Bridge and Kansai International Airport remained undamaged as a result of the earthquake?

Get Active

Read 'What to do if a big earthquake hits' from the Tokyo Metropolitan government. In groups, rank these actions from 1 to 9, giving Rank 1 to the action that you feel is the most important thing to do.

Immediate and long-term action after the earthquake

An increased number of seismic instruments to record and measure Earth movements were installed in the region.

In the late 1990s laws were passed that meant all buildings and transport structures had to be even more quakeproof:

- high-rise buildings had to have flexible steel frames
- small buildings had to have concrete frames with reinforced bars to absorb shock waves
- houses were to be built from fire-resistant materials, not just bricks and wood
- new buildings had to be built on solid rock, not clay or landfill material.

Get Active

Kobe is an example of an earthquake that happened in an MEDC some years ago. Your task is to investigate a more recent (in past 12 months) earthquake that happened in an MEDC:

- You could begin by visiting the following website: http://earthquake.usgs.gov/eqcenter/recenteqsww/.
- You could Google 'earthquakes in the last 12 months' and follow the links.
- Choose the event that is of interest to you.
- Organise your research findings in a PowerPoint presentation. Your slides should include text and visuals:
  - location map
  - photographs
  - date and time of earthquake
  - casualties
  - damage
  - impact on people
  - impact on the environment.
- Present your case study to the rest of the class.

weblinks

www.absconsulting.com/resources/Catastrophe_Reports/Kobe,%20Japan%20EQ%201995.pdf – This website gives information about the lessons learnt after the Kobe earthquake. It has many good images.

case study

An earthquake event in an LEDC: Indian Ocean earthquake 2004

On 26 December 2004, as many people went about their normal business and holidaymakers started to make their way down to the sun-soaked beaches, a magnitude 9.2 earthquake occurred off the west coast of Sumatra, Indonesia, in the Indian Ocean. Some of the people that the earthquake's effects later killed would not have even known the earthquake had happened. It was the second largest earthquake ever recorded on a seismograph and had the longest recorded duration, lasting almost 10 minutes.

Causes

There is a major fault line where the Australian plate meets the smaller Sunda plate at the Sunda trench. It is part of a subduction zone. A 15-m slippage along this fault line happened in two stages and led to this prolonged earthquake. As well as the plates moving sideways, the ocean floor rose by several metres and caused the devastating tsunami that marked this infamous earthquake.

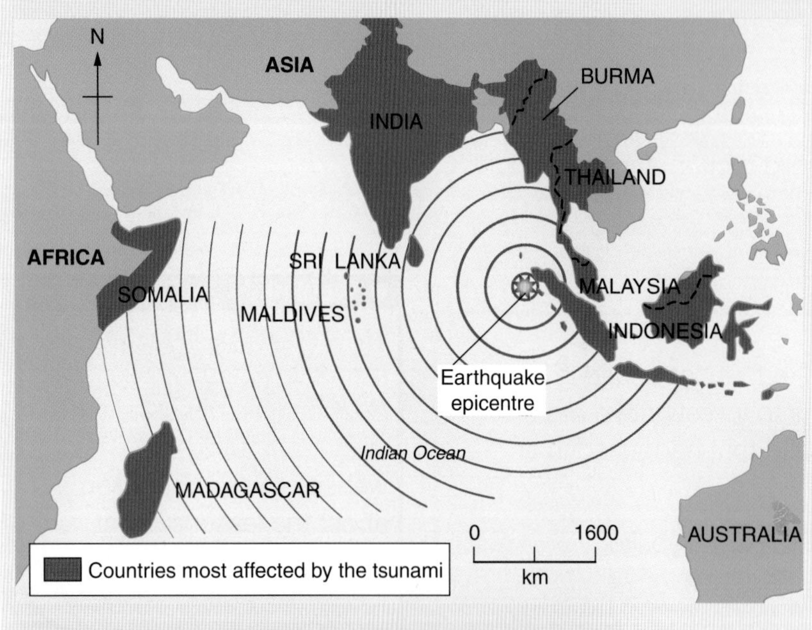

◄ **Figure 25** Location map showing the epicentre of the 2004 Indian Ocean earthquake

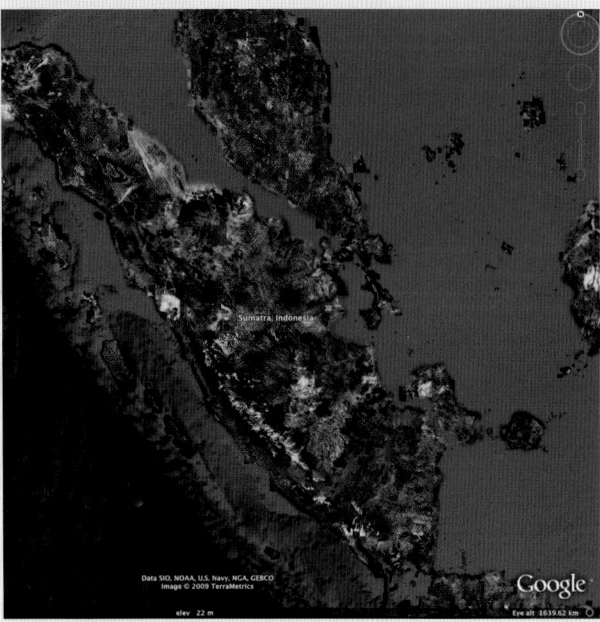

▲ **Figure 26** Satellite image of the Sundra trench region

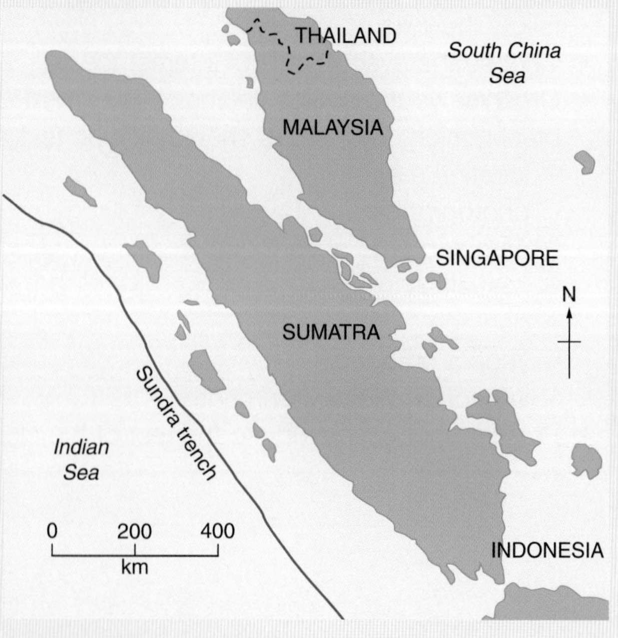

▲ **Figure 27** A map of the Sundra trench region

KEY

RED = IMPACT ON PEOPLE
GREEN = IMPACT ON ENVIRONMENT

▲ **Figure 28** Emergency aid was needed to rescue people of all ages. This photograph shows South Korean firefighters who came to help in the search of ruins of hotel buildings in Khao Lak beach resort on Thailand's western coast

Short term

Sixty-six per cent of the fishing fleet of Sri Lanka was destroyed. This had important economic implications as fishing provided direct employment to a quarter of a million people on the island.

Conservative estimates record over 125,000 people were injured.

A tsunami wave reaching 30 m high travelled in a circular motion from the epicentre affecting countries on all sides of the Indian Ocean.

The whole Earth vibrated by 1 cm due to the energy released by this slippage. The energy released on the Earth's surface was the equivalent of 1502 times that of the atomic bomb exploded in Hiroshima.

Aftershocks triggered by the main earthquake continued to shake the region for another 3–4 months.

Just over 1.1 million people were temporarily displaced due to coastal devastation.

Long term

The raising of the seabed reduced the capacity of the Indian Ocean and raised global sea level by 0.1 mm.

The confirmed death toll was just under 187,000. About one-third of this total were children.

The coastal ecosystems of the areas affected by the tsunami have been severely damaged, including mangrove and coral reefs.

In the Maldives, 17 coral atoll islands had their freshwater supply contaminated by seawater after being overwhelmed by waves. This has rendered them uninhabitable for decades.

There has been widespread mental trauma as it is a traditional Islamic belief that relatives of the family must bury the body of the deceased, but in many cases no body has been retrieved for such a burial.

The massive release of energy is expected to shorten the length of a day by 2.68 microseconds because of a change made to the shape of the Earth.

One positive result was that the tragedy became the reason why a rebel group declared a ceasefire with the Indonesian government.

case study

What was the management response?

Although the area affected by this earthquake is within a zone of activity which is used to minor quakes and volcanic eruptions, it is made up of poor LEDCs and they lack the resources to have the scale or quality of response that MEDC areas like Japan can afford.

Before the earthquake: prediction and precautions

Prior to this earthquake there was no early warning system in place to record such underwater quakes within the Indian Ocean. One island called Simeulue did evacuate its coastal areas. People felt the tremor and fled to inland hills before the tsunami struck. In northern Phuket, an island west of Thailand, a young geography student called Tilly Smith recognised the warning signs of an approaching tsunami wave. She and her parents warned others and the beach was safely evacuated. Most places had no such warnings, so thousands of people were on the beaches enjoying a holiday or preparing to begin a day of fishing. Watch her story on http://movingimages.wordpress.com/2007/10/10/geography-lesson-that-saved-many-lives-the-story-of-tilly-smith/.

◄ **Figure 29** Tilly Smith, shown with former US President Clinton, recognised warning signs and persuaded her parents to alert people to evacuate the beach before the tsunami struck

Know the warning signs of a tsunami

An earthquake is a natural tsunami warning. If you feel a strong earthquake do not stay in a place in a coastal location.

If you see the ocean pulling out unusually rapidly or far, it is a good sign that a big wave is on its way. The sea may even bubble or froth. Go to high ground immediately. In the Indian Ocean quake people had about 5 minutes between the sea receding and the wave arriving.

A tsunami is a series of waves, so do not go back to the coast until you are told it is safe to do so.

When on holiday or at home keep a store of emergency supplies that include medications, water and other essentials sufficient for at least 72 hours. Any natural disaster can come without any warning.

Immediate and long-term action after the earthquake

Immediately after the earthquake the world pulled together to provide aid and expertise to the stricken areas. Over US$7 billion dollars were donated from nationals and non-governmental organisations (NGOs)

Many countries such as Sri Lanka, Indonesia and the Maldives declared a state of emergency to allow strict laws to be implemented to keep order and help with humanitarian aid distribution.

A review of the poor earthquake and tsunami warning system in place around the Indian Ocean took place and in June 2006 25 new seismographic stations became operational relaying information to national tsunami information centres.

◀ **Figure 30** One task that faced countries was clearing up the beaches and burying the dead to reduce the threat of disease. Elephants were even used to help

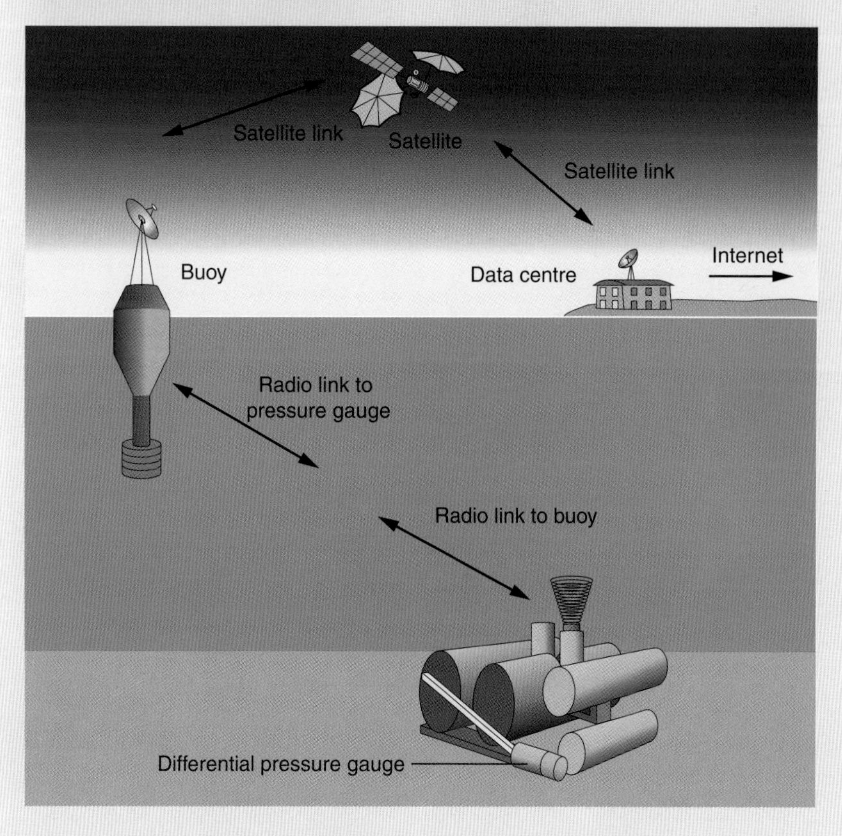

◀ **Figure 31** Diagram showing one positive outcome of this earthquake: a tsunami warning system for Indonesia

Get Active

1. With a partner, look at and discuss what the spidergram shows.
2. Working together, create a similar spidergram for the Indian Ocean earthquake.
3. Look at those created by others.
4. Revise your original attempt to show what you now know about the Indian Ocean earthquake.

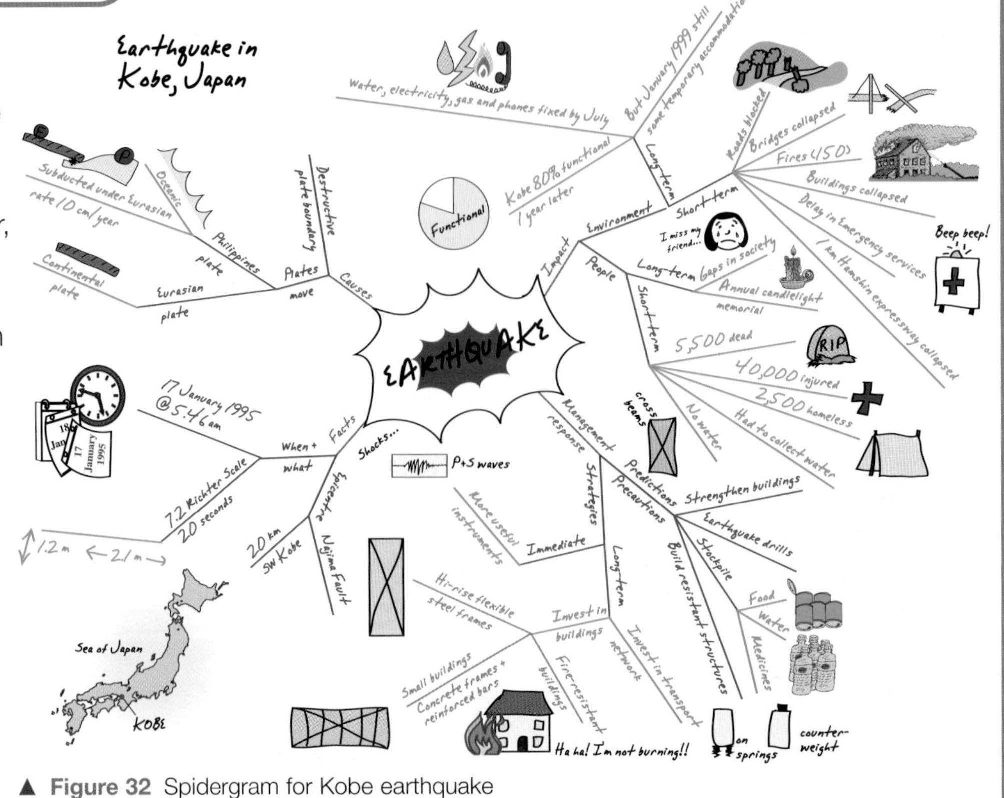

▲ **Figure 32** Spidergram for Kobe earthquake

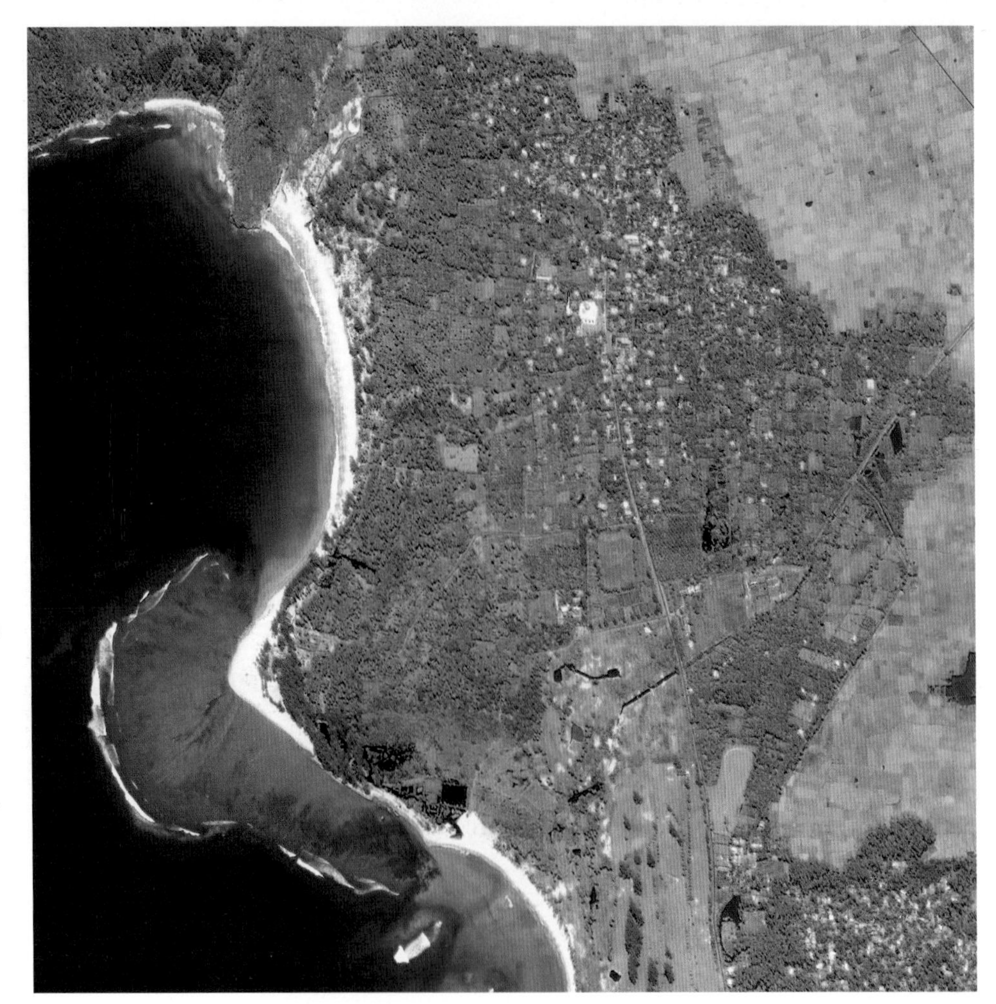

► **Figure 33** Stages of mapping the 2004 tsunami showing the use of GIS to show the impact of the tsunami on one small area of coastline. The town of Lhoknga, on the west coast of Sumatra, Indonesia, was completely destroyed by the tsunami, with the exception of the mosque (white circular feature) in the city's centre. This page shows the region before the tsunami struck and on the opposite page the same area after the tsunami hit

As fast as a commercial jet

- Where the ocean is deep, tsunamis can travel unnoticed on the surface at speeds up to 500 mph (800 km an hour), crossing an ocean in a day or less. Scientists are able to calculate arrival times of tsunamis in different parts of the world based on their knowledge of water depths, distances, and when the event that generated them occurred.
- A tsunami may be less than 30 cm in height on the surface of the open ocean, which is why they are not noticed by sailors. But the powerful shock wave of energy travels rapidly through the ocean, as fast as a commercial jet. Once a tsunami reaches shallow water near the coast, it is slowed down. The top of the wave moves faster than the bottom, causing the sea to rise dramatically.

Get Active

1 How do you explain a tsunami like the one that happened on 26 December 2004? Look at the animation at the following website: http://news.bbc.co.uk/cbbcnews/hi/newsid_4130000/newsid_4132400/4132491.stm.
   - Go to: 'Guide to Earthquakes'.
   - Scroll down to: 'Tsunami: animated guide'.
   - Watch the animation.
   - Explain what happened in nine steps.

2 Tell the story of how the tsunami affected one person or a family.

Sample examination questions

1 Basic rock types

Foundation Tier

(i) Name the two igneous rocks from the list below

Slate Sandstone Basalt Limestone Granite [2]

(ii) Explain how limestone is formed [4]

Higher Tier

(i) Name two igneous rocks. [2]

(ii) Compare the formation of slate and limestone. [6]

2 Plate tectonics theory

Foundation Tier

(i) Complete the following statements about plate tectonics. Choose your answers from the list below.

Crust Fold Destructive Core Liquefaction

- A plate is a piece of the Earth's ________________. It moves because heat from the ____________ of the planet makes the mantle move.
- The largest ____________ mountains are found at collision zones. [3]

Study the diagram below which shows the destructive plate margin where the Nazca plate meets the South American plate. Use it to help you answer questions (ii)–(iv).

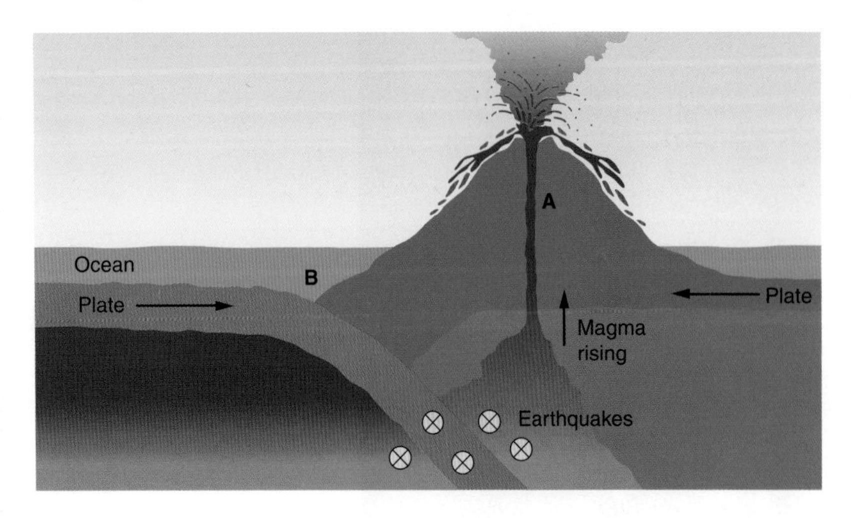

(ii) State the meaning of the term **plate**. [2]

(iii) Write out and complete **Table X** by matching the letter to the feature named.

Table X

Feature	Letter
Volcano	
Ocean Trench	

[2]

(iv) State whether the following sentences are true or false.

(v) Explain how an ocean trench is formed at a destructive margin. [4]

Higher Tier

(i) Explain why plates move. [4]

	True/false
The Nazca and South American plates are moving apart	
Earthquakes and volcanic eruptions happen at destructive margins	
The South American plate is made of continental crust	

(ii) Describe and explain the formation of two landforms associated with a destructive margin. [8]

3 Tectonic activity in the British Isles

Foundation Tier

(i) Describe and explain the causes of an earthquake you have studied which happened in the British Isles.

Name of place and date of earthquake

____ [1]

Causes of the earthquake [4]

(ii) State one difference between a lava plateau and basaltic columns. [2]

Higher Tier

Describe and explain the formation of a volcanic plug. [6]

With reference to an earthquake which happened in the British Isles, explain the causes of the earthquake and outline its main impacts. [9]

4 Earthquakes: can they be managed?

Foundation Tier

(i) Explain why earthquakes often happen at plate margins. [4]

Study the diagram below which shows part of a Red Cross Home Earthquake Plan for Americans. It gives people tips on how to prepare for an earthquake. Use it to help you answer question (ii).

How to prepare for an earthquake

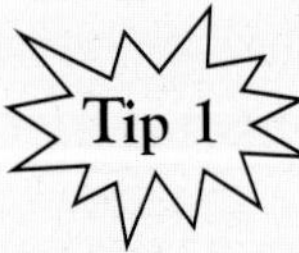

Learn how to use a fire extinguisher.

Bolt bookcases, china cabinets, and other tall furniture to a wall.

Have lots of bottled water stored in a safe place.

(ii) Choose **two** of the tips shown and explain how they would help reduce the amount of damage or deaths caused by an earthquake. [6]

(iii) For a named area you have studied, describe the precautions taken to reduce the impacts of earthquakes:

- named area [1]
- precautions [4]

Higher Tier

Study the diagram below which shows the destructive plate margin where the Nazca plate meets the South American plate. Use it to help you answer the two questions.

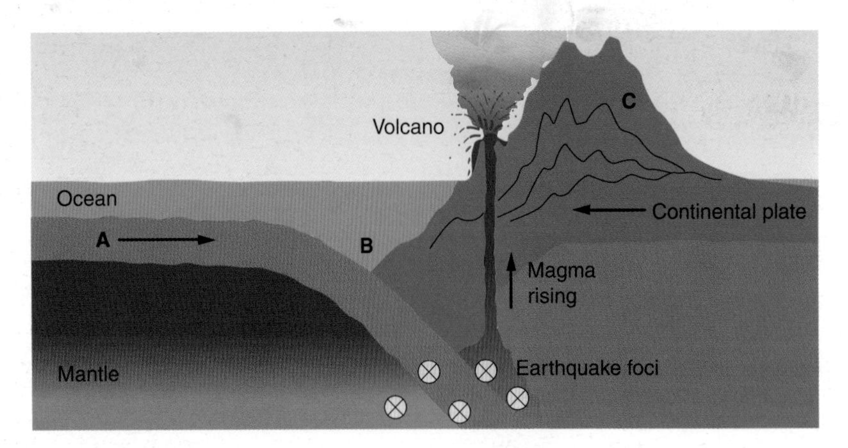

(i) State the meaning of the term **plate**.

(ii) Copy out and complete the table below by naming the features seen at a destructive plate margin. [3]

Letter	Feature
A	
B	
C	

(iii) Explain why liquefaction may be a hazard associated with earthquakes. [4]

(iv) Compare the immediate and long-term strategies taken after an earthquake you have studied in an MEDC and an earthquake you have studied in an LEDC. [9]

UNIT TWO

Living in Our World

People and Where They Live

Learning outcomes

In this theme you will learn:

- why the world's population is growing
- how to use a GIS
- the impact of migration into a country
- what population structure is
- what settlements are and how they work
- the reasons settlements grow
- how settlements can be planned
- how settlements can be made sustainable.

People and Where They Live

Population growth, change and structure

Birth and death rates

The population of the world is growing rapidly: there are now over 6.5 billion of us on the planet. Population growth occurs when **birth rates** are greater than **death rates**. Birth rate is the number of live births each year per thousand of the population in an area. A high birth rate would be 40 per thousand. Death rate is the number of deaths each year per thousand of the population in an area. The reason that these are measured per thousand rather than per hundred (per cent) is so that whole numbers can be used.

The world's population changes according to the difference between birth rates and death rates. When birth rate is higher, this is called **natural increase**. For thousands of years the world population grew very little as both birth rates and death rates were high and they cancelled each other out – a similar number of people were born compared to those who died each year. By 1650 there were only about 500 million people on the whole planet.

From 1700 the population began to grow quite rapidly and then, in the twentieth century, the speed of growth increased even further (see Figure 1).

In the past 50 years, world population has multiplied more than ever in history and we can see that this enormous growth of the human population is set to increase in the coming years. Approximately 300 babies are born around the world every minute. Although some people will have died, this still adds up to

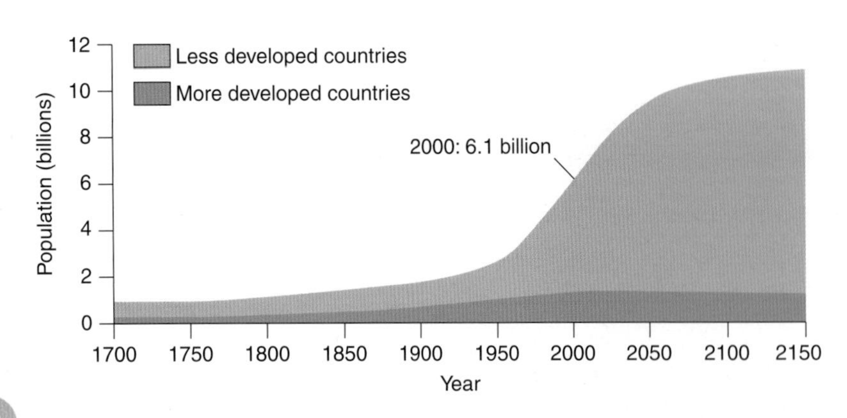

▲ **Figure 1** World population growth 1700–2150

more than 76 millon extra people in a year.

The world's population in 1980 was about 4.4 billion people (a billion is a thousand million). By 1999, the planet had reached six billion. It is expected that there will be 9.3 billion people by 2050.

Where most of these people live has also changed. In 1800 places like Europe contained a high proportion of the world's population. Most of the recent growth has been in less economically developed countries (LEDCs). The 48 least developed countries in the world are forecast to triple in size from 658 million to 1.8 billion.

The reason for the growth of population is that the death rate in many countries has fallen dramatically. Many of the diseases which commonly caused death, for example smallpox, have been eradicated or controlled owing to improved medicine and sanitation. The birth rate has fallen too, partly due to more widespread use of birth control, but not as quickly as the death rate.

▲ **Figure 2** Is the world overpopulated?

In 1950, in the African country of Namibia, 168 of every 1000 children born died as infants. By 2005, this had fallen to just 48. In 1950 a typical child in Namibia was born in the countryside far from medical care, into a poor family with a mother with limited education. Should the child fall ill, the poor communications and poor medical services in rural areas meant that the chances of survival were low. In 2005, many more Namibians live in cities. These cities have a modern health service which will provide a supply of medicine that the family will be able to use if they can afford it. It is also more likely that the mother will have a higher educational level than 60 years ago and incomes may also be higher. The result is that more children survive through infancy.

It is still not great. One out of every six children in Africa dies before the age of five. Partly for this reason, the birth rates are still high in these countries. As birth rates are still quite high, the levels of natural increase are very high and the population of countries such as these is increasing rapidly.

● weblinks

www.un.org/popin/ – United Nations Population Information Network website.

www.census.gov/ipc/www/idb/ – US Census International Database.

http://news.bbc.co.uk/1/hi/sci/tech/4584572.stm – A six-part series looking at the biggest problems facing the Earth.

Get Active

Think about the fact that the world's population is currently rising by about 76 million per year. What will be the challenges in providing housing, food/clean drinking water, education, employment, medical care and infrastructure (transport, power, water, communications, waste disposal) for a number of people larger than the population of the UK, and keep on doing it each year, year on year for the foreseeable future? Can the Earth cope?

- Working in six groups complete a *carousel* activity to consider the challenges for our planet in providing for increasing numbers into the future and suggest some ways in which these problems may be solved:
  - housing
  - food/clean drinking water
  - education
  - employment
  - medical care
  - infrastructure.
- To complete this activity you will need six large flip-chart pages and six different coloured markers. Each group needs a sheet with one of the six challenges written on the top. Each group has its own colour marker.
- Select a scribe, time-keeper and reporter.
- Write down your responses, thoughts and ideas about the challenges and possible solutions (you have 5 minutes to do this).
- When your 5 minutes are up, move on to another sheet, taking the colour marker your group has been given. Read the responses of the previous group and discuss whether you agree or disagree. If your group agrees put a tick with your marker beside that point. If you disagree, write why or pose a question. Then write down any new thoughts raised by your group on the sheet. If any of your ideas stemmed from the previous groups' responses, connect them with an arrow.
- Continue the carousel until you have had the opportunity to see and respond to each of the six headings. You should finish up at the sheet you started with.
- Read over all the responses now on the sheet. Agree the main points.
- The reporter gives a 1-minute feedback to the rest of the class.

Homework

Individually, answer the initial question:
What are the challenges in providing for a world population increasing by 76 million per year and can the Earth cope?

Extension

- Form four groups. Discuss one of the questions below:
  1. What sort of lifestyle can the Earth sustain?
  2. How many of us can continue to live at the current consumption levels of more economically developed countries (MEDCs), and what level should everyone else be expected to settle for?
  3. How can we expect poor people to respect the environment when they need to use it to survive?
  4. Are ecofriendly lives a luxury for the rich or a necessity for everyone?
  5. How do *we* need to change our lifestyles if we are going to make our contribution to this change?
- After the group discussions, report back to the rest of the class.

Migration

When examining population change for parts of the world instead of the whole planet, more than just birth rates and death rates are important. This is because people can move into or out of areas.

This movement is called **migration**. Migration is a permanent change of residence across a boundary, for example the border of a country. There are a number of terms used when describing different types of migration:

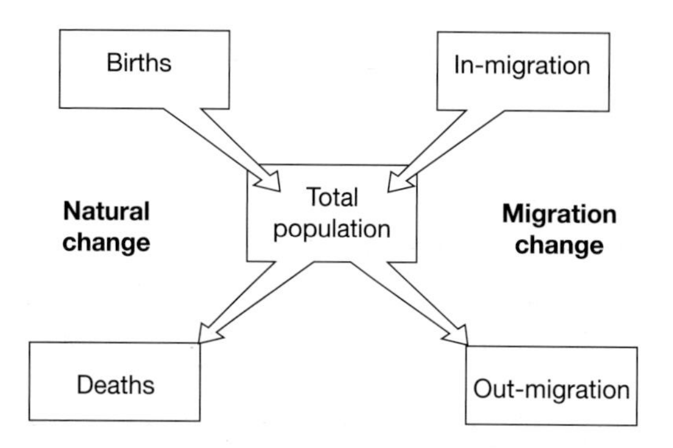

▲ **Figure 3** Factors leading to population change

- International migration: movement between countries, for example moving from Northern Ireland to Canada.
- Internal migration: movement within a country, for example moving from Northern Ireland to London. (This affects the distribution of the country's population.)
- In-migration: the movement into a place or region, for example moving to London.
- Out-migration: the movement away from a place or region, for example moving away from the Sperrins.
- **Emigration**: moving away from a country, for example you emigrate from Ireland.
- **Immigration**: moving into a country, for example you become an immigrant in Australia.

Why people move is often because of personal factors. Most people have factors which would encourage them to stay in their 'home' place. For some this might be family ties, familiar surroundings, a friendly environment and so on. There might be other things about their home place which are not so pleasant. Unemployment, poor wages, few opportunities, poor educational opportunities, war with another country, civil war, drought/famine, poor social life and so on might be some of the features of the 'home' place that might encourage someone to leave. These are called **push factors**.

The potential place to which migrants might move also has an impact on their decision. There might be aspects of it which do not attract migrants: it might be very distant, there may be language barriers, it may be seen as dangerous and unfriendly. However, there might be more positive aspects to it. It may offer economic opportunities, more social freedom, higher wages, and guaranteed employment, family and friends may have already moved. These are called **pull factors**. Whether a person migrates or not is largely caused by whether the push and pull factors are strong enough to overcome the ties with home and the fear, cost and hassle of moving.

Get Active

In pairs, draw up lists of the most important push and pull factors.

Get Active

This is a GIS activity: you will use a GIS to investigate the scale and origins of in-migration to parts of Northern Ireland.

Much of the information collected in the Northern Ireland census is found on the Northern Ireland Neighbourhood Information Service (NINIS) website, where you can access a selection of interactive maps.

1 Go to: www.ninis.nisra.gov.uk/mapxtreme/InteractiveMaps.asp (select 'People and Households'). A number of datasets from the census are available. A dataset is just a list of all the information.
2 For the purpose of this activity, we are most interested in 'Country of Birth' as this will give us an indication of migration. We can see maps with various levels of detail: LGD (Local Government District) is least detailed and SOA (Super Output Area) is the most detailed.
3 Select View Map SOA Level. You will see a coloured (shades of blues and greys) map which you can zoom into and move around in using the navigation arrows. Clicking on Reset will zoom you fully out again. Right clicking the mouse also works.

If you hover over an area on the map the details of that area appear on the left. In this case they provide details of the country of birth of all the people who lived in that area in the last census, when they were last counted. The categories are Northern Ireland, England, Scotland, Wales, Republic of Ireland, other EU countries and elsewhere.

The map shows the proportion from Northern Ireland but you can change that by changing the 'Select Measure' on the left-hand side of the screen. Each of these produces different patterns.

Once you are familiar with the maps and how they work, you are ready to do this research.

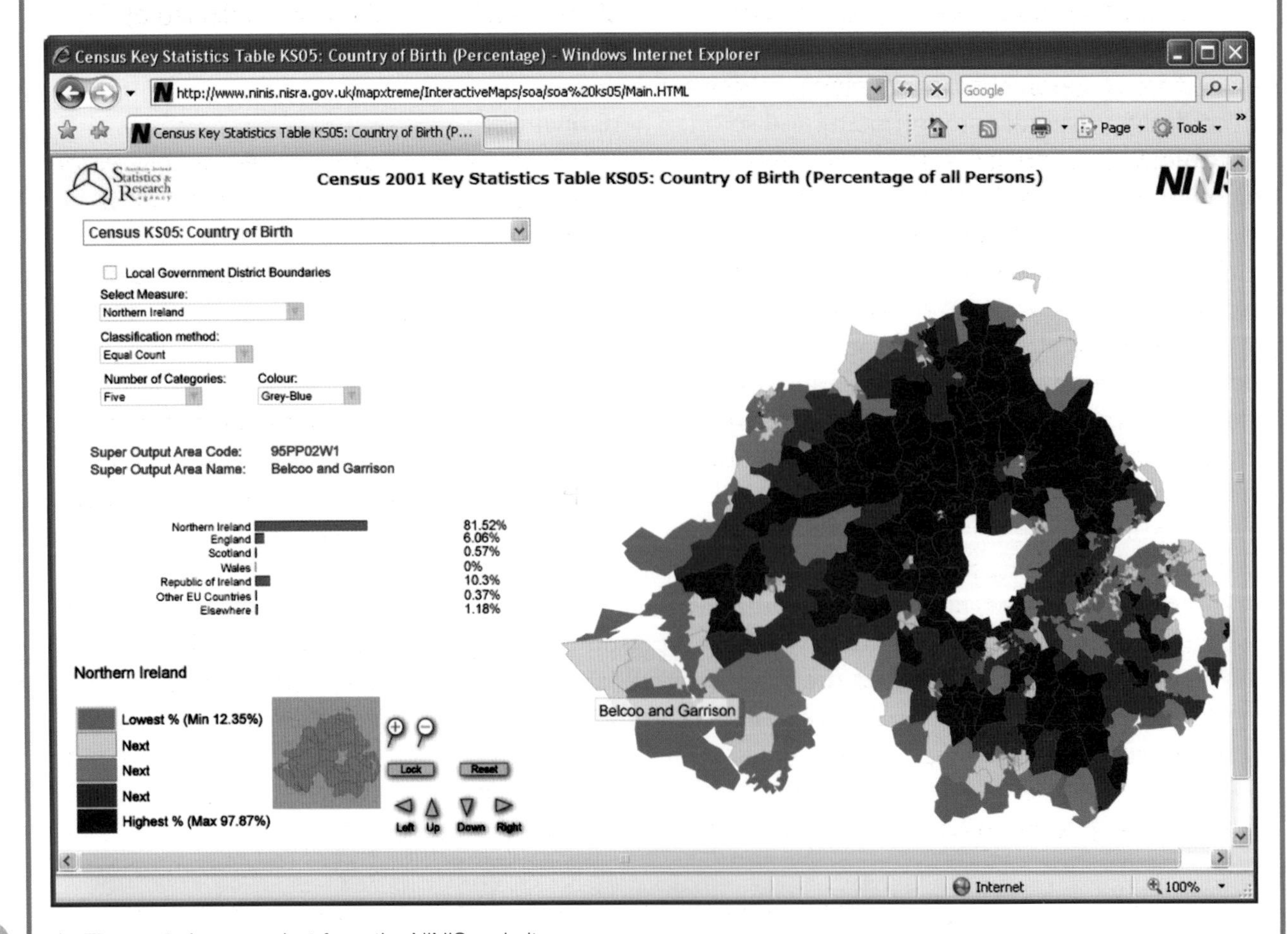

▲ **Figure 4** A screenshot from the NINIS website

Get Active

4 Find the area you want to examine in detail. You might do this as a whole class, using a data projector for example and researching a few places together, or in small groups of perhaps three people around a computer. If you are doing this with others, remember that everyone has to take part and everyone has to make notes and write this up.
5 Get a map of the area you are studying and print it out or put it into a presentation as a slide. You can put the information you are researching around it:
   - Find out the population of the area you are examining elsewhere on the NINIS site and note this figure. Try some of the tabs on: www.ninis.nisra.gov.uk/mapxtreme/viewdata/Census/CensusKS01.xls.
   - From the map note the countries of birth of the residents of that area: you could do a screenshot of the map and the graph. You can do the mathematics to convert from percentages into numbers using the population figure you found earlier. Are the numbers different from what you expected?
6 Try to find some more information elsewhere on NINIS which might give more detail. For example you should be able to find the number of people in each Local Government District on the Worker Registration Scheme (Data Catalogue, Population and Migration, Worker Registration Scheme). This is a means of recording the numbers of workers in Northern Ireland who come from the eight countries that joined the EU in May 2004: Poland, Czech Republic, Estonia, Hungary, Latvia, Lithuania, Slovakia and Slovenia. These are often called A8 counties. A8 nationals have similar rights to people from other EU countries but there are some restrictions on their rights to work, apply for benefits and/or to get help with housing. These restrictions do not apply to people from Malta and Cyprus, which also joined the EU in May 2004:
   - Note any of this information around your map also.
   - If you are going to make sense of the area that you are investigating you really have to compare it with another place. If you are doing this in a small group present your findings and note the findings of others. Is there anything surprising about what you found out?
   - The GIS should make it easier to retrieve information about places but you still need a geographer's skill to make sense of it.
7 What does your research tell you about migration into the area or areas you chose?

Extension

You can extend your knowledge and understanding of migration into Northern Ireland even further. Read the news release of 31 July 2008 from the Northern Ireland Executive found at: www.northernireland.gov.uk/news/news-dfp/news-dfp-july-2008/news-dfp-310708-new-migrants.htm.

1 Between 2004 and 2007 by how many did immigration into Northern Ireland exceed emigration?
2 Since 2007 has the flow continued at the same rate? What is the evidence for your answer?
3 Which nationality made up the greatest proportion of immigrants? What percentage of the total number of immigrants came from this country?
4 Why has Northern Ireland received fewer immigrants from Bulgaria and Romania?
5 From which non-EU countries did most immigrants come from?
6 In 2007, what percentage of births were to mothers born outside the UK and Ireland? How has this figure changed in the course of this century? Quote actual figures to support your opinion.
7 What percentage of schoolchildren did not have English as a first language?
8 What were the three main reasons immigrants gave for coming to the UK?
9 What impact might this immigration have on the education and health services?
10 Quote actual figures from the news release to support the assertion that Dungannon in Co. Tyrone is not typical when it comes to immigration.

case study

Positive and negative aspects of international migration in the UK

The United Kingdom of Great Britain and Northern Ireland, or the UK as it is better known, had a total population of 60.6 million in 2006. The birth rate and death rates are about the same (10.7 per thousand and 10.1 per thousand, respectively) but the population has been growing because immigration is higher than emigration. In the UK between mid-2005 and mid-2006, 385,000 people left on a long-term basis (for more than a year), mostly to Australia and Spain, and 574,000 entered the UK on a long-term basis. So the population rose by about 189,000. In total 1.5 million people have been added in the past 10 years, two-thirds of them from Asia or Africa. It has been calculated that, if immigration continues to exceed emigration as it does now, the total population of the UK will be 70 million in 2031 and, by 2081, will be 85 million.

Despite these seemingly large figures, the number of people in the UK who were born overseas is only about 10% of the total population. While this was only 6% in the UK in 1981, in Australia the figure is 24% and in Canada 19%. Switzerland has 23% of its population born overseas. Denmark, on the other hand, has only 7% of its population born overseas.

Between 2004 and 2008, 700,000 people from the A8 countries (remember that these are eight countries that joined the EU in May 2004: see page 115) came to the UK, many from Poland. The economic downturn which started in 2008 had prompted many of these people to return to their countries of origin.

Many migrants go to particular areas for reasons of employment or to be close to similar migrants. International immigrants largely concentrate in the UK's biggest cities. In the 1950s through to the 1970s, most international migration was to cities in the Midlands such as Birmingham or further north such as Leeds and Sheffield. At that time those cities had a range of industries and a need for workers which made them attractive to these migrants. More recently cities in the south of the UK have attracted most migrants. London, as the capital city with the largest range of opportunities, has the highest proportion of migrants, with almost 45% of the population of the city not having been born abroad.

Get Active

- Using ICT, draw a graph to show the percentage of the population born overseas in the UK, Australia, Canada, Switzerland and Denmark. Think carefully about the type of graph that best shows this kind of information for comparison purposes.
- Rank the countries from 1 to 5 (Rank 1 has the highest percentage born overseas).
- How do you account for the fact that countries like Australia and Canada have almost one-quarter of their population born overseas?

Get Active

1. Figure 5 shows that immigration brings a net gain of £2.5 billion to the UK's chancellor of the exchequer (the government's chief financial minister). Think of a visually attractive way of representing this.
2. Look at the work of everyone in the class and decide which one best gets this message across.
3. Why did you choose this one? What attracted you to it?

Impact of migration

The impact of the migration of people into an area is controversial. It is very difficult to say whether one effect or another is due to migration or not and there are very different views about how good or bad migration is for an area. You should look carefully at the source of any of these arguments and make a judgement as to whether they are reliable or not, or whether they have reasons for using facts inaccurately.

Tax income. Some studies have looked at whether migrants pay more in taxes than they cost in public services. But this is very difficult to calculate. For example, when do you decide that a newcomer is a UK native? A British-born child of an Indian immigrant consumes public money when he is at school but becomes a taxpayer when he gets a job. What about the Philippino nurse who spends 3 years working in a care home tending Northern Irish pensioners? Does such a person count for the income tax that they pay or the social care they provide? It is very difficult to distinguish between the possible benefits such people bring and the possible costs on the people of the country.

Research by the UK government found that, in 1999/2000, £28.8 billion of public money was paid to overseas-born migrants in benefits and public services. However, in the same period, they paid £31.2 billion in taxes. This meant that they contributed £2.5 billion more in taxes than they used.

Production. Most immigrants add to production of the country into which they move and this creates earnings for the country. Many of the recent immigrants from eastern Europe, for example, work in industry where they increase production.

On the other hand, some studies have suggested that any such increase in production is tiny and the main benefit may be to the immigrants themselves. They are able to send home about £10 million a day from the UK.

Housing. Some people suggest that the rise in population through immigration will lead to many more houses being needed in the UK.

Some say that continued inflows of migrants will push house prices up by 10%, but this is estimated to take 20 years to happen. In any case, it is very possible that changing economic circumstances will mean that migrants may no longer find the UK such an attractive place to come to, or to stay in 20 years from now.

Employment rates. A recent publication reported that while migrant workers had increased the supply of labour in the UK, this had not reduced the chances of British-born workers getting jobs. This was because migrant workers have filled important skills gaps in the UK labour market – doing jobs that local people could or would not do – rather than taking jobs away from UK-born workers.

However, another view is that employing migrant workers, such as those from Romania and Bulgaria, in an open-door policy could mean that UK-born workers would not be able to develop their skills in time to compete for jobs. This could risk damaging social cohesion causing difficulties between people of different backgrounds.

It is broadly agreed that immigration seems to have reduced unemployment in the UK over the past few years. But there is some uncertainty about what will happen to unemployment in the future, particularly if the economy falters.

There is some evidence that if there have been losers as a result of migration, then this has been among those in low-paid jobs who compete with migrant workers for employment. However, it has not been possible to calculate exactly how large or small this group is. There is some evidence in certain areas, such as the building trade in some cities in the south of England, that UK-born workers in low-paid jobs may have lost out.

On the other hand, immigration to the UK has made a positive contribution to the average wage increase experienced by non-immigrant workers. It would seem that as immigrants get jobs being paid the national minimum wage, non-immigrant workers tend to get wage levels higher than this.

Social costs and benefits. Large numbers of immigrants coming to an area can put pressure on some services such as schools. Planning of school places is very difficult in these circumstances as unexpected arrivals put pressure on admissions, often during the school year. Sometimes the immigrant families need additional support, particularly if there is a language barrier.

However, because of the work that these immigrants do, all of us benefit through lower prices. In addition, as the immigrants pay tax, this reduces the need to raise tax from the rest of us.

In the short term at least, immigration may create winners and losers: the biggest winners have been immigrants and their British employers. We might all be losers if the recent migrants did decide to return to their countries of origin. Society has come to depend on them for our labour and the question is being asked 'What would we do if they did go home?'

▲ **Figure 5** The impact of migration

Get Active

Has the recent wave of migration into the UK had a positive or negative impact on the country?

Part 1

To begin with, in groups, complete a *plus*, *minus* and *interesting* (PMI) exercise to help you consider all sides of the argument:

1 tax income
2 production
3 employment rates
4 housing
5 social costs and benefits.

Make a copy of a PMI sheet like the one below and record the thoughts of your group:

PMI for tax income		
Plus	**Minus**	**Interesting**
•	•	•
•	•	•
•	•	•

Each group should complete five PMI sheets, one for each of the areas that are impacted by migration.

Part 2

Complete a *consider all factors* (CAF) activity by making a copy of the template below and filling it in:

CAF template	
Question to be discussed: Has migration into the UK had a positive or negative impact?	
Factor 1 Tax income	**Plus**
	Minus
	Interesting
Factor 2 Production	**Plus**
	Minus
	Interesting
Factor 3 Employment rates	**Plus**
	Minus
	Interesting
Factor 4 Housing	**Plus**
	Minus
	Interesting
Factor 5 Social costs and benefits	**Plus**
	Minus
	Interesting
After discussion of all factors, we think that …	

A new migration?

A number of politicians are beginning to recognise that some voters are disturbed by the pace of change and, as a result, many are pressing for further restrictions in immigration to the UK.

Research has shown that average immigrants to the UK have higher levels of education than their UK counterparts. However, they tend to work in jobs that are less skilled and pay lower wages than a typical UK-born worker with a similar level of education.

Many of these recent migrants do not want to become British, or even to stay in Britain for very long. They come to the UK, they work here, and some stay for a while, while others go home quite quickly. This is a new type of migration: not as a one-off move to form a new life in a new country, but a movement of people backwards and forwards between countries. In the past migrants tended to emigrate to a new country and settle there, like Irish people to Canada. Nowadays a migrant is more likely to go to a country for a year or two with no intention of settling, like Polish people to the UK did in the early 2000s.

Nicholas Soames MP, the Conservative Party's co-chairman, expressed his view: 'We must be sure that industry can continue to compete as markets get more difficult. But we must balance the needs of industry with those of society. Failure to curb immigration would mean having to build seven cities the size of Birmingham in England in the next 25 years for new immigrants. That would not be acceptable to the public.'

People moving from one area to another can produce a multicultural society. This is a society which contains people from different backgrounds. There may be differences in culture, race, religions, language or national background. Living in a multicultural society can bring about many opportunities and many challenges.

The challenges that might exist in some multicultural societies can affect the immigrant community or the host community or both. These can include racial discrimination, physical and verbal abuse, employment problems, language difficulties, human rights abuses, misunderstanding, fear, intolerance, lack of trust, suspicion and hatred.

Of course, there are a great many positive aspects of living in a multicultural society, which again can be experienced by both the immigrant and the host community. These include experiencing different foods, different restaurants, music festivals and different types of entertainment and cultural events, as well as the opportunity to meet people from a range of different backgrounds and learn from them.

Get Active

Working in a small group, prepare a presentation that would respond to Nicholas Soames' argument. You should aim to highlight the positive contribution that Polish and other recent migrants have made to life in the UK.

To get some good ideas read the two newspaper articles from the *Independent* and the *Daily Telegraph*:

- The new immigrants: 'If you don't want us here, we'll take our skills and go' (*Independent*, 27 August 2006): www.independent.co.uk/news/uk/this-britain/the-new-immigrants-if-you-dont-want-us-here-well-take-our-skills-and-go-413557.html.
- Polish immigrants leaving Britain: what the Poles did for us (*Daily Telegraph*, 23 October 2008): www.telegraph.co.uk/news/worldnews/europe/poland/3248852/Polish-immigrants-leaving-Britain-What-the-Poles-did-for-us.html.

1. Print out the newspaper articles.
2. Divide your group in two, in order to read the two articles and to discuss them in some detail.
3. Use a highlighter pen to highlight the key points.
4. Note these key points.
5. Share them with the other half of the group.
6. Collate the key points from both groups.
7. Agree on the way your group will make its presentation.
8. Prepare the presentation, taking care to keep it within the time limits set by your teacher.
9. Present your response to the politician's argument.
10. Agree which group put forward the best response.
11. Identify and note the reasons why this was the best response.

Population structure

One way of showing the population of a country or region is a population pyramid. This shows two main population characteristics: the age and sex of the people living in the area. This is also known as the composition or **population structure**. A population pyramid is sometimes called an age–sex pyramid.

The pyramid is divided into two: usually the left-hand side shows the male population and the right-hand side the female. The bars that make up the pyramid represent the age of the population, generally divided into 5-year groups or cohorts: 0–4, 5–9, 11–14 and so on. The numbers along the bottom of the pyramid represent the percentage of the total population in each category. Sometimes, population pyramids show total numbers instead of percentages. Percentages are generally better as this allows easy comparisons to be made between regions or countries.

Figure 6 is a population pyramid for the UK for 2010 which displays the population in thousands for each individual year group. The points labelled explain how to interpret what the pyramid is showing.

In general:

- Less economically developed countries (LEDCs) have a wider base to the pyramid showing higher birth rates, and rapidly decreasing sides indicating a lot of infant deaths (high infant mortality) and a high death rate. They also come up to a sharp point, indicating very few elderly people. This is as a consequence of rapid growth – the bulk of the population are young – and short life expectancy.
- More economically developed countries (MEDCs) have a narrow base indicating lower birth rates. They have relatively even sides showing low rates of infant mortality, good health care and a relatively stable population. They tend not to taper until older age groups as there is a generally a long life expectancy.

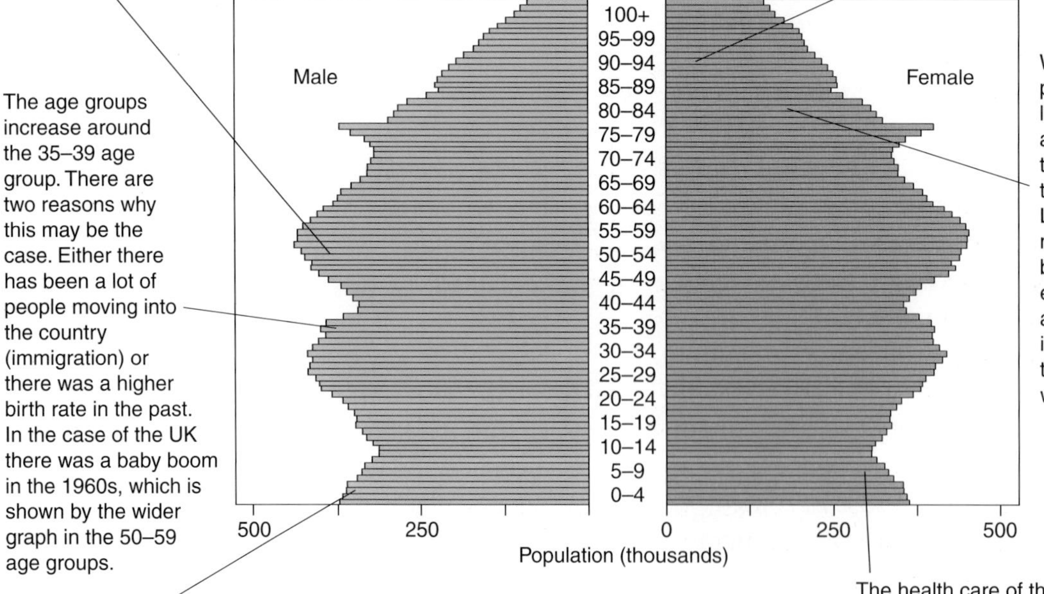

▲ **Figure 6** Population pyramid of the UK for 2010 (projected)

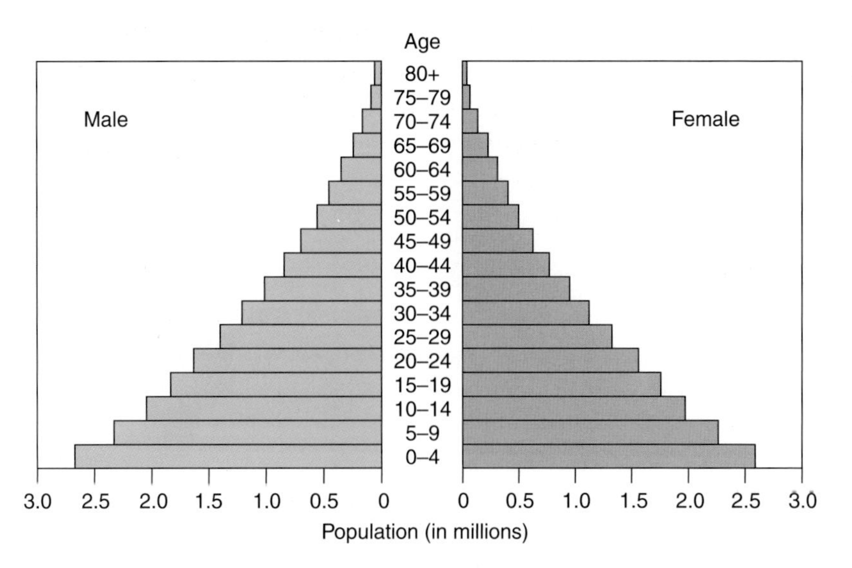

◀ **Figure 7** Population pyramid of Afghanistan for 2010 (projected)

Get Active

Watch the interactive age–sex pyramid for UK at: www.statistics.gov.uk/populationestimates/svg_pyramid/default.htm.

Work with a partner to work out the answers to the following questions:

- Play the animation of the UK population pyramid and pause it at 1977:
  - Note what happens to the numbers of young people between 1971 and 1977. What would explain that?
- Play the animation until 1991 noting what is happening to young people:
  - What would explain the changes shown?
  - Place the computer cursor over the bar of children born in 1997: how many were there?
  - How many 14 year olds are there: those born in 1977?
  - What effects might that difference make?
  - Look at the number of 44 year olds in 1991. These are 'baby boomers' who were born after the Second World War which ended in 1945. Why do you think birth rates rose after the war ended?
- Can you spot another group which seems to mark the same effect at the end of an earlier war? Do you know which war it was and can you predict when this group might have been born? Keep an eye on this group and play the animation until 2003. What happens to them and why?
- Between 2004 (16 year old) and 2018 (30 year old) the numbers of people in this young adult group increases. Can you think why this could be the case?
- Play the animation to the end. What do you notice about the shape of the pyramid?
- What could change in the UK to make these predictions wrong?

Population pyramids and migration

Out-migration: Albania

Albania is one of the poorest countries in Europe. This former communist state relies heavily on foreign aid and has a lot of debt. As a result of poverty and the need to escape from political upheaval there has been significant out-migration with between 300,000 and 400,000 Albanians working outside of the country and sending money back home. These remittances help to support the families left behind, but the migration has a significant impact on the population structure of the country.

- There is a significant gap in the pyramid in the 25–39 age groups. This emphasises that males are generally more migratory than females and that migration usually is more attractive to certain age groups.
- The migrants are economic migrants.
- Younger adults are more migratory than older adults.
- The migration leaves a male/female imbalance in the country.
- Often the most healthy and active members of the population leave.
- The loss of the most active population damages how productive a country can be.
- Since it is mainly males who migrate, it could be assumed that they will return home to their families at some stage.

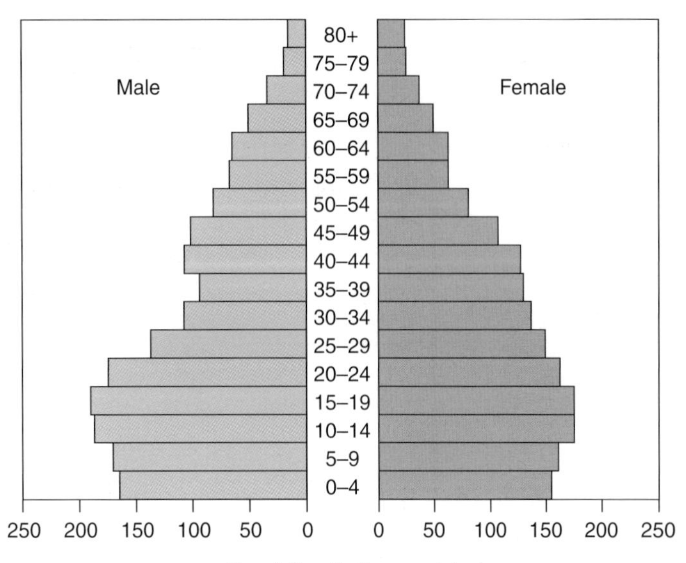

▲ **Figure 9** Population pyramid of Albania for 2003

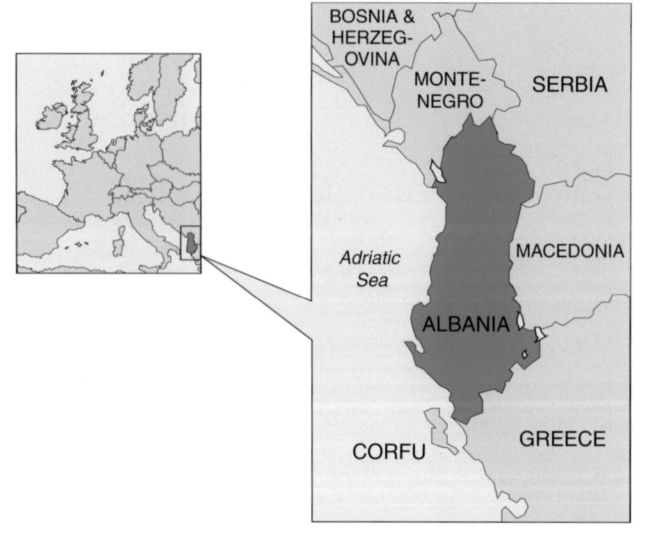

▲ **Figure 8** A map of Albania

In-migration: United Arab Emirates

The United Arab Emirates (UAE) is a federation of seven independent states lying along the east central coast of the Arabian Peninsula. It currently has a population of fewer than two million. The population grew significantly during the 1970s and 1980s as a result of in-migration. It is estimated that, today, only 25% of the population are nationals originally from the UAE. Migrant workers have come mainly from India, Pakistan, Bangladesh and Iran, as well as other countries. Migration has occurred because of the employment opportunities in the oil industry and in natural gas exploration as well as in construction, education and nursing.

- There is significant in-migration, especially of males.
- There has been an increase in the birth rate in the recent past as a result of the increasing population.
- The migrants are economic migrants.
- The pyramid is unbalanced because of the higher numbers of males attracted.
- Money is being taken out of the economy helping the economies of other countries.
- The mix of different cultures creates tensions between different groups.
- There is evidence of decreasing numbers of males in the older age groups, suggesting that migrants may have returned home on retirement.

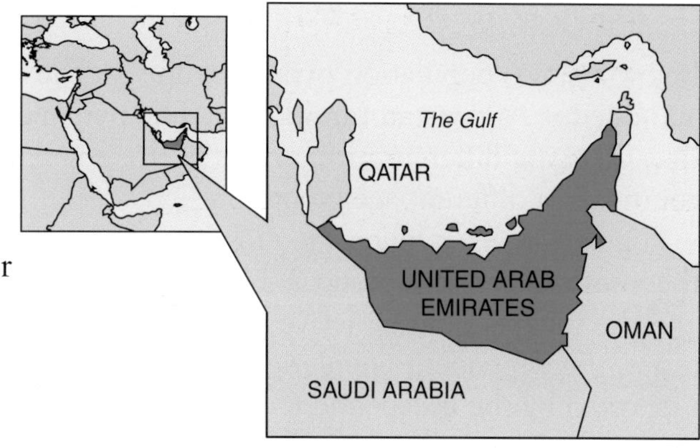

▲ **Figure 10** A map of the UAE

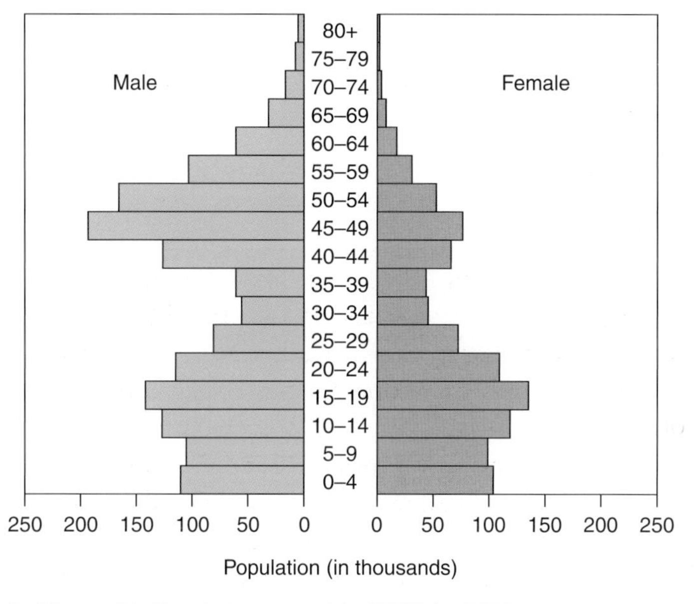

▲ **Figure 11** Population pyramid of UAE for 2003

Get Active

How would you think that the population pyramids for Albania (Figure 9) and the UAE (Figure 11) might change over time?

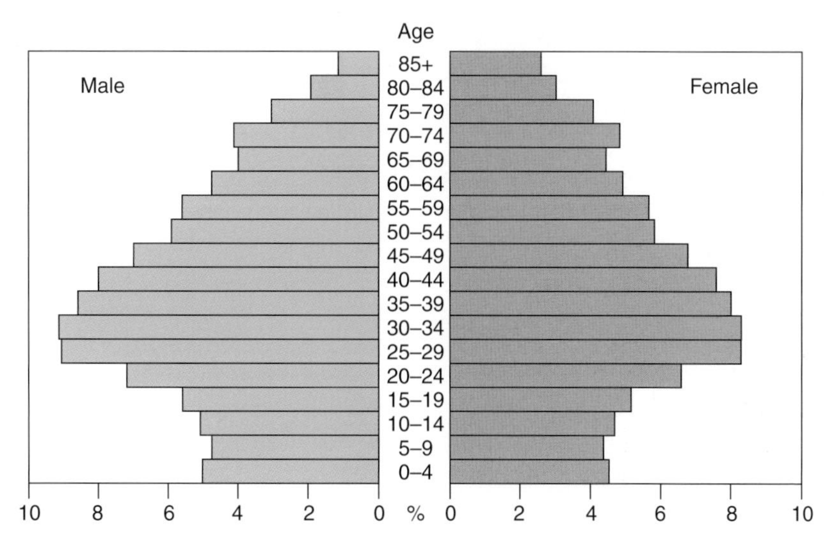

▲ **Figure 12** Population pyramid of Spain for 2005

Get Active

Look closely at the population pyramid for Spain (Figure 12).

1. Note the key features of the population pyramid for Spain.
2. In what ways is it similar/different to the population pyramids for Albania and the UAE?
3. How do you explain any differences you see?

Dependency

Below are two population pyramids: one for the UK (an MEDC) and one for Afganistan (an LEDC). The pyramids show clearly that there are different proportions of the population of the countries in different age groups.

Population geographers are most interested in three age groups: the **youth-dependent** group 0–14, the **aged-dependent** group 65+ and the independent or active population 15–64. In general terms, the dependent population of any country has to be supported by the independent or working population. One way the level of dependency is examined is through the dependency ratio.

The dependency ratio of a country is calculated by dividing the number of the dependent population by the active population and multiplying by 100. This is shown by the following formula:

$$\text{Dependency ratio} = \frac{\text{youth-dependent (0–14) + aged-dependent (65+)}}{\text{working population (15–64)}} \times 100$$

Usually MEDCs have a dependency ratio of between 50 and 75. In other words every 100 people of working age have to create enough to keep themselves and up to 75 dependents. LEDCs often have a dependency ratio of over 100. Usually this is because of a large youth dependency.

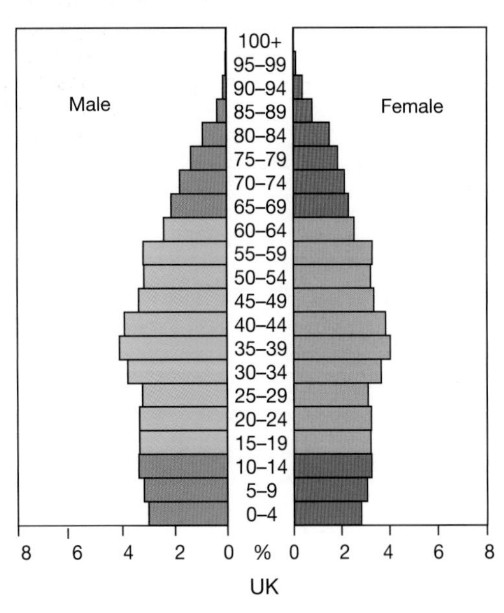

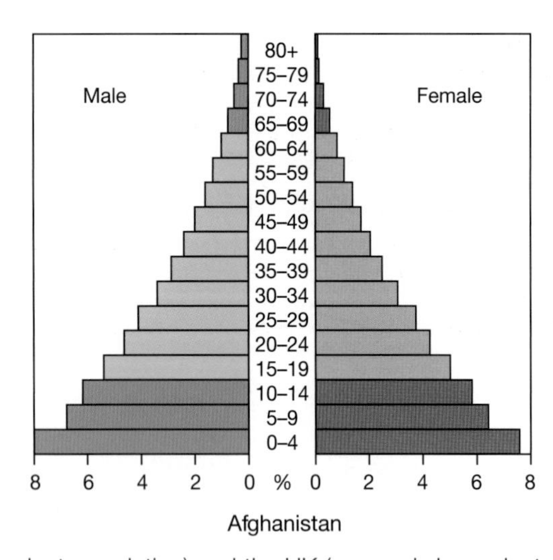

▲ **Figure 13** Population pyramid for Afghanistan (a youth-dependent population) and the UK (an aged-dependent population) for 2003

Aged-dependent population

- The aged dependent population depends on the working population for pension contributions as well as health care and other social service benefits.
- In MEDCs with an increasingly elderly population, there is an increasing burden on the working population to pay for health care and pensions. As people have a longer life expectancy then pensions have to be paid for longer periods of time. Some governments such as the UK's are encouraging people to work beyond 65 so that they can support themselves for longer.
- While an elderly population is not a major problem for LEDCs at present, a growing proportion of older people in the future will have to be planned for. A previously high birth rate and improved health care will increase numbers in an LEDC's aged-dependent population over time.

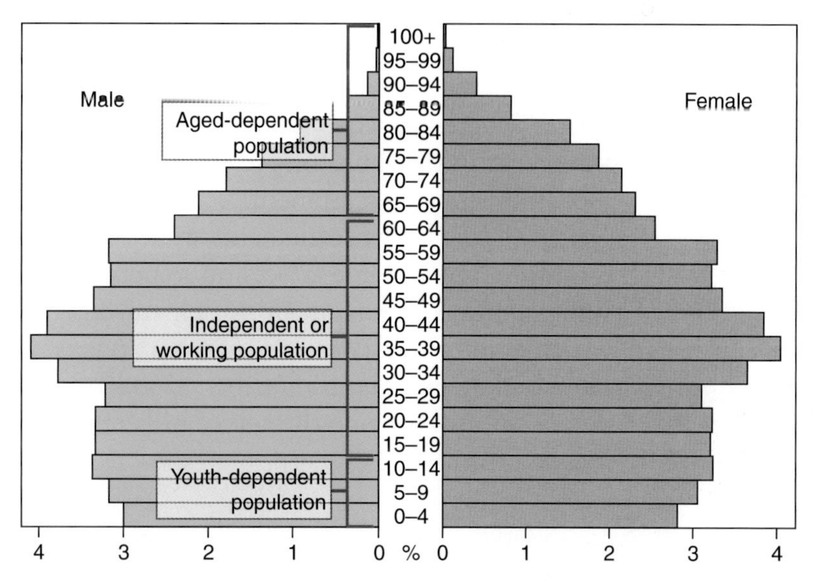

▲ **Figure 14** An example age–sex pyramid

Youth-dependent population

- The youth-dependent population is the youngest group of the population. They are usually dependent on parents or guardians for food, water, clothing and shelter. They are also dependent on the independent population for education and health care which is usually provided by the government from taxes paid by the working population.
- This population tends to be much larger in LEDCs than in MEDCs because of higher birth rates and larger proportion of young people in the population. However in many LEDCs, as birth rates fall, the proportion of youth-dependency ratio is falling also. Countries with a high youth-dependency ratio have to provide a lot in terms of education and medical provision.

Independent or working population

- The independent or active or working population is those aged 15–64. It seems strange for us in Britain to consider 15 year olds as in the working population, but for many parts of the world starting work at this young age is quite normal.
- The government collects taxes from the working population which are then used to pay for health care, education and social services such as child benefit or unemployment benefit. The working population may also be making pension contributions which will be used to support the population when they retire from work.
- The amount that is taken from the working population in taxes and pension contributions varies from country to country. The difference between that provided in an MEDC such as the UK is vastly different from that which is provided in an LEDC such as Somalia. In LEDCs where there is a large working population there may not be enough jobs to go round. This leads to problems of unemployment, underemployment and an informal economy.

Get Active

Working in groups, look back at the population pyramid for the UK. Think about how it has changed over recent years, with increasing numbers of people in the older age groups.

1 Discuss the consequences of such change on the following:
   - services
   - employment
   - health care
   - education
   - pension provision
   - society.
2 Note the key points that you agree on.
3 What are the challenges of an ageing population for the UK? Write individual extended answers.

Settlement site, function and hierarchy

Settlements

Settlements are places where people live. They can be isolated settlements of just one building right up to large cities or conurbations or megalopolises which are many cities that have grown to merge together.

No matter what size a settlement is, it has grown up on a particular site – the site is the land that the settlement is built on. Most settlements have an older centre which marks where the settlement was first established. Many of the settlements in Ireland are thousands of years old and their sites reflect the needs of the people at the time the settlement was first built. Most of these were related to the physical geography of the site: shape of the land (relief), closeness to water, shelter and defence.

Three of the most common settlement sites:

- *Wet point site*. The most important factor influencing the siting of the settlement is closeness to a water supply. Before piped water became commonplace in the countryside less than 100 years ago, people had to fetch it by hand from wells and springs and carry it to their homes. Particularly in areas where springs were uncommon, it made good sense to site your settlement next to a water source – a wet point site. In limestone areas of Ireland many settlements were located at the resurgence springs where the water which had seeped into the cracks in the limestone resurfaced at the foot of limestone escarpments.
- *Defensive site*. Many settlements were established by a single tribe, and sometimes it was important to have your settlement on land which could be easily defended from attacks launched by neighbouring tribes. Good defensive sites include the top of hills or inside a wide meander.

Get Active

Study a map of Belfast and the diagram below. Identify and explain the main locational factors related to its site.

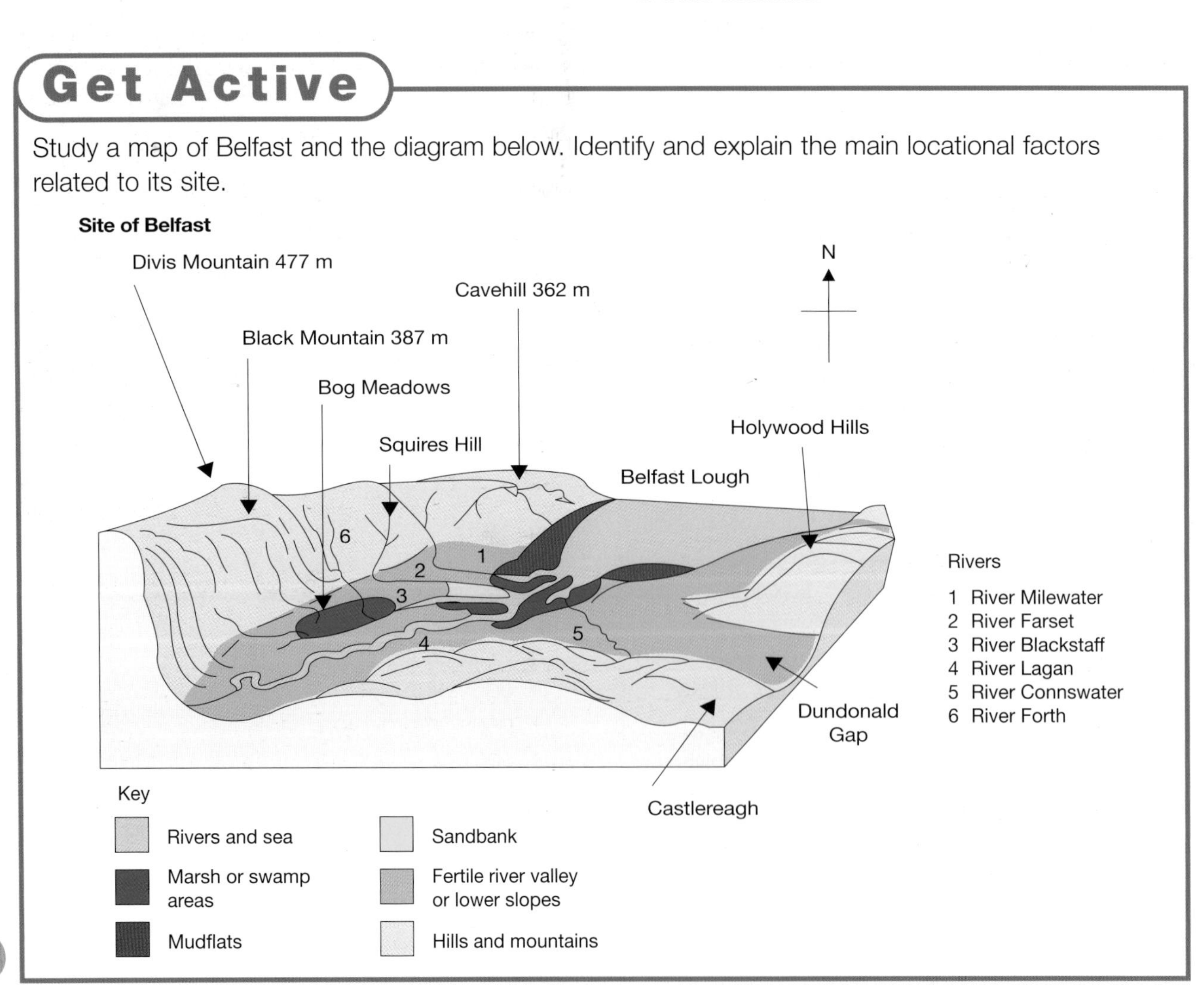

- *Bridging point site*. Such settlements are on a place because it is easy to cross a river. Many settlements have grown up on such sites, for example Newcastle and Glasgow. Belfast was built at a bridging point site as well. The original site of Belfast is close to the Queen's Bridge, next to the Lagan Lookout. Here a large sandbank allowed travellers to cross the River Lagan when it was exposed at low tide. Crossing points of main rivers are also useful to defend and are places where trading routes converge, so they make particularly good settlement sites. When the Normans invaded Ireland in the late twelfth century they built a castle in Belfast near the bridging point. It has long since disappeared although it is still remembered in some of the street names such as Castle Street.

Settlement location is very different from the settlement site. Location is where a **settlement** is compared to other things around it. A settlement might be said to be in the middle of a large plain some kilometres from another settlement. That is its location. It might have grown up around a source of fresh water. That is its **site**.

Get Active

Use *NI maps* (which used to be called InfoMapper) to examine a range of possible settlement sites. These are available via the links area of the LearningNI home page.

It is normally easier to spot the site of a smaller settlement as larger settlements have grown so big that the original reason for them growing up is no longer clear.

- Using the 1:10,000 scale maps, find a village or a small hamlet somewhere in Northern Ireland. Are there any clues as to why it grew up there? Work with a partner to find another place that may have grown up for a different reason.
- Using the maps can you spot where springs are found? Are settlements located close to these?
- Is there any evidence in some larger settlements of the original reasons for them being sited where they are?

Even today clues to the original sites of places can sometimes be traced from their names:

Gaelic word	Meaning
Ard	Height or high
Ath	A ford in a river or stream
Beag	Small
Cluan	A meadow
Coill	A wood
Dun	A fortress
Doire	An oak grove or wood
Druim	A large ridge or long hill
Garvaghy	Rough land
Gleann	A glen or valley
Cnoc	A hill
Machaire	A Plain
Mor	Big or great
Rath	A ringfort
Sliabh	A mountain
Anglo-Saxon word	**Meaning**
Dun	Hill
Ham	Homestead
Ingas (ing)	The people of
Mere	Lake
Thorpe	Outlying farmstead
Tun/ton	Enclosure or farmstead
Roman word	**Meaning**
Castra (chester)	A Roman town or fort
Colonia (coln)	A settlement
Welsh word	**Meaning**
Bach	Small
Bangor	Enclosed church settlement
Cwm	Valley
Drum/trum	Ridge
Gwyrdd	Monastery
Mawnog	Peat bog
Yswydd	Shoulder of a mountain

Settlement hierarchies

A hierarchy is when things are placed in order of importance. You get hierarchies in schools and in factories. Settlements too are arranged in hierarchies. In a **settlement hierarchy** the most important settlement probably has the largest population and covers the largest area of all the settlements. It is the most important settlement for that area with specialist services not found elsewhere. Lower down the settlement hierarchy are large numbers of settlements which have smaller populations and services that are common in other settlements of a similar size.

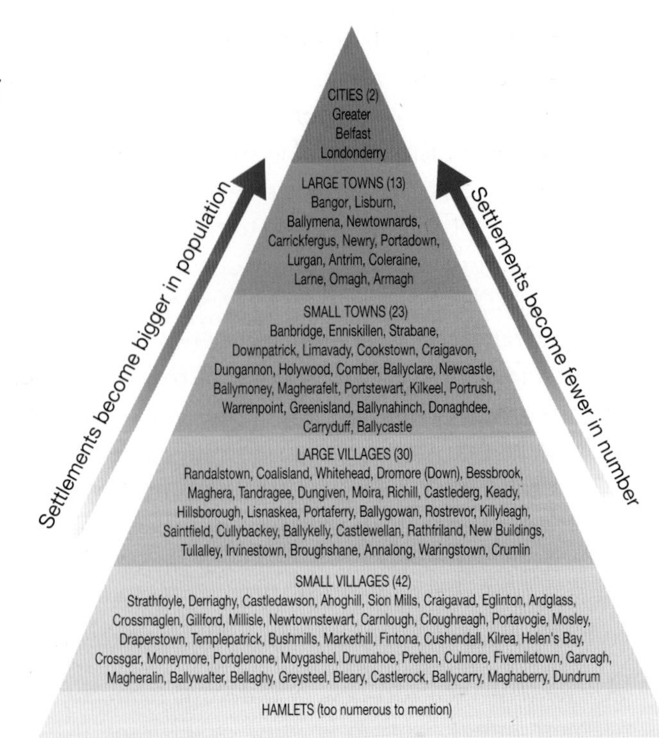

▲ **Figure 15** Settlement hierarchy for Northern Ireland (selected)

Order of goods and services

It is useful to put goods and services into one of three categories by examining how often we use such a service.

- **Low order**: these are goods and services that we usually buy or use every day or every other day. These include buying milk or newspapers.
- Middle order: these are goods and services that we generally buy on a monthly or fortnightly basis. This might include buying clothes or going to the cinema.
- **High order**: these are goods and services that are only bought or used rarely. This might include taking an international flight or buying a suite of furniture.

We can also examine goods and services by looking at how far people will travel to use the service and how many customers are needed to keep the service profitable.

Capital city or conurbation	Cathedrals, large hospital, national sports stadium and teams, out-of-town superstores, international airports, national museums and galleries, main local government buildings and all other services listed below.
City	One cathedral, full range of shops including department stores, main bus and train stations, large hospitals, university, local airport, court buildings, theatres, national sports teams and all other services listed below.
Large town	Wide range of shops, including the well-known high street shops, shopping centres, supermarkets, local bus and/or train station, small hospital, hotels, banks, opticians, furniture and electrical stores, solicitors, main police station and all the services listed below.
Small town	Small supermarket, health centre, dentists, several churches/chapels, restaurants, bus station, bank, small secondary school and all the services listed below.
Village	One or two churches/chapels, public house, primary school, convenience goods shop, small post office, village hall and all other services listed below.
Hamlet	Bus stop, post box and public telephone, if any services at all.

▲ **Figure 16** Settlement hierarchy by service

The **range** of a product or service is the maximum distance that people will travel to buy or use it. Convenience goods, which are low-order goods, have a short range. Few people would want to travel 10 km to buy a pint of milk. On the other hand, comparison goods have a larger range. Comparison goods, such as televisions, are those which people often want to look at in order to pick the one which suits them best. Many people would be happy to travel 10 km or more for comparison goods.

The **threshold of a product or service** is the number of customers needed to make an enterprise profitable. It is possible to state the threshold for each good or service. For example, if a settlement needs 15,000 people living in and around it to have a viable cinema, a settlement of 32,000 people will be able to have two. A settlement with just 12,000 people might have a cinema but it is likely to be unprofitable and will probably close.

Settlements higher up the hierarchy provide more services than those lower down. Settlements at the top of the hierarchy will also have more high-order services as their higher populations can support their large threshold populations. They will also have more middle- and low-order services than places further down the threshold. In relation to retail, high-order services often include comparison goods. Low-order services may include convenience goods.

Each settlement attracts people from the area around it to use its services. This is known as the sphere of influence of the settlement. Large settlements that offer a variety of high-order goods and services attract people from a wide area because the closer, smaller settlements cannot offer those services. In Northern Ireland, for example, universities or international airports or specialist hospitals are only found in or close to very large settlements. People are willing to travel great distances to get to these high-order services so the settlements have a wide sphere of influence. Smaller settlements with low-order services such as primary schools, grocery shops or petrol stations do not attract people from far away. These settlements have smaller spheres of influence.

Get Active

1. Name three services you might find in a village.
2. Name three services that might be found in a city, but not in a village.
3. Explain why one of the services you gave as an answer to the previous question would not be located in a village.
4. Name three services that might be found in a large town, but not in a small town.
5. In the context of Northern Ireland, can you think of any settlements that do not fit into the settlement hierarchy by service (look at Figures 15 and 16).

Other factors that affect the sphere of influence

There are a few other factors which have an impact on the size of the sphere of influence:

- *The **function of a settlement**.* The function of something is what it does. Some settlements are tourist settlements – it is what they do, their main function. Tourist settlements often have quite large spheres of influence. A dormitory settlement is where commuters to a large city sleep. Such places often have few services and would have a small sphere of influence.
- *Accessibility*. A settlement which is easy to get to, in other words is accessible, may have a larger sphere of influence as a result.
- *Level of competition from rival settlements of the same size or larger*. If a town is close to a city, people will use the city as it has the biggest variety and number of high-order goods and services. This will reduce the sphere of influence of the small town.

Ways of assessing the sphere of influence of a settlement

- Find out where people have come from to shop in the settlement's centre.
- Look at the catchment area of the largest school in the settlement.
- Examine the bus routes.
- Find out the boundary of the local authority.
- Look at the sources of advertisements found in the local paper.
- Find out where the people live who buy the local paper.
- Find out the service areas of the police station, hospital or fire station.
- Find out where spectators to local sporting occasions travel from.

Get Active

- Name a tourist settlement in Northern Ireland.
- Name a dormitory settlement in Northern Ireland and its nearby city.
- With a partner, think of other settlement functions and give examples from Northern Ireland.

Get Active

Study Figure 17 which shows the official spheres of influence of the main towns in Northern Ireland.

1. Name the three towns with the largest spheres of influence.
2. Name the three towns with the smallest spheres of influence.
3. Is there a geographical pattern?

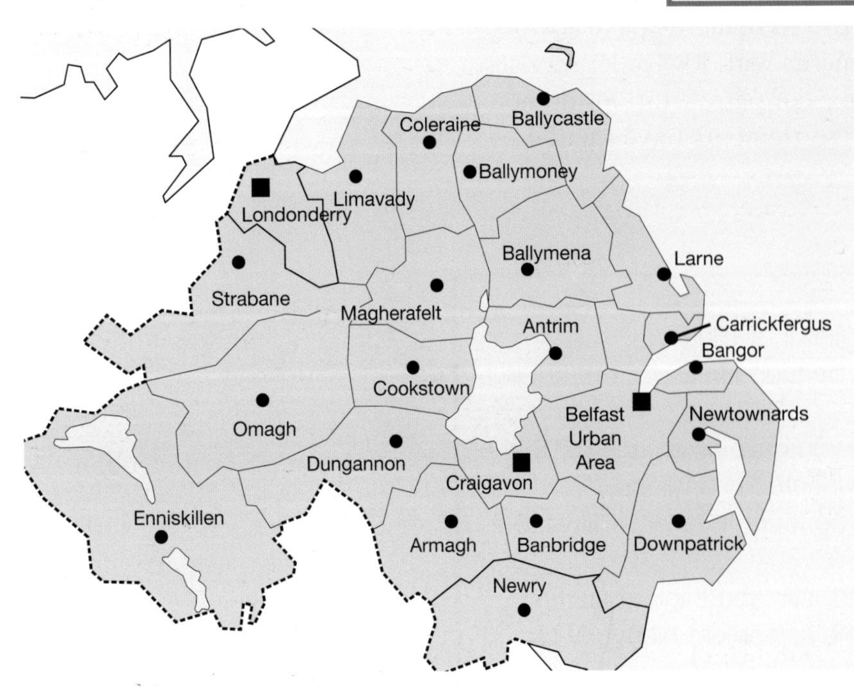

▲ **Figure 17** The official spheres of influence of the main towns in Northern Ireland as defined by the Government's Development Strategy 1975–95

Get Active

- Use *NI maps* by InfoMapper or Google Earth to identify settlements with a number of different functions.
- Publish a series of photographs about a settlement near to you, showing the main functions of that settlement.
- Annotate your photos.

Land use zones in MEDC cities

▲ **Figure 18** The central business district (CBD) of Hong Kong

Larger settlements such as cities have areas with specialised land uses. This means that there are areas which have developed mainly as commercial, residential, industrial and so on. These are called functional land-use zones.

At the centre of many cities is the **central business district** or CBD. This is where the main shops and offices are found, making it the centre for commerce and entertainment. All transport links lead to it so it is the most accessible part of the city. Because of this, it is the most useful place for many different land uses. As the land that it covers is relatively small, and the demand for space in it is high, the rents that people would be willing to pay to locate there are the highest in the whole settlement. As a result many properties build upwards and so it is in CBDs that skyscrapers are built. For many people the CBD *is* the settlement as it is the only place in the settlement that they visit. However, it is only a part of the settlement.

With increased traffic the CBD can become very congested and this has led to streets being pedestrianised. Car parks are now found around the CBD and there are often 'park and ride' car parks located at the edge of the city to reduce traffic in the CBD.

Around the CBD in many cities is a residential area with a high population density. This is called the inner city and is often a place where there is urban decay and dereliction. It is a term generally used for places where the inhabitants are poor, crime rates are high and unemployment is common. The inner city often has high levels of deprivation. Multiple-occupancy homes are common, where houses have been subdivided into flats. In some cities these areas may be in such a bad condition that they are called ghettos or slums. In some cities, parts of inner cities can become dominated with student accommodation (see Figure 19). This definition for inner cities works for places like London, Toronto, Dublin or New York. However, in some other cities such as Paris, Rome or Sydney, the inner cities are the most prosperous parts of the settlement where housing is most expensive and where the richest people in the cities live. In those cities the poor live in the suburbs.

Even in cities where the inner areas were places with the poorest quality housing and the most unemployment, changes can happen. Some parts of inner cities may become attractive to more wealthy people who start to live there again. As richer people move in, the character of the areas start to change, the area becomes more desirable, prices rise and the poor who were living there have to move elsewhere. Following the new people will be services such as upmarket supermarkets and delicatessens, restaurants and shops catering for this new population. Sometimes old buildings are taken over and converted to residential properties. These might already be residences or they may be old industrial buildings with some character. Sometimes new housing is built to cater for the wealthier incomer. This process is called gentrification and has taken place in many cities.

▲ **Figure 19** Inner city terraces, Belfast's Holy Land

Suburbs are residential areas at the edge of settlements. They are characterised by detached single-family homes and low population densities. Most house people who travel to work in the CBD although some suburbs are now areas of employment themselves as service and light manufacturing industries have grown up there.

▲ **Figure 20** Suburbs in east Belfast

Cities with an industrial base will contain industrial zones. The older industries may now be located in the inner cities as the city has grown around them. They are often associated with transport links such as railways or canals. They are likely to be in older buildings and will be surrounded by housing which originally would have accommodated their workers. This would be the case with many mill towns in Ireland and the UK. More modern industrial zones would be found on the outskirts. Here the buildings will be more modern and will rely on motorway transport to bring in raw materials and the workers and to distribute the finished product.

▲ **Figure 21** An old industrial landscape in Belfast of shipyards and terraced houses

Around the edge of many modern cities is an area which is not rural but not fully urban either. It is called the **rural–urban fringe**. Typically it is a place where recycling facilities are found and where park and ride facilities are provided. Airports and large hospitals are often located there too. However, despite these urban uses, the rural–urban fringe is largely open countryside although generally it is of poor quality with badly maintained hedgerows and woodland.

Urban sprawl is when a city or town spreads out into the surrounding countryside covering what was once farmland, woodland or wetlands with buildings such as roads, carparks, houses, shops and offices. This has a major impact on the environment as much of the wildlife is lost and water can no longer seep into the ground so easily, which can lead to flooding. Cities with large amounts of urban sprawl often have problems with transport also, with the people at the edge trying to get into work and into the shops and other services in the centre of the settlement.

▲ **Figure 22** Rural–urban fringe near Belfast

Get Active

Use *NI maps* to identify the various functional land use zones of Belfast.

1. Can you see the edge of the CBD? How do the buildings seem to change there?
2. What is the inner city characterised by in the aerial photograph? How does the map show this area? What does it look like on the historic mapping?
3. Can you see suburbs? How different do they look on the map and on the aerial photograph?
4. Are there industrial zones in the settlement? What do they look like on the aerial photograph and on the maps?
5. Is there an urban–rural fringe? Can you make out how the land is used there?

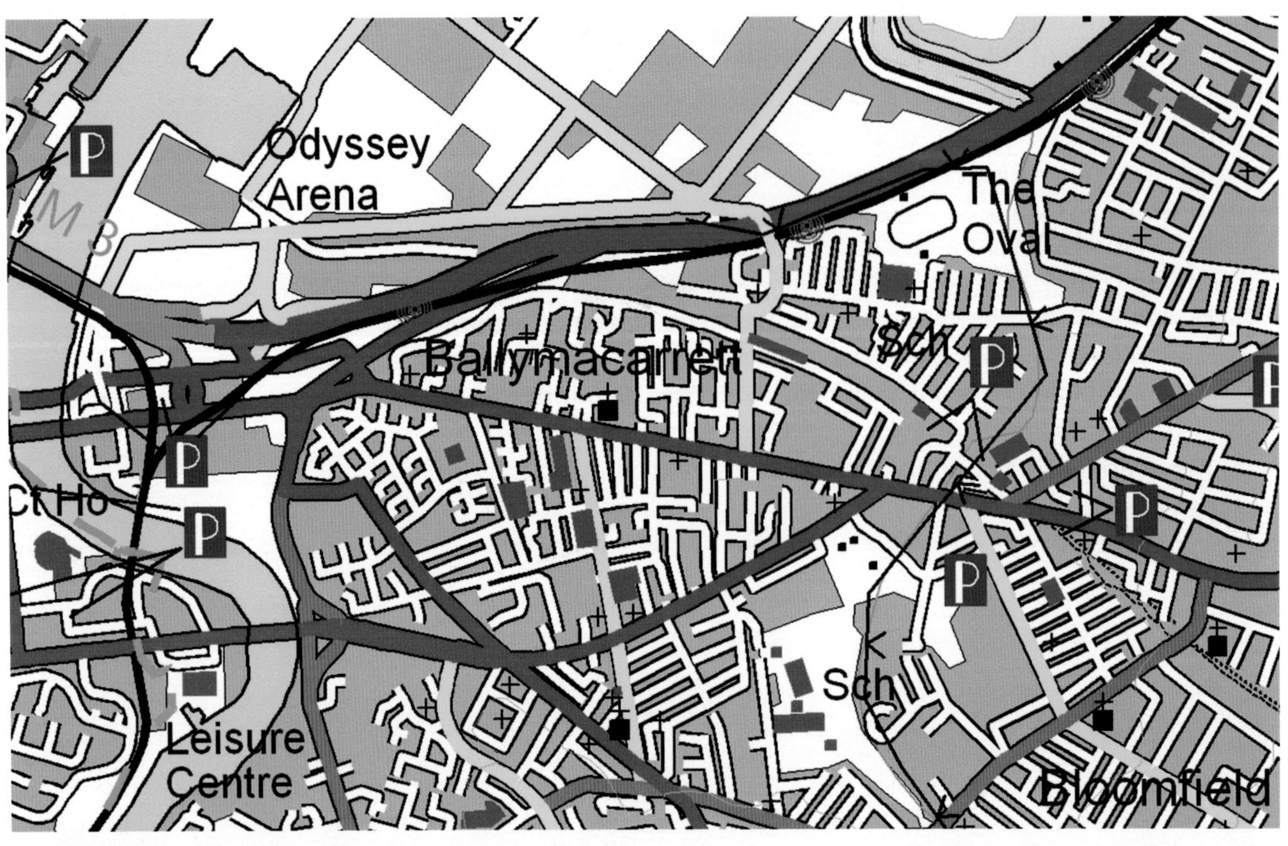

▲ **Figure 23** OS map extract of east Belfast

▲ **Figure 24** Aerial photo of east Belfast

▲ **Figure 25** Aerial photo of Culmore Road, Derry

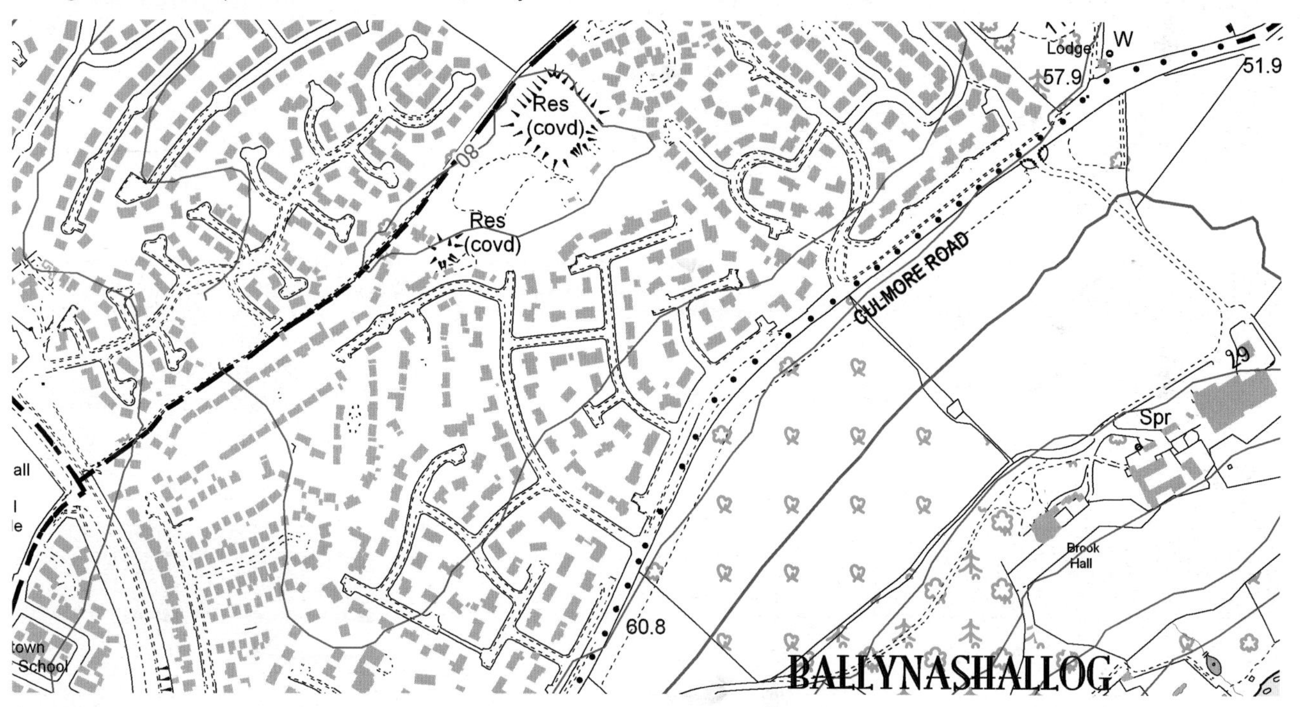

▲ **Figure 26** Map of Culmore Road, Derry

Get Active

1 In what ways are the two maps and aerial photographs in Figures 23 and 24 and Figures 25 and 26 similar or different?

2 How would you classify the land-use zones, site characteristics, general features and position in the hierarchy in the two areas? What is the evidence on the maps and photographs to support your opinion?

3 Using evidence from the maps and aerial photographs, describe both areas in terms of:
- communication networks
- housing
- leisure facilities
- green space
- industrial activity
- services.

Urbanisation in LEDCs and MEDCs

Urbanisation

Urbanisation is the increase in the proportion of people living in towns and cities. Before the 1950s most urbanisation happened in MEDCs. The rapid industrialisation which occurred in Europe and North America in the nineteenth and early twentieth centuries required large cities, and many people were attracted from the countryside to live in towns and cities. Since then urbanisation has slowed in these places and now many of the larger cities are losing population as some people move out of the cities to live in the countryside around them. This is called **counterurbanisation**.

Since 1950 most urbanisation has been in LEDCs in places such as Latin America, Asia and Africa. While more of the population of these continents still live in the countryside, their cities are growing very rapidly.

By 2030 the United Nations predict that 60% of the world's population will live in urban environments.

Causes of urbanisation

- People may be 'pushed' from the countryside for many reasons:
  - Mechanisation of agriculture reduces the need for labour in the countryside, leading to depopulation.
  - Natural disasters such as drought or crop disease in the countryside may push people towards cities.
  - Traditional land inheritance systems may divide the farmland up between children, generally the sons, so that the amount of land gets less and less. Alternatively if the land goes to just one son, the others may move away from the countryside.
  - Lack of investment by the government in rural areas.
  - Harsh farm life and poor working conditions.
  - Crop failure which results in food shortage and hunger.
- People may be 'pulled' towards the city for many reasons:
  - The standard of living is seen as higher there for many, particularly if you can get access to piped water and electricity.
  - The chances of getting a job may be greater.
  - The pay may be much higher than it is in the countryside: if a migrant is lucky enough to get a job in a factory, it can pay up to three times as much as they could earn as a farmer.
  - Access to health care and education is much more possible in cities than in the countryside.
  - Hearing stories of success from people who have moved to the city can attract many people.

Factor	MEDCs	LEDCs
Time	Nineteenth century/early twentieth century	Post-1950
Industry	Urbanisation linked to the growth of industry during the industrial revolution.	Urbanisation not necessarily linked to industrial change.
Technology	Labour-intensive machinery introduced in new factories at this time.	Technology not necessarily labour intensive – especially if inappropriate.
Employment	Rural migrants moved to city and found work in new factories.	Very few migrants find jobs in the 'formal sector'. Many find jobs in the 'informal sector', e.g. selling fruit on the streets.
Population growth	Death rates fell slowly, then birth rates rose in cities.	Death rates are falling rapidly, but birth rates remain high, resulting in high natural increase in urban areas.
Trade	Many European countries had access to colonies to allow trade and the means to feed the expanding population.	Debt and unfavourable trading relationships. Imported food is expensive.

▲ **Figure 27** Differences in urbanisation between LEDCs and MEDCs

- Natural increase in the countryside. Because birth rates remain high while death rates may have fallen, the pressure on the land increases. This leads to many people moving away from the countryside to live in towns and cities instead.

Urbanisation is also increased because the pushes and pulls often affect young people most, and they are often more able to make the enormous change from living in the countryside to living in a big city. Because the population of many cities is fairly young, the birth rates are often higher there than in the countryside. So, as well as an increase through migration, there is often a high natural increase in cities. In addition, because the numbers in the city are growing, this itself leads to more opportunities. These people will need more services, more transport, more items to buy, more schools, more clinics, more of everything. This provides employment opportunities which sucks in more in-migrants and so it goes on.

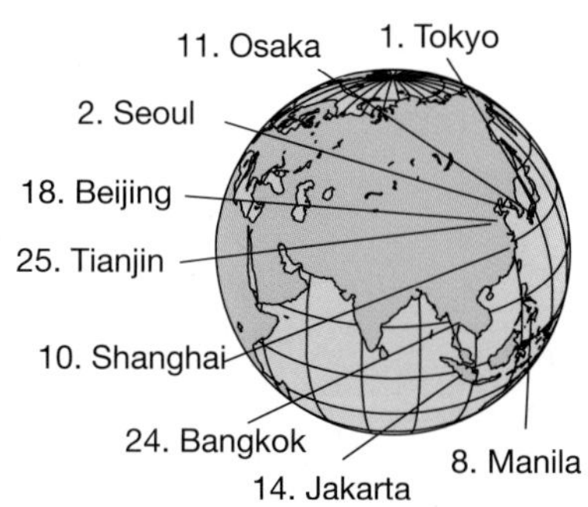

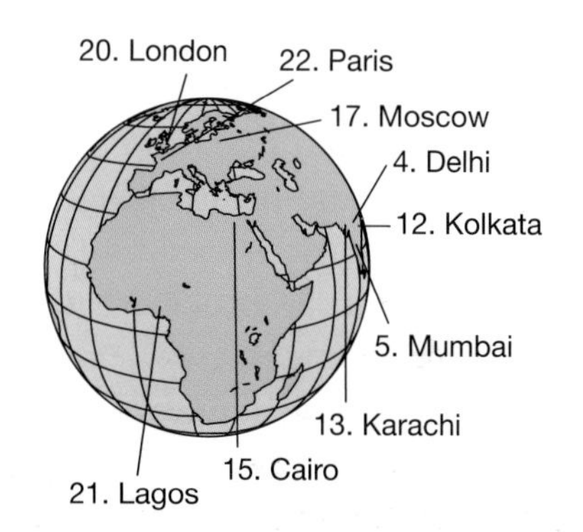

City	Country	1950	1990	2009
1. Tokyo	Japan	6.7	18.1	33.8
2. Seoul	South Korea	1.0	11.0	23.9
3. Mexico City	Mexico	3.1	20.2	23.9
4. Delhi	India	1.4	8.8	22.4
5. Mumbai	India	2.9	11.2	22.3
6. New York	USA	12.3	16.2	21.9
7. São Paulo	Brazil	2.4	17.4	21.0
8. Manila	Philippines	1.5	8.5	19.2
9. Los Angeles	USA	4.0	11.8	18.0
10. Shanghai	China	5.3	13.4	17.9
11. Osaka	Japan	3.8	8.5	16.7
12. Kolkata	India	4.4	11.8	16.0
13. Karachi	Pakistan	1.0	7.7	15.7
14. Jakarta	Indonesia	2.0	9.3	15.1
15. Cairo	Egypt	2.4	9.1	14.8
16. Buenos Aires	Argentina	5.0	11.5	13.8
17. Moscow	Russia	4.8	8.8	13.5
18. Beijing	China	3.9	10.8	13.2
19. Rio de Janeiro	Brazil	2.9	10.7	12.5
20. London	UK	8.7	7.4	12.3
21. Lagos	Nigeria	0.3	7.7	11.4
22. Paris	France	8.0	8.5	10.0
23. Chicago	USA	4.9	7.0	9.9
24. Bangkok	Thailand	1.4	7.2	8.8
25. Tianjin	China	2.4	9.4	8.2

LEDC

MEDC

(Figures are in population millions)

Trends to note:
The biggest cities are getting bigger – the top city in 2000 has over 25 times more residents than the top city in 1800. More and more of the world's largest cities are to be found in LEDCs – notably Latin America, coastal Africa and South-east Asia.

▲ **Figure 28** The world's 25 largest cities, listed in their order of size in 2009, and their positions on the globe

Growth, location and characteristics of shanty towns

Almost a billion people, or 32% of the world's urban population, live in slums, most of them in LEDC cities. These people live in overcrowded areas of housing, known as **shanty towns**, with very few services such as piped water, street lighting and so on. Usually the shanties are situated on land which is of limited value, perhaps at the edge of a railway track or canal or even land on which it is dangerous to build. The waste from the shanty towns not only is not removed, it builds up in the area and affects the health of the inhabitants, particularly that of the children who live there. Residents of shanty towns have more health problems, and less access to education, social services and employment, than other urban dwellers. Most have very low incomes.

The number of slum dwellers is projected to increase to about two billion over the next 30 years if action is not taken.

Shanty towns have grown up for a number of reasons, depending on the history of the city in which they are found. Most are a starting point for people who have just moved to the city, perhaps from the countryside, or for people who are temporarily in financial trouble. They provide a place where people can live cheaply for a time. Most residents of shanty towns aim not to stay there but to make enough money to afford a better place to live. While a number succeed, a high proportion do not. Life is difficult and uncertain for shanty town dwellers, particularly those who are not in stable employment but who work in the informal sector, a precarious existence. This sector is not like formal employment but may include trading at street corners or hawking goods to lines of traffic. Shoe shining or other occupations are also part of this informal sector of employment. The residents of many shanty towns have no legal right to live on the land on which their shacks are built and this makes their life insecure as they could return to see their houses bulldozed at any time. Often the residents live in poverty and despair.

case study

Shanty towns in Kolkata, India

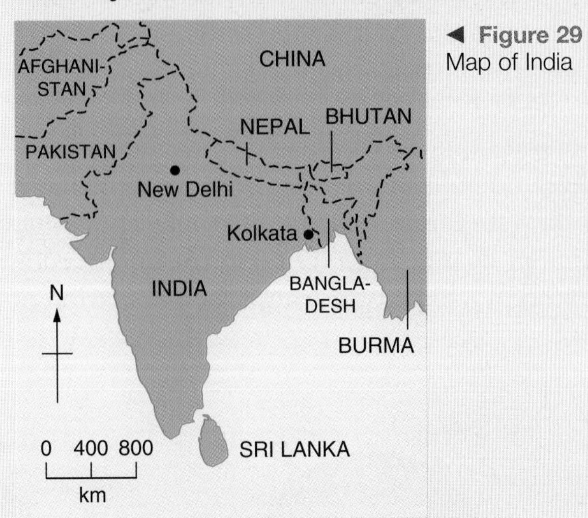

◀ **Figure 29** Map of India

Kolkata, formerly known as Calcutta, is a rapidly growing Indian city with a population which is not known exactly but is probably about 12.3 million. It grew up on flat swampland on either side of the River Hooghly, part of the Ganges Delta. There are three areas of poor-quality housing in Kolkata:

- In the centre of the city are poor quality houses dating back up to 150 years which grew up as the city urbanised.
- Around industries and at road intersections and alongside roads and railways are shanty towns which grew up 60 years ago.
- More modern shanty towns on unoccupied lands and along roads and railways.

In 2001, there were 5500 shanty towns in Kolkata of which only 2011 were registered. One-third of all of Kolkata's population are thought to live in these slums. The Indian government defines a slum as a place 'unfit for human habitation'.

Registered slums are called bustees in this part of India. They are recognised by the city authorities, and the people who live there have a right to live on the land they occupy. While bustees are the best quality of Kolkata's slum properties even they are built of poor-quality materials and tightly packed together. The residents of unregistered slums are much worse off. They have no rights to occupy the land on which their shacks are built, often along the

▲ **Figure 30** A shanty town in Kolkata

sides of roads and canals or on other vacant land. The quality of these houses is very poor.

Over 40% of the inhabitants of shanty towns in Kolkata have been there for two generations or longer. Most of them have migrated into the city from the surrounding countryside, partly pulled by the prospects that a large city would seem to offer and partly pushed by low wages, and mechanisation in the farms. Most inhabitants of the shanty towns work in the informal sector, and have an average household size of five or six people. Their average monthly earnings are between 500 and 1700 rupees (between £7 and £24), so about 75% of the Kolkata shanty town population are below the official poverty line.

The number of poor people forced to live in these shanty towns is set to increase considerably in the near future because of natural increase in the urban population and also because of in-migration. On average the urban slum population of India grew by over 21% between 1981 and 1991. In Kolkuta it has grown by almost 32%.

The standard of living of the shanty town residents was a cause for concern even during British colonial rule. The slums were seen as a nuisance and an eyesore which threatened the security and the health and hygiene of the city's rich population. Successive governments tried to deal with them by removing them but each time this was done, they just sprang up again.

Since 1974 the emphasis changed to trying to improve the living conditions of the slum dwellers. This scheme, called Environment Improvement in Urban Sector (EIUS), has been partially successful in the shanty towns where it was put into operation. However, the continued rise of population in the city has led to new slums being built.

Despite some success, Kolkata has a long way to go to solve the problems of the bustees and the unregistered slums. Clear long-term strategies are needed to reduce poverty, involve local people in developments, deal with the problem of unauthorised new slums growing up and provide further improvements to bustees. The problem is of such a scale that it would challenge an urban planner anywhere in the world.

● weblinks

http://en.wikipedia.org/wiki/Geography_of_Kolkata – Some details of the geography of Kolkata.

www.ess.co.at/GAIA/CASES/IND/CAL/CALmain.html#clim – A detailed look at Calcutta: not 'the city of joy'.

Photo 1

Photo 3

Photo 2

Photo 4

▲ **Figure 31** Bustees of Kolkata

Photo 5

Photo 6

Get Active

Working in small groups, look at and discuss the photographs of the bustees found in Kolkata (Figure 31). Each group works on a different photograph.

1 Describe what you see in your photograph. What is happening? Are there people in the photograph? What are the natural and built environments like?
2 For your photograph, what did you find most surprising or shocking and say why? Are the homes, other buildings, roads, etc. as you expected?
3 Write a selection of captions for your photograph which will illicit a variety of responses, for example, hope, despair, charity, pity, shock.
4 Agree what caption would be used if the photograph were used in the following contexts: a tabloid newspaper (e.g. the *Sun*), a charity advertisement (e.g. Oxfam), a geography textbook (e.g. *Geography Pathways*) or an encyclopaedia (e.g. Wikipedia).
5 List the ways photographs and captions are used in the media.
6 Think about things the people, including children, in your photograph might be thinking or feeling. Write appropriate speech bubbles to convey these thoughts and feelings.
7 Imagine you all live in this bustee in Kolkata. Use your photograph to identify the needs of your community, and especially the young people. List all the needs identified by your group. Agree on a rank order for (i.e. prioritise) these needs. Suggest ways in which the needs you have identified could be met.
8 Write a list of questions that you would like to ask about your photograph.

An urban planning scheme in the inner city: Titanic Quarter, Belfast

Urban planning is when people try to shape settlements so that they work more effectively. It is possible to study for a degree in town and country planning at university. Town planning courses are also very popular with students who have studied for a different degree, often in Geography. If you enjoy the human side of Geography, this might be a career that you would want to consider.

Increasingly planners are considering sustainability in their decisions. If cities are to meet the needs of the present residents, but also the needs of future residents, settlements must be developed sustainably.

Titanic Quarter

For many generations the River Lagan was vital to the people of Belfast. It was the focus of trade and of industry, bringing wealth into the city. The river allowed Belfast to act as a port and the trade passing through it made Belfast into a powerhouse of the Industrial Revolution. It was also the place where ships were built and launched. In the 1800s Belfast boasted the world's largest shipyard (Harland & Wolff), rope works and linen mills in the world.

Over the years since its heyday, Belfast had largely turned its back on the river and the riverside areas became derelict and polluted. Many of the people who formerly lived there moved away. The shipyard declined as large passenger ships and tankers began to be made in other parts of the world, such as in Asia.

One large-scale example of urban planning is a 75-hectare area of inner city Belfast where the shipyards were located, now called Titanic Quarter (TQ).

Titanic Quarter Ltd aim to make this part of Belfast an exciting waterfront development, transforming a derelict industrial site into an area which combines residences, businesses, educational facilities, offices, and research and development enterprises. There will also be hotels, restaurants, bars and other leisure facilities. Over 7500 apartments are planned, and 900,000 m^2 of space are being set aside for the other land uses. It is estimated that it will cost £5 billion.

▲ **Figure 32** Top: work in progress; below: the architect's model of the planned TQ

The developers hope that TQ will become a major social and business area of the city. The mix of offices, residences and art galleries, theatres, parks and water-sports facilities will all combine to create an exciting, modern area. All of this is within easy reach of Belfast's thriving commercial centre. Landscaped areas and open spaces will be an important part of the new development. A new major square for Belfast will be created in front of the former Harland & Wolff headquarters and other squares and green spaces are an integral part of the plans. The aim is to create an urban environment which is pleasant to live and work in, and attractive for leisure and tourism too.

Development strategy

TQ is planned as a grid of streets of similar scale to those in Belfast's city centre, with a mixture of land uses including the following:

- dwellings, including apartments and townhouses
- leisure and business areas
- the Titanic Signature Project
- a major third-level education campus (Belfast Metropolitan College)
- a cruise liner berth and other facilities for tourism
- local services and business support including local shops, health care, crèches and day nurseries.

(Adapted from www.titanic-quarter.com.)

How sustainable is it?

The TQ developers are business people and it is primarily being developed to make money for the investors involved. However, business people increasingly accept that sustainability is a challenge that the business community has to address. Often they recognise that sustainability can actually offer opportunities for business. As a result, sustainability has been made central to the development.

The developers identify five main aspects of the development where sustainability can be achieved:

- *Regeneration*: this old shipbuilding area is a brownfield site and building there reduces pressure on greenfield sites. Most jobs in cities are in the centre while the workforce lives around the edge of the city or outside it. This results in long commuting times, traffic congestion and increased pollution. If the population were to live, work and play in the same areas, as is encouraged in TQ, such problems would be reduced.
- *Accessibility and transportation*: TQ is very close to the CBD of Belfast and can become an extension of it. This makes it easily accessible for work, living and for leisure, particularly with public transport. There will be dedicated bus services, but the area will be built to allow light rapid transport systems to be introduced in the future. There are also pedestrian walkways and cycle routes in the plans.
- *Environmental protection*: some of the area is heavily contaminated as a result of industry in the past and this will be restored. Where possible, construction materials will be reused, reducing the need to use fresh materials. Locally available, recyclable and environmentally responsible materials will be used in the construction, where possible.
- *Energy and climate change*: all of the buildings in the development will be constructed so as to reduce carbon dioxide emissions as much as possible. Careful design and siting and the use of energy conservation measures will ensure this.
- *Biodiversity*: TQ is located in an important coastal site in Belfast Lough. The company aim to support and improve biodiversity by creating landscaped areas and habitats.

Sustainability is not just about the buildings

For true sustainability, the local communities which grew up around the shipyard and were employed in it have to be included in the new Titanic Quarter. TQ wants to ensure that communities across Belfast can benefit from and be involved in the development.

They say: 'We are committed to engaging with the people of Belfast, particularly those from socially disadvantaged communities … encouraging them to avail of opportunities in Titanic Quarter.' To do this, TQ are involved in a range of projects. One of these initiatives is the Newtownards Road 2012 project, regenerating one of Belfast's busiest routes into the city, and strengthening links between TQ and east Belfast. TQ also helps ventures such as the 'Stepping Stones Project' which helps the long-term unemployed to find work.

TQ will also bring jobs to Belfast as a whole. It is anticipated that the scheme will result in more than 15,000 jobs in construction and 20,000 new jobs after it has been established. There will be a wide range of employment opportunities in industries such as ICT and environmental technology. Opportunities in finance, business, tourism, hospitality and leisure are also likely.

case study

● weblinks

www.titanic-quarter.com/ – The Titanic Quarter website contains images and movies showing what the development will look like, when it is finished.

http://news.bbc.co.uk/1/hi/uk/8025036.stm – A video clip showing some of the construction.

▲ **Figure 33** Photographs of the TQ before the development

Get Active

- Would you like to live in TQ? What are the good points? What are the not so good points?
- Is it certain that TQ will be sustainable? What might happen that would make it less so? Is the way of life in places like TQ something for rich people or is it a way of life that everyone on the planet should aspire to? Give reasons to explain your answer.
- Use *NI maps* (available in the Links area of LearningNI) to research what the TQ area used to look like. The historic mapping should show you what it was like in 1880 or so, although some of the historic mapping, which does not show railways, is from the 1830s/1840s. The 1:10,000 map is from the 1970s and the 1:10,000 colour is modern. Use the aerial photography to see what it looked like in 2006, before the current building. You could publish into *NI maps* some word-processed documents giving your ideas about what you think about TQ. Google Earth will also provide good images of this part of Belfast.
- Over 100 years ago TQ was a world-leading industrial area, launching famous ships such as the *Titanic*, *Olympic* and *Britannic*. After a period of decline it is being reborn as a modern mixed-use area. What might it be like 100 years from now?

Sample examination questions

1 Population growth and structure

Foundation Tier

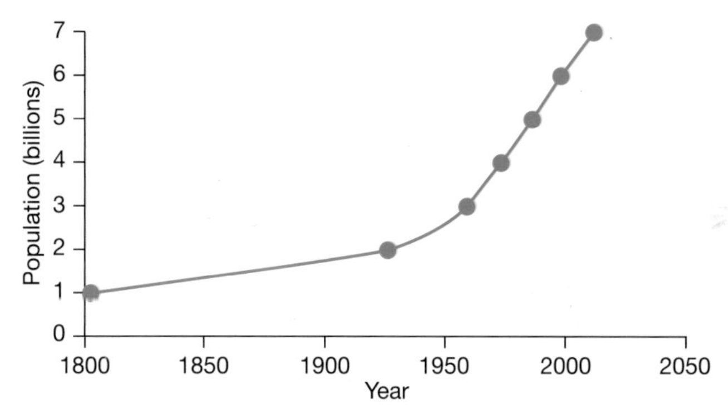

▲ Figure 34

(i) Complete the following sentences about the graph of population growth since 1800 using words and numbers from the list below. [4]

Increased	decreased			
6	7	1900	1950	2000

- World population has ______________ by approximately ______________ billion from 1800 to 2025.
- The most rapid growth occurred after ______________.
- The population passed six billion in ______________.

(ii) Explain why birth rates have fallen in MEDCs. [4]

(iii) For a named EU country you have studied, describe the impacts that international migration has had on its services:

(a) country [1]
(b) impacts [4]

Higher Tier

(i) Using information from the graph (Figure 34), describe world population growth since 1800. [4]

(ii) Explain why birth rates and death rates have fallen in MEDCs. [6]

(iii) Evaluate the positive and negative impacts that international migration has had on one EU country which you have studied. [9]

2 Settlement site, function and hierarchy

Foundation Tier

Study Figure 35 which shows a model of urban land use. Answer the questions which follow.

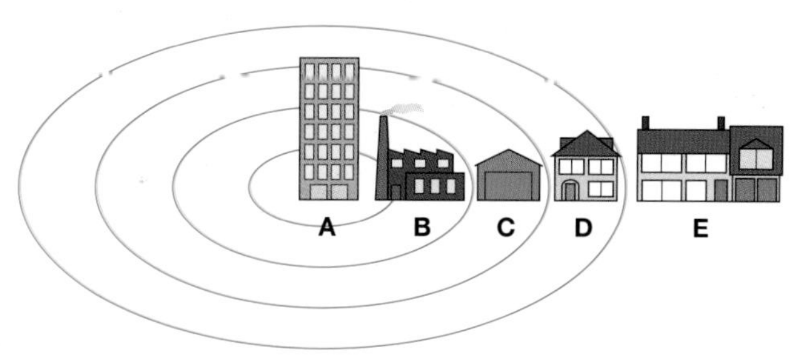

▲ Figure 35

(i) Create a key in Figure 35. Include the following labels in your answers. [2]

Village CBD Suburbs

(ii) State what the letters CBD stand for. [2]

(iii) Buildings in the CBD are usually tall. Explain why this is so. [3]

(iv) Study the map of San Francisco (a city in the USA) in Figure 36 and state three functions it shows that this settlement has. Choose your answers from the list below. [3]

Coal mining Fishing Recreation
Treasure production Education

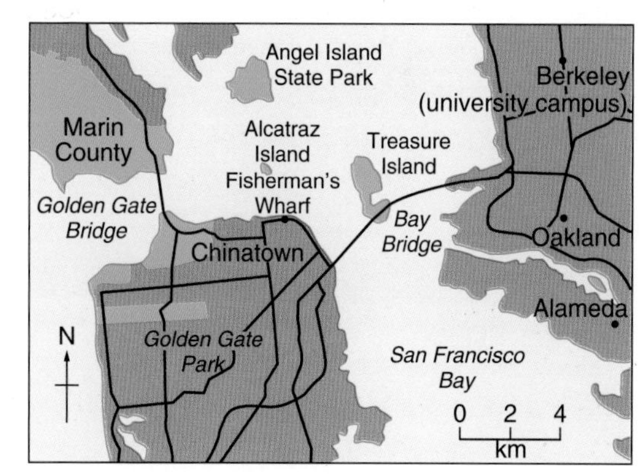

▲ Figure 36

Higher Tier

1 Study the map of San Francisco (a settlement in the USA) in Figure 36.

(i) Identify one site characteristic of this city. [2]

(ii) State two functions of this settlement shown by the map. [2]

(iii) Use map evidence to justify the classification of this settlement as a city. [2]

2 (i) State three characteristics of the central business district. [3]

(ii) For a named MEDC city, describe how a planning initiative has improved the housing and employment opportunities of the inner city area and evaluate the sustainability of this initiative. [9]

3 Urbanisation

Foundation Tier

(i) Write out the two causes of urbanisation shown on the list below. [2]

Natural increase	Urban sprawl
Aerial photography	Migration

(ii) Study Figure 37 which shows some possible features of a sustainable city.

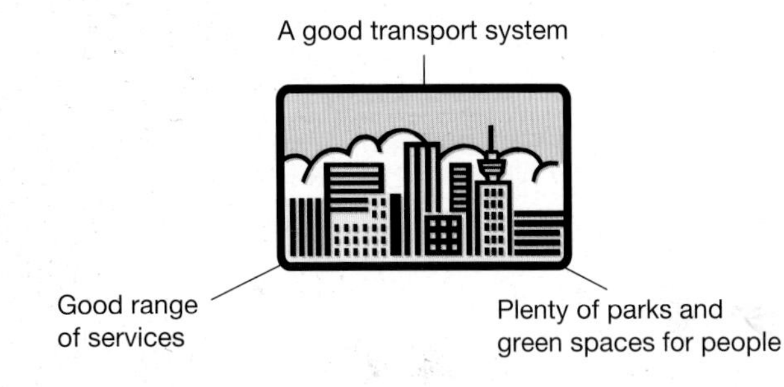

▲ **Figure 37**

Match the headline to the evidence for sustainability. One has been completed for you.

Headline		Evidence
Five new city parks to open •		• A good transport system.
More people are using public transport •		• Good range of services.
New city building to have shops, offices, a cinema and a gym •		• Parks and green spaces for people.

[2]

(iii) Describe two changes which could be made to improve the inner city area of MEDC cities. [6]

(iv) For a named urban planning scheme which you have studied, explain how sustainable the changes are:

(a) scheme [1]
(b) sustainability [4]

Higher Tier

(i) Explain two causes of urbanisation [4]

(ii) For a named LEDC city you have studied, describe and explain the growth of its shanty town areas. [9]

(iii) For a named MEDC city you have studied, describe changes made to housing and employment opportunities by one urban planning scheme. [6]

(iv) Evaluate the sustainability of an urban planning scheme which you have studied. [5]

UNIT TWO

Living in Our World

Contrasts in World Development

Learning outcomes

In this theme you will learn:

- how variations in levels of development have been caused
- how development can be measured and the effectiveness of a range of indicators
- what globalisation is and what its consequences are
- how international trade works and how it can be unfair
- about the role of appropriate technology in development
- what the different forms of aid are and their consequences
- to investigate a strategy to reduce the development gap between MEDCs and LEDCs.

Contrasts in World Development

The development gap

Indicators of development

Geographers are interested in differences in levels of **development** in different countries around the world. They are also interested in variations in levels of development within countries. There are many ways in which 'development' can be measured and each indicator of development has its own advantages and disadvantages. In the past, development was measured in economic terms only, usually in gross national income (GNI) per person. This is the total that a country produces every year, converted into US dollars for easy comparison, divided by the population of the country. The UK's GNI per person was about US$31,000 in 2006. This compares to Burundi's GNI per person of just US$96. This is an enormous **development gap**.

Based on wealth, countries can be divided into the rich, industrialised 'north' (**MEDCs**), including Canada, the UK and Germany and the economically less developed 'south' (**LEDCs**) such as Sierra Leone, Nepal and Burkina Faso.

Figure 1 shows the north–south divide which illustrates the economic difference between the rich 'north' and the poor 'south'. Note, however, that this is a generalised map and it places countries which in economic terms are expanding rapidly,

Get Active

Find out more about this GNI for countries by visiting the website: http://en.wikipedia.org/wiki/List_of_countries_by_GNI_(nominal)_per_capita.

1 Create tables to show:
   - the 10 countries with the highest GNI and note the actual value in US dollars
   - the 10 countries with the lowest GNI and note the actual value in US dollars.
2 Locate the 20 countries on a blank world map.
3 Give your map an appropriate title and key.
4 Can you identify any discernible pattern or trend?

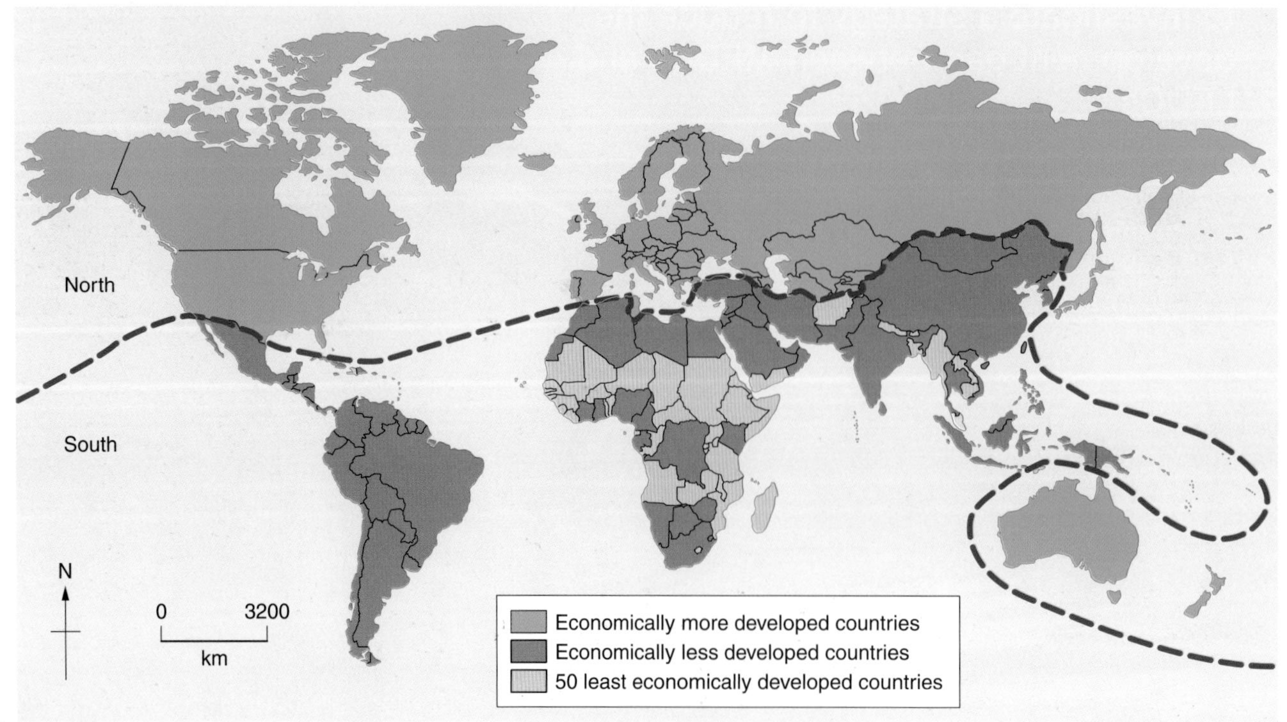

▲ **Figure 1** The global north–south divide

Get Active

How does Figure 1 compare to the map you completed in the previous activity? What are the similarities and differences? Write two sentences to describe the 'industrialised north' and the 'less developed south' in terms of GNI.

such as India and China, in the economically less developed part of the world. Also oil-rich countries such as Saudi Arabia are classified as this too.

Measuring development by wealth alone is not entirely satisfactory. Some economically wealthy countries might not be considered 'developed' in other ways. To measure development in this way alone reduces development to just one variable – economics. Increasingly it is seen as important to consider other factors too when measuring development, especially indicators of the social welfare of a population. This will produce a figure that tries to measure the **quality of life** of the people who live there.

The indicators of development can be subdivided into **social indicators** which relate to people's well-being, that is they measure *human welfare*, and to **economic indicators** related to *wealth*. Figure 2 shows some socio-economic indicators of development for a range of countries. The table suggests that there are clear links between wealth and a range of social factors. More economically developed countries have a longer life expectancy, a slower natural population increase, higher literacy rates and fewer people per doctor than countries that are economically less developed.

Get Active

With a partner, look closely at the table of data in Figure 2. Discuss what it shows about one or two individual countries.

Quoting the names of countries, and actual figures from the table, draw out the relationship between wealth and different social factors. Was there anything that you found surprising, and if so, why?

Key indicators of development:

- *GNI per person*: this is the gross national income – all the money earned by a country each year, divided by the number of people. In this case the figure has been adjusted according to how expensive each country is and how far the earnings might go (purchasing power parity).
- *Life expectancy*: the number of years that a person would be expected to live, on average, at birth.
- *Annual population growth rate*: calculated by subtracting the death rate from the birth rate. A minus figure shows a falling population.
- *Urban population*: the proportion of the population which lives in towns or cities.
- *Adult literacy*: the percentage of people in a country aged 15 or over who can read and write.
- *Human development rank*: the position of a country on the human development table produced by the United Nations (see the most recent at http://hdr.undp.org/en/statistics/).

Country	GNI per person (US$) 2007	Life expectancy (years) 2007	Annual Population growth (%) 2007	Urban population (%)	Adult literacy (%) 2007	Doctors per 100,000 people 1992–5	Televisions per 1000 people 1996–8	Internet users (%)	Human development rank 2008
Ireland	37,090	78.1	1.1	58.1	99.0	167	456	41	5
UK	33,800	78.9	0.3	89.4	99.0	164	645	66	21
Canada	35,310	81.2	0.8	76.9	99.0	221	715	84	3
Italy	29,850	80.1	–0.1	66.8	98.8	n/a	486	55	19
Brazil	9,370	71.7	1.2	80.2	88.6	134	316	25	70
China	5,370	73.2	0.6	32.7	90.9	115	272	19	94
Lesotho	1,890	40.1	0.1	26.4	84.8	5	24	3	155
Bangladesh	1,340	63.2	2.0	20.0	43.1	18	7	0.03	145
Nepal	1,040	60.9	2.1	11.2	48.6	5	4	1.1	147
Sierra Leone	660	40.9	2.3	35.3	35.1	n/a	26	0.02	179

▲ **Figure 2** Socio-economic indicators of development

Problems with indicators

One major problem with social indicators is that the information is often obtained from a census or household survey which may not be accurate. In addition, some social indicators are directly related to the wealth of a country. For example, the wealthier the country, the more likely it is that people will have televisions and access to the internet, the more doctors there will be and the better the health of the population.

Get Active

- What is a census?
- How often is it completed in the UK? What about Ireland?
- Why might the census not be accurate?
- Why does the government pay particular attention to the census and make it compulsory for people resident in the UK to complete it?
- For what purposes might the government use the information collected by the census?

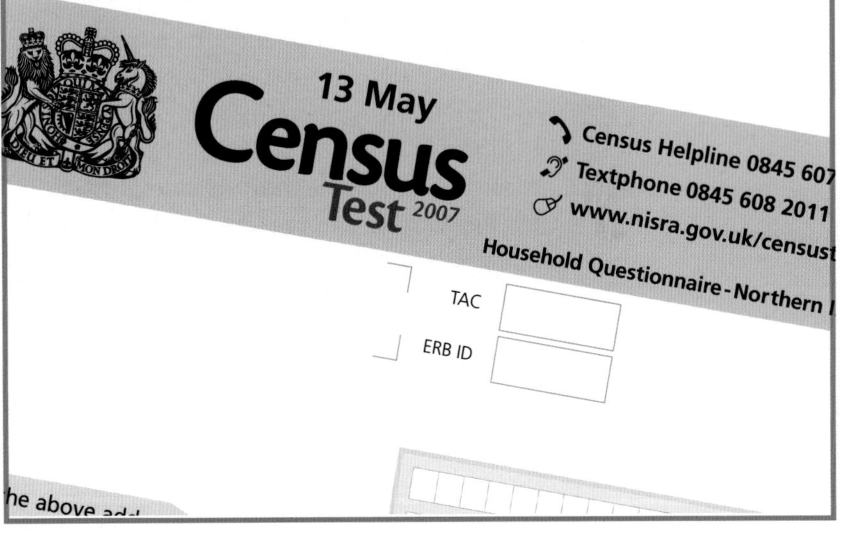

The use of separate indicators can also disguise variations in development. For example, when comparing GNI per person, countries, with high levels of subsistence agriculture (when farmers generally do not sell their crop for money but use it to feed their families) will seem to be worse off than they are, despite the population being well fed.

For these reasons some composite measures have been developed by the United Nations Development Programme (UNDP) which combine a range of indicators. Three of these measures are:

- the **human development index**
- the human poverty index
- the gender-related development index.

The human development index (HDI)

This index is expressed as a figure between 0 and 1 (see Figure 3). Countries can be ranked according to their HDI score. The closer the score is to 1 the more developed the country is. The index combines measures of health, wealth and education as follows:

- Life expectancy at birth measured in years.
- Adult literacy rate and the combined primary, secondary school and third-level education enrolment.
- GDP per person, measured in US$ (GDP is gross domestic product, similar to GNI).

Some geographers feel that the HDI still puts too much emphasis on wealth and suggest that other measures should be incorporated, for example, freedom of speech. However, the HDI for many countries around the world is improving with the exception of Sub-Saharan Africa (partly because of HIV/AIDS) and the new countries of Central Asia, for example Kazakhstan, due to worsening education provision and high mortality rates.

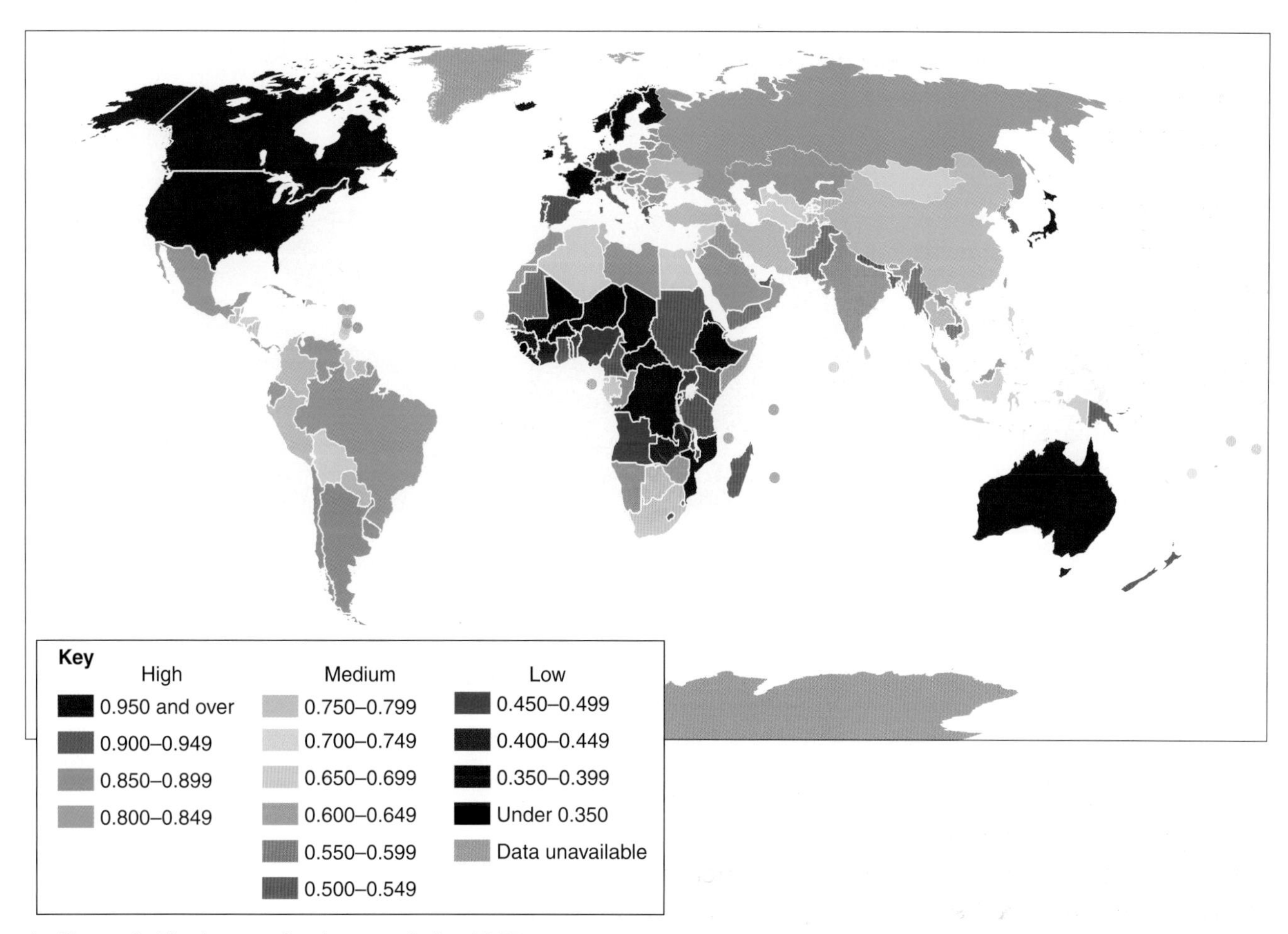

▲ **Figure 3** The human development index 2007

Get Active

In groups, compare the world map showing HDI to the initial world map showing the north–south divide:

- In general terms, how are the two maps similar?
- In more subtle terms, how are the two maps different?
- Which of the two maps is the most useful? Why?

Further information on indicators

The human poverty index (HPI)
Poverty is not just about income. The HPI uses indicators that measure non-financial aspects of poverty, in other words, deprivation. It is made up of these factors combined:

- Early death rate: the probability of not living until the age of 40.
- Adult illiteracy: the proportion of adults unable to read or write.
- Living standards: the percentage of the population not using improved water sources and the percentage of children under 5 years who are underweight.

Countries with high scores where there is much poverty include Burkina Faso, Mozambique, Sierra Leone and Burundi. Countries with low scores in deprivation include Japan, Sweden, Norway and the Netherlands.

Gender-related development index
This index measures the same characteristics as the HDI, but this time the facts are considered on a gender basis by looking at the inequalities between men and women.

The scores are largely similar to the HDI values with similar countries appearing in the highest and lowest categories. There is some variation in the middle development countries.

▲ **Figure 4** Deprivation in Mozambique. A child plays in a pool of stagnant water

Summing up the indicators

In conclusion it can be seen that there are vast differences between countries in terms of their development. However it is measured, the gap is ever widening and cannot be sustained environmentally, politically or economically. Gustave Speth of the UNDP suggests:

> 'Sustainable human development is development that not only generates economic growth but distributes its benefits equitably [fairly]; that regenerates the environment rather than destroying it; that empowers people rather than marginalising them. It gives priority to the poor, enlarging their choices and opportunities, and provides for their participation in decisions affecting them. It is development that is pro-poor, pro-nature, pro-jobs, pro-democracy, pro-women and pro-children.'

Get Active

1 Read the list of terms below and agree a meaning for each with your partner.

1.	birth rate	2.	most people in primary industry
3.	Asia	4.	Europe
5.	high life expectancy	6.	subsistence agriculture
7.	low GNP	8.	natural increase
9.	high birth rate	10.	low infant mortality
11.	MEDCs	12.	South America
13.	little trade	14.	migration
15.	agribusiness	16.	high GNP
17.	death rate	18.	high death rate
19.	LEDCs	20.	Africa

a Each of the numbers in the sets of four below relates to the topic development. With your partner work out which is the *Odd One Out* and what connects the other three.

Set A	14	17	1	8
Set B	17	11	10	16
Set C	7	19	9	5
Set D	2	15	13	6
Set E	20	3	4	12

b Still with your partner, find *one more* from the list to add to each of the sets above so that *four* items have things in common, but the *Odd One Out* remains the same. Think about why you have chosen each one.

c Now design some sets to try out on your partner! Choose three numbers that you think have something in common with each other and one that you think has nothing to do with the other two. Get your partner to find the *Odd One Out*, then do one of theirs. Try a few each, but remember to be reasonable.

d Organise all the words into groups? Create between three and six groups. Each group must be given a descriptive heading that unites the words in the group. Try not to have any left over. Be prepared to rethink as you go along.

Source: *Thinking Through Geography Material*, Interboard Geography Group, LNI Library.

2 a Use the internet to obtain the latest GNP and HDI figures for the UK, the Russian Federation, Germany, Sri Lanka, Columbia, South Africa, Botswana, Saudi Arabia, China and Sierra Leone. Rank all of the countries according to their GNP per capita: the country with the highest GNP should be ranked 1 and the lowest 10. Now repeat for the HDI, ranking the country that performs best as 1 and the country that performs worst 12.

b Plot the results on a scattergraph like the one shown below:

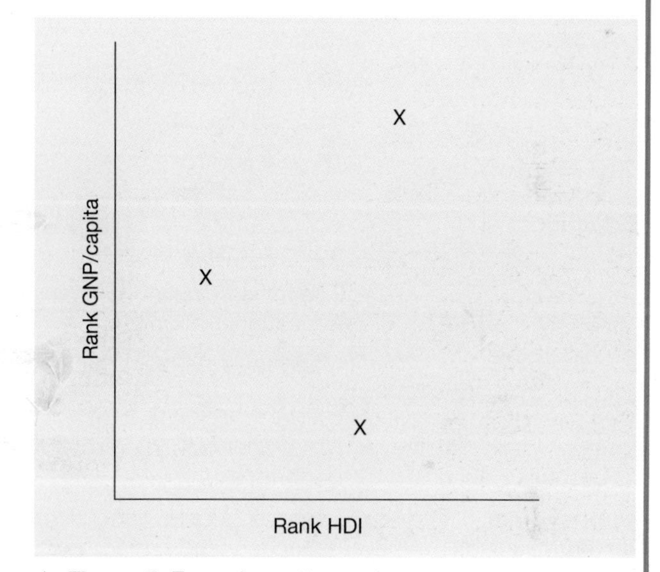

▲ **Figure 5** Example scattergraph

c Describe and account for the resulting pattern.

d If you were designing an index to show development what factors would you consider?

	MEDCs	LEDCs
Gross national product (GNP)	• The majority have a GNP of more than US$5000 per year. MEDCs have 83% of the world's income.	• The majority generate less than US$2000 per year. Collectively, LEDCs have only 17% of the world's income.
	• High percentage of population is above poverty line; that is, they have an income of more than US$14.4 per day.	• High percentage of population is below the poverty line; that is, they have an income of less than US$1 per day.
Life expectancy	• Over 75 years.	• Under 60 years.
Population and population growth	• 25% of world population.	• 75% of world population
	• Relatively slow growth, for example 25% of population doubles in 80 years.	• Fast growth, for example 75% of population doubles in 30 years.
	• Effective family planning.	• Little or no family planning.
Disposable income spent on consumer goods	• High – large numbers of consumer durables per 1000 people due to large disposable income.	• Low – few consumer durables per 1000 people.
Health	• Good – relatively few people per doctor.	• Poor – large numbers of people per doctor.
	• Account for 94% world health expenditure.	• Account for only 6% of the world health expenditure.
	• Well-equipped hospitals.	• Inadequate hospital provision and medication.
Education	• Account for 89% of the world's education spending.	• Account for 11% of world's education spending.
	• The majority have full-time secondary education.	• Few have formal education opportunities.
	• Good teacher–pupil ratio in schools.	• Poor pupil–teacher ratios.
	• High adult literacy rates.	• Low adult literacy rates.
	• No gender bias in educational opportunities.	• Females disadvantaged in educational opportunities.
Employment structure	• Large % of population involved in secondary and tertiary industry.	• High % of population involved in primary industry.
	• 75% of world's manufacturing industry.	• 25% of world's manufacturing industry – much of it MNC owned.
Levels of technology/ mechanisation	• Highly mechanised.	• Mostly manual labour and animal power.
	• Large investment in research and development.	• Little native investment in research and development.
	• 92% of world's industry.	• 8% of world's industry.
Diet/access to clean water	• Balanced diet but increasing obesity.	• Much malnutrition.
	• High animal protein diet.	• Low protein diet.
	• 70% of world's food grains.	• 30% of world's food grains.
	• Majority of population have access to clean water.	• Many people do not have access to clean water.
Energy	• High levels of consumption, use 75% of world energy.	• Lower consumption rates, currently 25% of world energy.
Communications	• Good communications infrastructure: roads, railways and airports.	• Communication infrastructure focused on urban areas. Limited elsewhere.
Exports	• 82% of world's export earnings.	• 18% of world's export earnings.
	• Mostly manufactured goods.	• Based on primary products and unprocessed raw materials.

▲ **Figure 6** Differences in development between MEDCs and LEDCs

Causes of variations in levels of development/factors that hinder development in LEDCs

We may know what development is, and something about how to measure it, but what causes contrasts in development levels in the first place? There are a number of reasons as to why economic development in LEDCs is hindered.

Historical reasons

Colonialism is the system in which many western European countries, such as the UK, France, the Netherlands, Germany, Spain, Portugal and Belgium took over the running of areas of land elsewhere on the globe and took resources and wealth from them from the sixteenth century onwards. This meant that colonies in South America, Africa and Asia provided raw materials which allowed the colonising country to develop their industries and become richer. Colonialism as a system had ended by the 1970s. For example, Malaysia became independent of Britain in 1957, Algeria independent of France in 1962 and Mozambique became independent of Portugal in 1975.

The development of these countries might have been helped a little by colonialism, and sometimes a good network of roads and railways and an efficient education sector may have been put in place by the colonial powers, for example. However, it had mainly a negative impact on the colonised countries, leaving them dependent on the markets in the MEDCs. People who believe this often point to the fact that MEDCs continue to get much of their wealth as a result of LEDCs being kept poorer.

Get Active

What does the cartoon in Figure 7 suggest one of the effects of colonisation has been? Who has gained? Why? Who has lost? Why?

▲ **Figure 7** 'Gold diggers'

Environmental factors

Natural hazards such as droughts, floods, hurricanes, earthquakes and volcanoes often hinder economic development. Disasters such as floods can make it difficult for countries to expand economically. On the other hand, floods bring rich sediments and volcanic areas are also very fertile. Of course, natural hazards are not restricted to LEDCs. There are volcanoes and floods in MEDCs too and hurricanes sweep the southern coast of the USA each year. However, LEDCs are less prepared for such hazards and they often lack the finances to reduce the effects for their populations.

There are also some diseases which thrive in tropical climates, where many of these LEDCs happen to be located. Malaria, once common in Europe, remains a problem in Africa because the illness restricts how effectively someone can work. HIV/AIDS too is a problem for many African countries.

The environment of many LEDCs is also under pressure from economic activities. Mining, forestry and, more recently, tourism can all put an environment at risk. This is particularly so when attempts are being made to access larger and larger profits. For example, deforestation earns a lot of money for a country but, when the trees have been removed, the land is vulnerable to desertification. Rainforests are vulnerable to the leaching of minerals because of the high rainfall and the land left behind may have little agricultural value as a result.

Get Active

Explain the following terms and how they impact on the environment:

1 deforestation
2 desertification
3 leaching.

Dependence on primary activities

Most employment in MEDCs is in **tertiary activities** – work in services such as teaching, nursing, refuse collection, banking, catering and so on. A very small percentage of people in MEDCs are employed in **primary activities** – work in extractive industries such as mining, farming, forestry and so on. LEDCs are very different, although they are changing. At present they usually have poorly developed tertiary industries. They often have very high proportions of their populations involved in primary industry, and depend on it for much of their earnings. For example, Zambia depends on its export of copper for 98% of its export earnings – almost everything they earn.

This is a problem for these countries as the prices paid for the primary products produced – things like cotton and copper ore – vary enormously from year to year. The result is that the countries find it very hard to plan ahead. If you want to build a motorway or a new hospital you have to be sure of your earnings. Many LEDCs are not sure from year to year. Figure 8 shows how copper prices varied over a five-year. This makes it very difficult for Zambia's government to plan ahead.

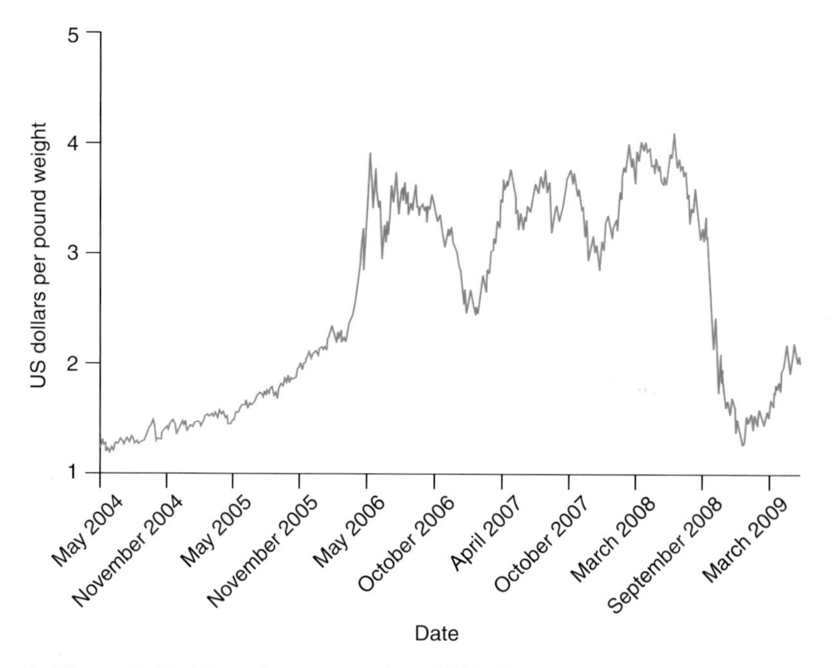

▲ **Figure 8** Variations in copper prices 2004–8

Get Active

In pairs, study Figure 8 and think of three questions that it would be worthwhile exploring. Then:

- Give feedback to rest of class.
- Listen to all the suggested questions.
- As a class, try to answer the questions.

Types of economic activity

There are four types of economic activity:

- Primary activities involve people getting raw materials or extracting them from the environment, either the land or the sea. Examples of jobs like this are fishermen, miners and farmers.
- **Secondary activities** involve the processing of primary products to make manufactured goods. Examples of this are in any of the manufacturing industries such as making cars, footwear or computers.
- Tertiary activities are services provided to people. Examples of jobs in this area include nurses, refuse disposal workers and social workers.
- **Quaternary activities** involve research and development into new designs and products. These normally require high levels of technology. They provide information and administrative services to other industries. Often governments do not separate tertiary and quaternary activities in their statistics.

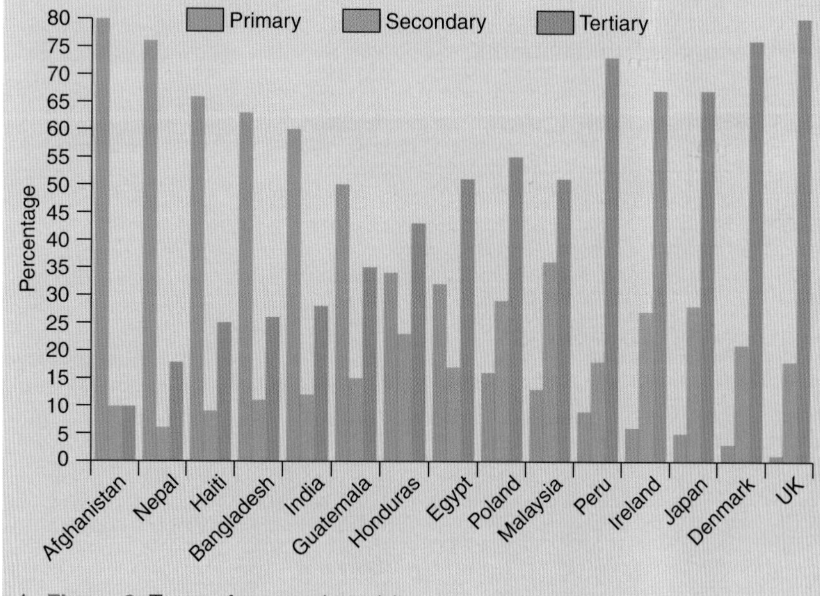

In terms of levels of economic development, generally the more developed a country is, the more its economic activities include tertiary and quaternary industries and there is a smaller percentage engaged in the primary.

▲ **Figure 9** Types of economic activity

Debt

Following the end of colonialism, banks in MEDCs lent enormous amounts of money to many LEDCs. Much of the money was destined to be spent on massive infrastructural developments such as dams, airports and roads. This was thought to be a good way of stimulating development.

Inevitably the scale of lending was such that many countries had difficulties in paying off the banks. One example should indicate what happened. Ecuador is a tiny country in South America, on the equator, hence its name. In the 1970s the government of Ecuador borrowed US$3 billion from international lenders. The government at that time was a dictatorship and spent much of the money on the military, to ensure that they retained power. Ecuador has been a democracy since 1979 but the debt still needs to be paid. As interest is charged on the loan, soon Ecuador owed more than it had borrowed in the first place. The debt is now more than US$10 billion.

There is a tremendous human cost to this debt as every dollar spent on paying it off means one less dollar for fighting poverty and improving the quality of life for people. In 2007, Ecuador paid $1.75 billion towards its debt, which is more than it could afford in total on social services, health care, the environment, and housing and urban development put together. In December 2008, the government of Ecuador said that it would not pay back the money. The president called the debt 'immoral and illegitimate'. However, the consequences for the country of not continuing to pay back the debt are very serious.

Here are some startling facts:

- The poorest 49 countries have debts totalling $375 billion.
- The poorest 144 countries have debts over $2.9 trillion (a trillion is a thousand billion or a million million).
- The world's poorest countries pay almost $100 million every day to the rich world.
- Total debt continues to rise, despite ever-increasing payments, while aid is falling. For example:
  - The poorest 60 countries have paid $550 billion in both principal and interest over the last three decades, on $540 billion of loans, and yet there is still a $523 billion debt burden.

Get Active

How true is it to say that the enormous debt repayments of poor countries are subsidising rich countries?

Would you agree with President Mkapa of Tanzania when he said: 'I encourage you in your advocacy for total debt cancellation for poor countries because, frankly, it is a scandal that we are forced to choose between basic health and education for our people and repaying historical debt.' Why? Why not?

In what ways do LEDCs suffer by having to spend so much on debt repayments?

Politics

Economic development is much easier if a country is peaceful and has a stable government: that is a government that is efficient and not liable to dramatic change. Those countries can more easily invest in national infrastructure and **trade**, leading to economic growth. A peaceful country is more likely to attract investors than one in which there is conflict. These investors can create jobs and wealth. Many governments try to attract multinational corporations into their countries as this should increase earnings and the wealth of the area. A political system that is corrupt often is less likely to develop. Aid money or money supporting inward investment may be embezzled by corrupt officials. As lack of corruption is now a requirement for receiving aid, a number of African countries particularly become ineligible for aid because of their corrupt governments.

A strategy for reducing the global development gap

In 2000, leaders from 189 countries meeting at the United Nations agreed to the Millennium Development Goals (MDGs). These are a set of eight ambitious targets designed to reduce global poverty and disease by 2015. As countries have agreed concrete targets, the MDGs have injected new momentum into the fight against global poverty.

Governments and international organisations, through agreements like the MDGs, have for a long time worked at reducing the global development gap. Increasingly ordinary people are becoming motivated to do something themselves and to make sure that the governments deliver on their commitments. ONE was inspired by campaigns such as the Jubilee 2000 *Drop the Debt* and *Make Poverty History*.

Eradicate extreme poverty and hunger

Around the world, over one billion people attempt to live on less than a dollar a day; each night one person in seven goes to bed hungry.

Provide universal primary education

Improved access to primary education helps development as a result of improved health and earnings and yet 72 million children across the world do not currently attend school.

Promote gender equality

It has been shown that, while women often bear the brunt of poverty and poor health, improving their lives is often the key to development.

Reduce child mortality

Nearly 10 million children die before their fifth birthday every year: one every three seconds. Nearly all of these deaths are from diseases like diarrhoea or measles which are easy to prevent or to treat.

Improve the health of mothers

For example, over half a million mothers die from complications arising from childbirth each year.

Combat HIV/AIDS, tuberculosis and malaria

These diseases are among the worst in the world in terms of their impact on people and with a devastating impact on opportunities for a country's development. In 2007, HIV/AIDS killed more than two million, tuberculosis 1.7 million and at least one million people died of malaria globally. The incidences of these diseases can be reduced considerably.

Ensure environmental sustainability

Across the world more than one billion people have no clean water and more than twice as many have no access to basic sanitation. Climate change and population growth is likely to increase these figures.

Build a global partnership for development

To succeed in all of these goals means that the world's governments will have to co-operate in prioritising development, whether MEDC or LEDC.

▲ **Figure 10** The Millennium Development Goals

case study

ONE: an American organisation that is attempting to reduce the global development gap

▲ **Figure 11** Musicians Damien Rice and Bono attend the 'Edun And ONE: The Campaign To Make Poverty History Launch' party in New York in 2006

ONE is a US advocacy organisation. This means that it argues its case, mainly with politicians. It advocates an end to extreme poverty by achieving the internationally agreed MDGs. One of the things that makes ONE a little different from other organisations is that it has used the internet to make its case in powerful ways. In the 2008 US presidential race between Barack Obama and John McCain, the ONE organisation formed ONE Vote 08 and used YouTube, Facebook, Flickr and MySpace to campaign to get global poverty and the MDGs talked about by the politicians. Action Against Hunger is another campaign that ONE is running.

ONE's website claims:

> ONE is Americans of all beliefs and every walk of life – united as ONE – to help make poverty history. We are a campaign of over 2.4 million people and growing from all 50 states ... As ONE, we are raising public awareness about the issues of global poverty, hunger, disease and efforts to fight such problems in the world's poorest countries. As ONE, we are asking our leaders to do more to fight the emergency of global AIDS and extreme poverty. ONE believes that allocating more of the US budget toward providing basic needs like health, education, clean water and food would transform the futures and hopes of an entire generation in the world's poorest countries.
>
> ONE is nonpartisan; there's only one side in the fight against global AIDS and extreme poverty. Working on the ground in communities, colleges and churches across the USA, ONE members both educate and ask America's leaders to increase efforts to fight global AIDS and extreme poverty, from the US budget and presidential elections to specific legislation on debt cancellation, increasing effective international assistance, making trade fair, and fighting corruption. Everyone can join the fight. The goal of ending poverty may seem lofty, but it is within our reach if we take action together as one. You can start now by joining ONE and pledging your voice to the fight against extreme poverty and global AIDS.

Since 2000, improvements have been achieved. The cancellation of some debts has saved African countries $70 billion, and this, along with targeted aid for education, allowed 29 million more African children to go to school for the first time. In addition, increased funding for health around the world helped almost three million HIV-positive people to get life-saving drugs. In combating malaria, 59 million bed nets have been supplied. This shows what can be achieved. However, there are other measures which would suggest that not enough is being done for all countries to reach the targets that they signed up to by 2015.

What impact ONE has had in the improvements is difficult to say. However, it is clear that ordinary people are increasingly not prepared to allow their governments to make decisions on their own. It is partly the internet that has allowed this to happen.

The Commitment to Development Index (CDI)

This is an index that rates 22 of the world's richest nations on how much they help poor countries build prosperity, good government and security. Individual countries are scored in seven policy areas, which are then averaged to produce an overall score. To find out more about the Commitment to Development Index have a look at: www.cgdev.org/section/initiatives/_active/cdi/_non_flash/.

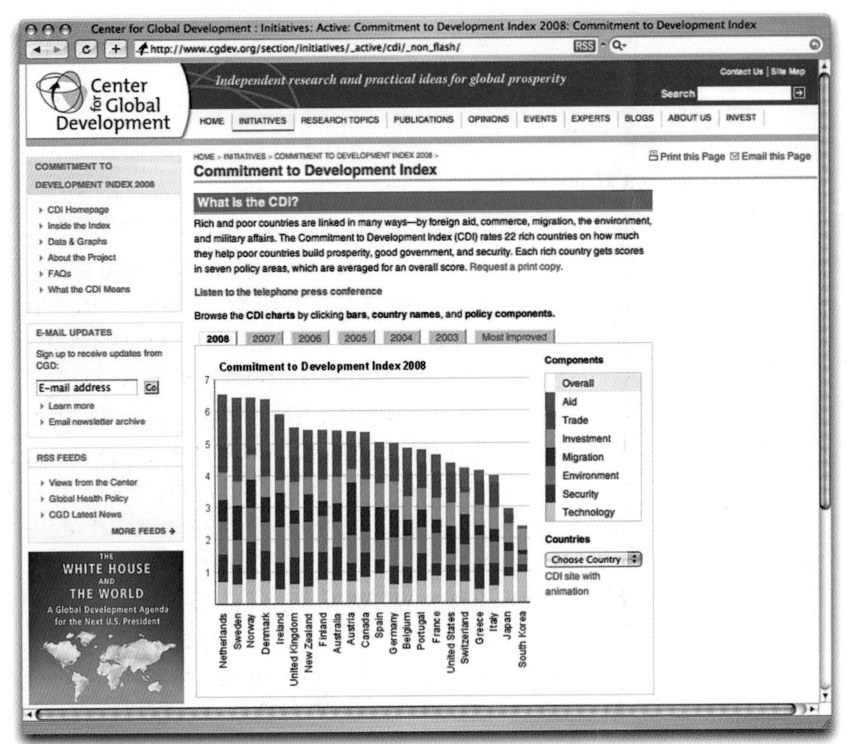

▲ **Figure 12** The Commitment to Development Index 2008

Get Active

1. What are the seven areas of policy used to produce the CDI?
2. Rank the top 10 countries for the most recent year available (put the country with the highest score first).
3. Did anything surprise you? What about the performance of the world's major economic powers: the USA and Japan?
4. Look more closely at the performance of two countries (USA and Ireland). You can do his by clicking on the divided bar graph for each of the countries or by using the *Choose Country* option box on the screen. How do you explain why Ireland was ranked 5 in the world in 2008 while the USA was only ranked 17. Use facts and figures quoted on the website to justify your opinions.

weblinks

Further information about fighting poverty can be found at these sites, or you may be able to find others. Do some research to find out how some of these campaigns work.

www.actionagainsthunger.org/what-we-do/one-campaign

www.jubileedebtcampaign.org.uk/

www.makepovertyhistory.org/

www.one.org/international/

www.micahchallenge.org.uk/

Factors contributing to unequal development

Globalisation

The world is shrinking in many ways. People can travel quickly and easily across the planet. The internet means that everyone can easily communicate within and between countries. World trade has opened up so that brands can now be sold around the planet. This is called globalisation. Many industries have globalised as well, with branches in a great many countries around the world. These are called multinational corporations (MNCs).

Many MNCs are household names: Coca-Cola, Nike, Nestlé, Levi, McDonalds and Adidas are a few. Others have names that are not household names but they are still enormously powerful around the world. These companies are often richer and more powerful than the countries in which they work. Most of the market in major products is controlled by only a few companies as shown in Figure 13.

Globalisation means:

- Companies operate in many countries and so international operations are increasingly important for people and companies.
- Decisions taken in one country can quickly affect other countries because of the improvements in transportation and the spread of global communications, such as email and videoconferencing.
- Economic power is concentrated in the hands of a few global companies or MNCs. Of the world's 100 largest economies, 50 are now MNCs and *not* countries.
- Countries are increasingly interdependent because they need to trade with one another and exchange goods – the lives and actions of people in one country are increasingly linked with those of people thousands of kilometres away.

Globalisation affects some places in the world more than others. The MEDCs usually are where the headquarters of the MNCs are located and this is where the profits are likely to end up. On the other hand, the LEDCs generally produce the raw materials. Sometimes the processing or assembly of the raw materials takes place in the LEDCs to take advantage of the low wages there.

Another impact of globalisation has been the increased movement of people, money and ideas which is generally seen as a beneficial change. However, this movement has also led to the increased movement of invasive species and of diseases. The swine flu pandemic, which started in 2009, is an example of this.

Multinational corporations (MNCs)

An MNC is a company with factories in many countries; sometimes they are called transnational corporations (TNCs). The business of the company is usually secondary manufacturing of products which are then sold worldwide. The headquarters of the company is in a MEDC, but the factories are in both MEDCs and LEDCs. Most of the high status and most profitable parts of the multinationals remain located in the MEDCs. The research and development parts, for example, may be more likely to be found in the richer countries. The scale of multinationals means that they have the money to run efficiently at low costs, which earns high profits. These can, in turn, be invested in more research and development and in advertising their products.

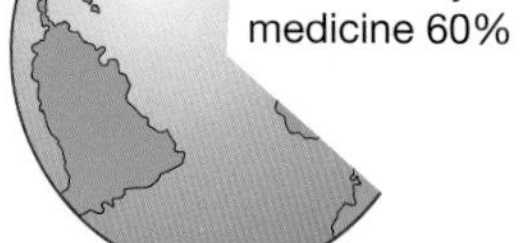

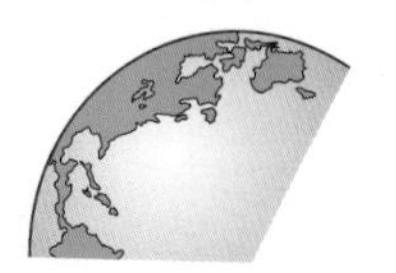

▲ **Figure 13** The market share of the top 10 corporations by sector

1. Global communications

It is becoming cheaper and easier to communicate. Jake in New York can Skype his cousins in Cork for as long as he likes for nothing. Ten years ago, the same call would have cost $3. In 1930, when Jake's grandfather first arrived in America from Cork, it would have cost him $245 to phone home. If Kathy in the USA saves a month's wages, she can buy the most up-to-date computer. A worker in Bangladesh would have to save 8 years' wages to buy a computer. Jake and Kathy can surf the web and understand four out of every five websites – because they are written in English. However, nine out of every 10 people in the world don't understand English.

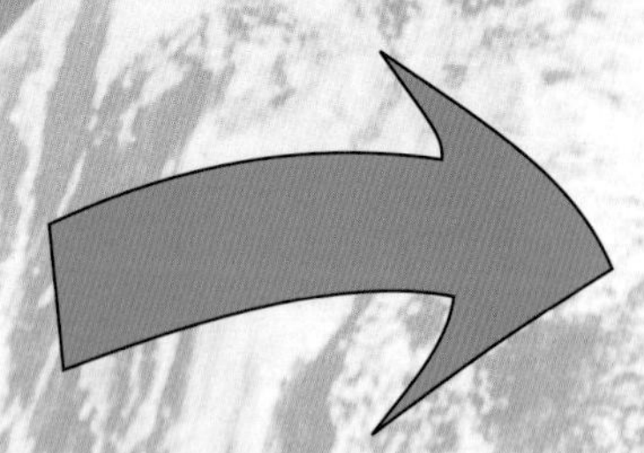

2. Global advertising

Advertisements for goods like Coca-Cola and Levis can be seen everywhere, from Belfast to Berlin to Beijing. In the 10 years from 1987 to 1997, Nike increased its spending on ads from $25 million to $500 million. Tiger Woods, the golfer, is paid $55,555 per day to advertise Nike products. Workers making Nike products in Indonesia earn around $1.25 per day. This is often not enough to live on.

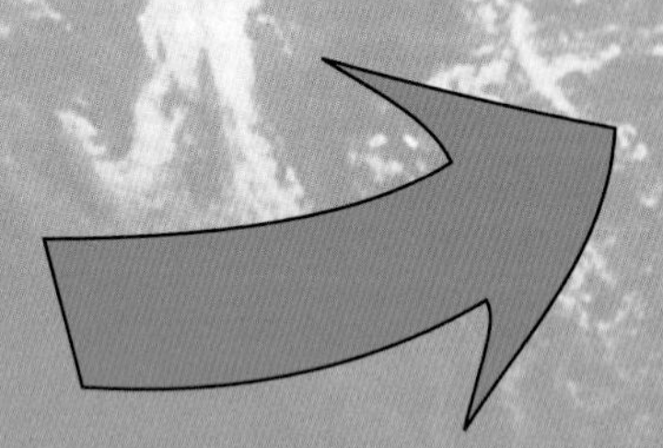

3. Trade is increasing

Three times more goods are shipped or flown between countries now than 20 years ago. Trade can create jobs in poor countries, but people often have to work in terrible conditions. On banana, coffee and flower farms, for example, workers get very low wages, work long hours and have to use dangerous pesticides or chemicals. Some countries are missing out on trade altogether: the 50 poorest countries are being left behind and making less and less money from trade compared to richer countries.

4. Global rules

The World Trade Organisation (WTO) was set up to write the rules for trade between countries and to make sure that all countries obey them. This could be very good – fair rules would mean that everyone would win. However, the rules are written to suit rich countries. This is because rich countries can afford to pay lawyers to debate the rules, while poor countries cannot. For example, Japan has 25 trade experts at the WTO, Bangladesh has one, and 29 of the poorest countries have none. There are up to 10 meetings every day. Poor countries cannot go to all the meetings and so important decisions are made without them.

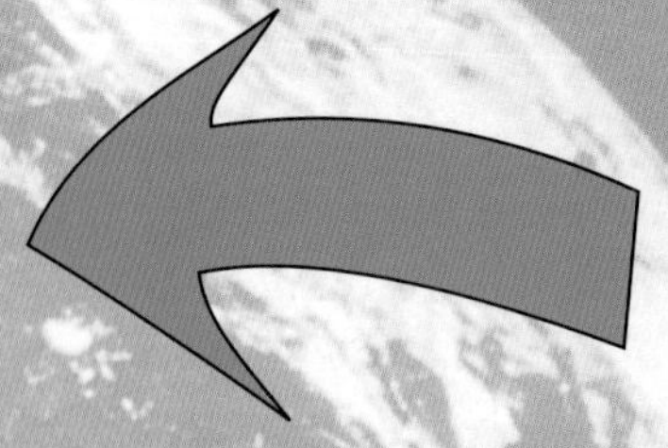

5. Travel and tourism

Travelling abroad for holidays can be interesting and exciting. People make friends from foreign countries and may discover many interesting things about other people's lives and the global environment. However, some people fear tourism can have a negative side. In many countries, local people look and dress in beautiful costumes and jewellery, such as the Maasai cattle farmers in Kenya. Sometimes, tourists may treat local people like objects to be photographed rather than human beings who can feel and talk.

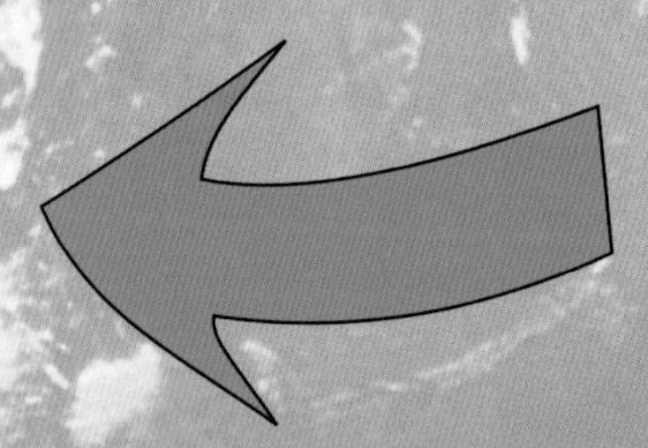

6. The media

Television, films, radio and newspapers can help people to learn about what is happening in other places and what it would be like to live there. On the other hand, the media may also give people a false impression of other countries. In India, many people think that life for everyone in Europe and the USA is exactly as it appears in the movies: rich and exciting. Meanwhile, news reports about Africa often only show images of desperate hungry people. However, most people in Africa have little money but find many ways to make their lives happy and full, and are certainly not helpless or starving.

▲ **Figure 14** Six situations in which globalisation affects people

MNCs have grown in size and influence so that some of the larger ones make more money in a year than all the African countries put together. They control most of the world's trade and investment, produce most of the world's manufactured goods and contribute to modern technology and scientific discoveries.

Investment is the capital or money attracted to one country from another country. Multinationals often invest in LEDCs, but foreign investment is very limited in the world's very poorest countries where 20% of the population live.

Relocation means the movement of one company or industry from one place to another. MNCs often move factories from an MEDC to a LEDC, or from one LEDC to another. Generally this is to find places with cheaper labour costs.

One local example of relocation is Avalon Guitars Ltd (formerly Lowden Guitars) of Newtownards, Co. Down (see Figure 15).

The main reasons for *not* building a new factory in Northern Ireland were:

- Being able to increase the profits without the need to invest capital in a new factory.
- Faster deliveries to customers from other countries (10 weeks instead of 16–24 weeks).
- Product range could be expanded using expertise of guitar makers abroad.

The following factors were important in the choice of location of partner factories by Avalon Guitars:

- The high levels of productivity and easy access to capital, especially in Korea, give it a competitive advantage.
- Cheaper labour costs, especially in China – a typical factory worker earns US$1 per day (and will usually have food and dormitory accommodation provided).
- High levels of investment in technology especially in Spain where skilled labour is available to make the specialist 'classical' guitar. The top model of classical guitar in Brazilian rosewood and Western red cedar was priced at £5999 in 2009.

This company specialises in hand-made guitars on a limited production basis at the rate of 1500 per year at its factory in Newtownards, where it employs 32 people. It also has a distribution centre based in Texas, USA as 50% of the products are sold in North America. The increase in demand is greater than the capacity available at the factory in Newtownards and so the company decided to extend the production of acoustic guitars to the Far East. After researching 20 factories abroad, four partner factories in Korea, China, the Czech Republic and Spain were chosen to make Avalon guitars. The HQ in Newtownards will continue to be involved in the design, research & development, marketing and the quality control of the product. The local company is becoming a design-led global brand in the acoustic guitar market.

▲ **Figure 15** Avalon Guitars

Get Active

1. Explain in your own words how MNCs manage to run efficiently at low costs to earn high profits.
2. What problems can arise in the search for ever lower labour costs?
3. Why are labour costs significant for MNCs?
4. Why do the research and development departments of MNCs remain in MEDCs? What would need to happen for these departments to be shifted to LEDCs?
5. Imagine you were a financial expert advising the directors of Avalon Guitars about locating their new production facility. You have one minute to make your pitch to the board of directors:
   - Pick out all the key economic data that you think are important in making the decision.
   - Use these points to make your pitch:
     a. make a draft of your pitch
     b. check that it lasts no longer than one minute
     c. practise your pitch
     d. make your pitch to rest of the class.
   - Class decides on the best pitch.

case study

Who really gains? How globalisation both helps and hinders development in India

Some countries like India have been affected greatly by globalisation. Since the 1990s the Indian economy has opened up, barriers to trade have been demolished, entrepreneurs have been encouraged and foreign investors welcomed. As a result India's economy grew at enormous rates. In 1996–7 growth rates of almost 78% have been claimed. This compares to a growth rate in the 1970s of just 3%. While the growth of India's economy has now slowed, its economy is still expanding. According to some reports, in 2007, India was set to become the world's third largest economy, overtaking Japan. Despite the global slowdown, India's Prime Minister was claiming that growth rates of close to 7% would be possible in 2009–10.

India is also finding itself a major player in the world. India will be expecting to land a permanent seat on the Security Council of the United Nations when it is reformed. They would become part of the club which at present comprises China, France, Russian Federation, the UK and the USA.

The supporters of globalisation believe that this has all come about because of the opening up of the economy. India's low labour costs and its huge English-speaking workforce combined with encouragement for MNCs have made it popular with them for everything from manufacturing to call centres.

The success of high-tech industries in India resulted in the return of large numbers of skilled Indians who had moved overseas to get work. This has been described as a 'brain gain', the opposite of 'brain drain' when people leave. These people form part of India's growing middle class, a potentially vast domestic market for Indian industry.

Get Active

Describe in your own words the terms 'brain drain' and 'brain gain'.

Average living standards appear to be increasing in India as a result of globalisation. Between 1990 and 2004, life expectancy rose from 59 to 63 years. Over the same period, adult literacy rose from 50% to 61%.

Mass consumption, once only found in MEDCs, is now available to more and more Indians. Enormous shopping centres are being built in the major cities and towns to allow the wealthy middle class to spend their money.

Get Active

1 Working in groups, make a list of factors that explain India's rapid economic progress.
2 Rank these factors in order of importance.

▲ **Figure 16** A Bangalore shopping mall

It has been suggested that if the economic growth continues, this will drive up living standards for the whole population of India, and globalisation is identified as the cause.

There is an alternative view. Despite globalisation and the claims made of it, 300 million Indians live on less than $1 a day and almost half of children under 5 years of age in India are malnourished. Less than a third of homes in India have a toilet. Of India's 500,000 villages, less than half have a connection to the electricity network.

Percentage (number) of Indians who are middle class	20–25% (200–250 million)
Increased spending by India's middle classes	$300 million
The increase in the 'super-rich' in next 5 years	17 million to 35 million
The number of Indians with the same spending power as US residents	40 million
Growth of consumer spending in last 10 years	6%
Percentage of India's population younger than 40 years of age	75%

▲ **Figure 17** Some facts about India. Source: adapted from findings from a Chesterton Meghra survey

Get Active

Imagine you are a 16 year old living in these kinds of conditions. What would life be like? Write a diary entry for one day in your life.

case study

Globalisation has been accused of widening the gap between rich and poor. Opening up trade between India and other countries has benefited those who have the skills to work in the high-tech industries and in the call centres, but has harmed the chances of many ordinary Indians as goods have come in from outside, damaging their chances of getting a job.

Some have blamed the opening up of trade by globalisation as something which has started to erode India's traditional values, putting consumerism above the family and community which were once so important in India. Globalisation has brought Western ideas of dress, diet and behaviour, some of which is shocking to older Indians. The shopping centres may be crowded but they are mocked by some as a place to buy scented candles and other tasteless articles by people with nothing else to do with their money.

India is a richer country because of globalisation, but the benefits of this wealth have been too slow in helping India's poor to have a better life. Average income per person is still just $720 (£365) a year in India. Remember that this is an average and there are a lot of billionaires in India. Many of the poor are in remote rural areas, far away from the rapidly growing city of Bangalore with its high-tech industries.

▲ **Figure 18** A homeless man begs outside a car showroom in Kalkutam. Globalisation has done little to reduce poverty in India

This is not just a problem for people with very low incomes but could threaten the future of India itself. As the gap between rich and poor widens, there has been unrest from communist militants in more than a quarter of India. According to India's Prime Minister, this threat is the single greatest security challenge that India has ever faced internally.

The communist guerrillas are not likely to beat India's government, but they can still cause problems in the poorest regions in India, where they are strongest. These areas may continue to get very little investment and so will not have much economic growth. This will further increase differences between the richer and the poorer parts of India. While globalisation cannot be said to have caused the rise in the guerrillas, the increased gap between rich and poor in different parts of India will make it more likely that the communist groups will get local support for longer.

It is unclear where globalisation will take India and whether the global slowdown which started in 2008 will affect the enormous changes which have taken part in the country.

Get Active

In groups:

1 Consider the statement: 'For India, globalisation widened the gap between the rich and the poor, making the rich, richer and better off, and the poor, poorer and less well off.' Note the key points of agreement.
2 List the possible outcomes of the campaign being waged by armed militants in parts of India.
3 What is the significance of describing the militant rebels as 'communists'?

weblinks

http://news.bbc.co.uk/1/hi/world/south_asia/6257057.stm – Key facts about the growth of India.

http://news.bbc.co.uk/1/hi/business/6288325.stm – Prosperity in Bangalore.

www.progressive.org/mag_apb091906 – Impact of globalisation on India's farmers.

www.un.org/esa/sustdev/csd/csd16/PF/presentations/farmers_relief.pdf – Pressure on India's farmers.

http://news.bbc.co.uk/1/hi/world/south_asia/3481855.stm – Is globalisation good for India?

http://news.bbc.co.uk/1/hi/world/south_asia/6195617.stm – India could suffer from globalisation.

Newly industrialising countries

Newly industrialising countries (NICs) are countries which have not yet become MEDCs, but their economies are growing rapidly, outpacing their LEDC neighbours. Rapid industrialisation in the cities of these countries is transforming them very quickly and causing social upheaval as people are sucked into the cities from the countryside around. Often these NICs have moved from an economy dominated by agriculture to one based on manufacturing, and multinational corporations are often operating there. There may be increased social freedoms as well. However, environmental, social and labour standards tend to be weaker in NICs than in MEDCs so sometimes they are criticised.

The first NICs were Hong Kong, South Korea, Singapore and Taiwan which developed rapidly from the 1960s. All four of these are now high income economies and with a HDI of over 0.9, comparable to many MEDCs. Which countries are currently NICs depends on the sources you read. Most lists include Turkey, South Africa, Brazil, China, India, Mexico, Malaysia, Thailand and the Philippines. Others include Indonesia and Russia in the list. It is widely believed that, by 2050, the largest economies in the world will include a number of NICs: China, India, Brazil, and Mexico.

Get Active

- Locate the countries termed as 'NICs' on a blank world map.
- Give your map an appropriate title.
- From a locational point of view, what do most of these NICs have in common?

World trade can create problems for LEDCs

Trade is the buying and selling of goods and services between one country and another. Trade takes place because no single country can provide everything that its population needs or wants, so goods and services are exchanged with other countries. For this reason, countries are dependent on one another in world trade – interdependent. Imports are the goods brought into a country from another. To pay for these a country has to sell goods or services as exports. Imports and exports include raw materials, energy resources and manufactured goods.

Trade is becoming more competitive as all countries want to increase the amount of trade but to be less dependent on imports at the same time. Countries try to reduce expensive imports and try to earn more from exports.

MEDCs and LEDCs have very different patterns of trade. While world trade has increased enormously with globalisation, it can create problems for LEDCs.

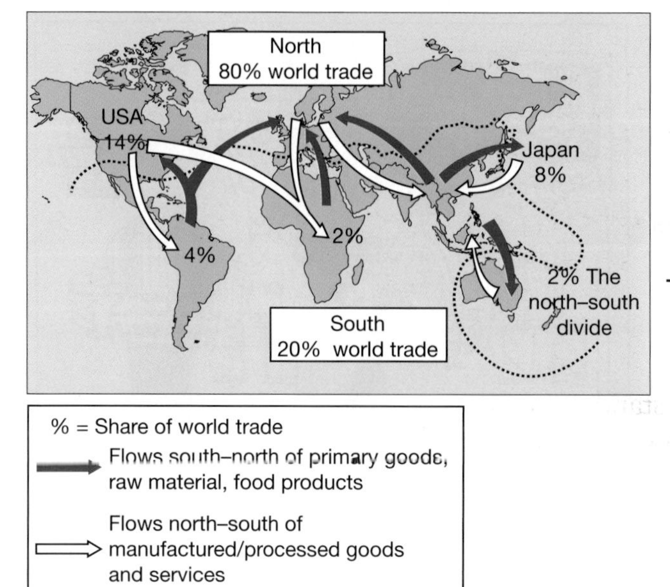

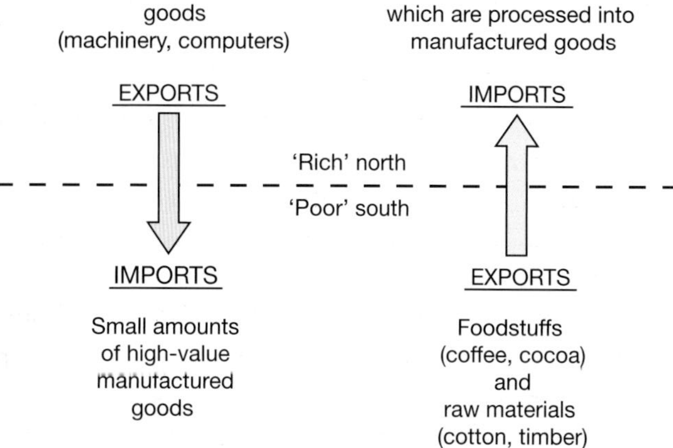

▲ **Figure 19** World trade patterns

The trade pattern of MEDCs

1 The share of world trade by MEDCs is increasing and MEDCs control 80% of the world's trade. Most of this is between MEDCs. The EU and the USA control over half of world trade.
2 Many of the MEDCs export more than they import.
3 Some countries join into 'clubs' like the EU and trade between themselves and less with other countries, including LEDCs.
4 MEDCs largely export processed manufactured goods such as machinery which fetches high prices when exported to LEDCs.
5 Many MEDCs put up trade barriers against other countries to protect the workers' jobs in the MEDCs. They do this by putting taxes or tariffs on imports and limiting the amount which is imported.
6 It is estimated that trade barriers in the rich MEDCs cost LEDCs US$700 billion every year.

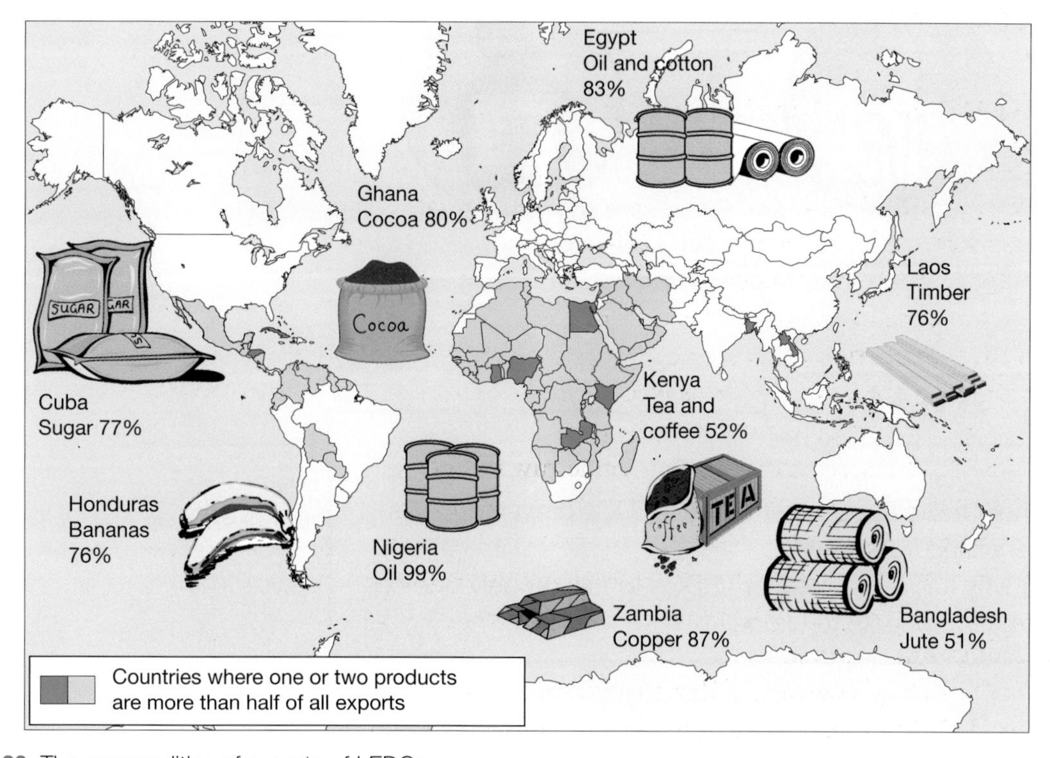

▲ **Figure 20** The commodities of exports of LEDCs

The trade patterns of LEDCs

1. LEDCs have a decreasing share of world trade and control only about 20%. Only the NICs have a larger amount of trade with MEDCs – examples are South Korea, Taiwan and Brazil. These countries have rapidly increased their exports of manufactured goods to MEDCs.
2. Most LEDCs have a trade deficit – they import more than they export – and do not belong to trading blocs.
3. Many LEDCs export primary unprocessed products or raw materials and foodstuffs which are sold at low and fluctuating prices. A total of 50 LEDCs depend on only three products for half of their export earnings – coffee, cotton and cocoa.
4. The trade gap between MEDCs and LEDCs is becoming wider as trade becomes more unbalanced.

▲ **Figure 21** Cartoonist's view of global trading

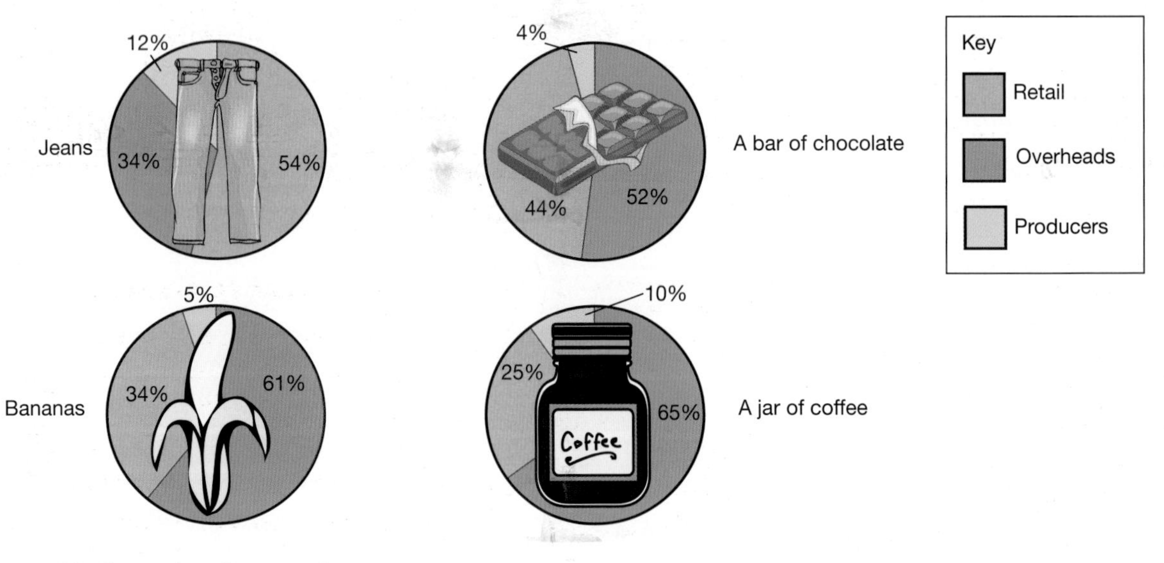

▲ **Figure 22** Share of profits to producers

Get Active

In pairs:

- Agree how trade barriers set up by MEDCs prevent LEDCs from benefiting from trade.
- Explain why it is a problem for LEDCs to rely on only one or two primary products to export.

Most do sell their crops abroad. This makes them very dependent on the world prices for their goods which fluctuate from year to year.

More money is earned by processing the goods, but this is done by MEDCs

Why don't LEDCs process their own goods?

Tariffs in many MEDCs make this difficult.

Surely their crops are needed by many countries? Why don't they get a good price?

Look Buddy, when the price of my coffee goes up I drink less!

Few of their products are really essential.

Why don't they stop growing for an overseas market and produce crops they need themselves?

Because they need money to pay off the debts ... both of individual farmers, and of governments.

- So, it is risky for LEDCs to be based on cash crops.
- Foreign exchange benefits only the small elite.
- Once countries and individuals are in debt it is difficult to stop growing cash crops.

▲ **Figure 23** Five trade traps for LEDCs

Sustainable solutions to deal with the problems of unequal development

Sustainable development

Sustainable development means 'meeting the needs of the present, without compromising the ability of future generations to meet their own needs' (from G.H. Brundtland's *Our Common Future*, 1987).

Sustainable development aims at maximising the economic, environmental and social benefits of development while minimising the economic, environmental and social drawbacks. There is often conflict between economic development and the protection of the environment. Traditionally, economic development was seen in terms of large-scale industrial projects such as dams, enormous factories or major road developments. Sustainable development is more likely to focus on small-scale projects that are for the well-being of local people and have the minimum impact on the environment.

Sustainable development should therefore improve:

- quality of life
- standard of living.

This can be done by:

- using natural resources in a way that does not damage the environment
- encouraging economic development that the country can afford and so avoid debt
- developing **appropriate technology**, that is, technology suited to the skills, wealth and needs of local people, which can be handed down to later generations.

Appropriate technology

This is technology which, in its design, considers the community that it is intended for and the environment in which they live. Typically appropriate technology uses fewer resources, is easier to maintain, costs less overall and has a lower impact on the environment in comparison to other technology.

A pump which requires petrol and spare parts from abroad when it breaks down is *not* appropriate technology. Something which uses locally available materials and could be fixed by the local people if it breaks is.

An example would be a solar cooker. These are appropriate in some places, depending on climate and how food is cooked. They reduce the amount of firewood used locally, improving the environment, do not give out smoke (a cause of ill-health in many countries) and cost very little to make, often costing as little as £4.

Another high-tech example of appropriate technology would be Loband (www.aptivate.org/Projects.Loband.html) which allows places with slow internet connections to use the World Wide Web. Loband simplifies webpages by reducing their size and this allows them to download much more quickly, bringing the internet to places where it previously could not be accessed.

► **Figure 24** Making tea with a solar cooker. A woman in Mongolia making tea for guests using a solar cooker made from a parabolic satellite dish covered in mirrors. By adjusting the position of the dish towards the sun she was able to boil a kettle of water in a few minutes using no fuel at all

Get Active

Research

Research another example of appropriate technology. You might begin with an internet search using a search engine like Google:

1 Provide a photo or diagram/sketch.
2 Explain how it works.
3 Outline the benefits to people.

Communication task

Present your research to the rest of the class.

Assessment of ideas put forward

As a class decide on the best presentation.

In August 2002 the second World Summit on Sustainable Development (WSSD) was held in Johannesburg, South Africa. It was an opportunity to review the progress of the sustainable developments planned at the first Earth Summit 10 years before, in Rio de Janiero.

The Johannesburg summit focused on sustainable development in five areas, together known as WEHAB. These are:

- Water and sanitation.
- Energy.
- Health.
- Agriculture.
- Biodiversity.

Although there have been improvements in some of these areas in the 10 years since the Rio Summit, there is still room for improvement. However, the fact that more than 22,000 people attended the meeting from 198 nations is positive, as it means that more governments and people will be encouraged to consider sustainable development projects.

Get Active

- In groups, decide if such global summits achieve anything concrete or if they become 'talking shops'.
- Do the world's major powers always take on board the agreements that are reached at global summits, like the one held at Kyoto in Japan?

case study

A sustainable development project: fishing in South-west India

Along the shores of Kerala and Tamil Nadu, which are the two most southern states of India, local villagers depend on fishing for their food and income. This area is one of the most densely populated areas in the world with a population density of 135 people/km^2. Of the working population, 70% are involved in fishing directly and 21% in fishing-related activities. These are some of the poorest people in India and they have a literacy rate of 31% which is much lower than the literacy rate of 64% elsewhere in Tamil Nadu.

▲ **Figure 26** A traditional southern Indian canoe

Get Active

- Define the term 'population density'
- How does the population density of Kerala and Tamil Nadu compare with:
  1 The UK?
  2 Ireland?
  3 The USA?
- Show your findings visually.

▲ **Figure 27** Fibreglass boats

▲ **Figure 25** The experiences of a Tamil Nadu fisherman

▲ **Figure 28** Kanyakumar, the southernmost point on the Indian subcontinent

The people fish from canoes made of hollowed out logs and rafts known as kattumarams. A unique feature of these rafts is that they can be changed into bigger or smaller units by adding or removing a log. The rafts are well designed to cope with the fierce south-west monsoon surf conditions.

Two problems decreased the income from fishing for the villagers:

- Owing to widespread deforestation in the area, there is a shortage of suitable tree trunks and light wood which is used to make the canoes and rafts. This has caused the traditional boats to become very expensive to make.
- The total catch decreased significantly between the mid-1970s and mid-1980s. It was felt that this was due to the increased use of trawlers fishing for prawns which disturbed the traditional fishing grounds.

In an attempt to address this problem, the fishermen then worked in consultation with European agencies on a number of development projects. Together they were able to devise ways of using the technology in a way more suited to the needs of the fishermen. The fishermen needed boats that were:

- unsinkable
- able to carry engines so that they could travel further and avoid trawler paths
- light
- easy to launch from surf-beaten beaches
- able to last 7–10 years
- more comfortable and able to carry more than boats powered by sail and oars.

A solution was found in the design of a new boat.

The new boat followed the traditional centuries-old designs but it was built in a different way. This preserved the uniqueness of the traditional boats in the region. The new building technology involved stitching and gluing. The method used the carpentry skills of traditional boat building and so was suitable for the local fishermen. Marine plywood and fibreglass were used as the building materials instead of the traditional tree trunks as this reduces the cutting down of trees that are already under threat. The new boat is easily adapted to many craft designs and therefore uses local people's skills while using technology to which the local industry can adapt.

The boats gained in popularity and the local fishermen, in consultation with the European agencies, have extended the range of designs. New job opportunities have resulted in the building of the boats and by the end of 1995 there were about 5000 plywood boats in operation in the area. Between 2000 and 2002, two-thirds of all boat-owning fishermen changed from the wooden kattumarams to plastic fibre boats and boats made of plywood. The transformation using appropriate technology played a vital role in the development process in this area of southern India.

Both the economy of the local community and the environment have been helped by this development as the scale of it is sustainable. The next generation of fishermen will not have their livelihoods threatened by the development of new boats, so long as overfishing does not happen.

The fishing communities, which had been faced with economic collapse and the movement of large numbers away from the fishing communities into urban areas, will now be able to continue. With a guaranteed income, these people will no longer be among the poorest population of India and, over time, their literacy rates may improve.

Get Active

Working in groups:

- Discuss the short-, medium- and long-term benefits of this new boat to the fishermen, their communities and the wider environment.
- Agree the main points and draw up three lists.

Fair trade

Fair trade means that people who make or grow a product are paid fairly for their work. Producers get paid directly at fair prices, cutting out the middlemen who would have taken most of the profit. Fair trade sales are increasing and now account for £500 million in the UK alone each year. Bananas account for £150 million, an increase of 130%. One in every four bananas sold in the UK is now fair trade and we consume three million fair trade bananas each day.

Fair trade in coffee

Many coffee farmers receive market payments that are lower than the costs of coffee production, which keeps people in a cycle of poverty and debt. The world price for raw coffee has dropped to just $1.30 per kilogram. When the market price of coffee drops below the producers' costs, people who produce coffee are working longer and harder for less money. The intensive production of coffee can cause other difficulties such as the loss of trees through deforestation to clear land for coffee production, and pollution from pesticides.

How fair trade has helped coffee producers:

- Fair trade guarantees a minimum wage for the harvests of small producers; this means they can provide for the basic needs for their families.
- Farmers are provided with credit facilities and paid a minimum price.
- Fair trade brings the product directly to the consumers and cuts out some of the intermediate costs of middlemen so that the benefits of trade are more likely to reach the producers.
- Fair trade develops long-term trade based on trust and respect.
- Fair trade works with co-operatives so that the producers control the business and the members of the co-operative share the profits and benefits fairly.
- The profits from receiving fair wages can be used by the producers to invest in health, education and the protection of the environment.

Some of the advantages of fair trade policies for a group of coffee producers in Mexico have been:

- In the village, farmers run a bus service to the nearest town which takes their children to the only secondary school.
- The farmers have bought a computer to track the sales of coffee and keep records on the crop.
- Fair trade encourages sustainable farming practices, for example organic farming, which does not use chemicals, and sustainable cultivation methods have been used to grow the coffee.

Farmer	1.5p	
Agent	1p	The producing country's total profit is a mere 11p
Haulage	1p	
Marketing and drying	7.5p	
Export cost	12p	
Packaging and marketing	25p	
Roasting and processing	62p	
Retailers	60p of which 30p is profit	
TOTAL COST:	**£1.70**	

▲ **Figure 29** How the coffee trade affects you. This is a breakdown of where your money goes when you buy a cup of coffee in a typical coffee-house or restaurant. The figures are based on the average price of a cup of coffee in the UK

Advantages of the fair trade system to MEDCs

- If producers in the LEDCs earn higher wages and are helped to develop in the long term, they will be able to increase their spending power. This means that they will be more able to afford to buy high-value processed products such as computers from the MEDCs. In turn this means that the MEDCs will expand their trade and will have new markets in which to sell their manufactured goods. This is becoming more important as 75% of the world's population lives in LEDCs.
- Consumers in MEDCs will be able to buy top-quality products knowing that the trade has been good for everyone.
- Consumers in MEDCs are able to keep their consciences clear as they know they have helped poor producers in LEDCs by trading in a moral way. People will feel that they are being good citizens by caring for other people. Trading in a fair way will contribute to people's well-being and development in other countries, so improving the quality of life for everyone.

Celestina from Tanzania

We get a higher price when we sell our coffee for 'Cafédirect' (a fair trade coffee). This means that our co-operative has been able to pay a doctor who will give treatment to our members.

(A co-operative is a group of people who have formed a business together. The members share the profits and benefits.)

The price difference has meant that I can afford more food for my family and send my children to school properly equipped with books for the first time.

Cafédirect stand by the agreed price for our coffee even when the international price of coffee falls on the world market.

Luis from Ecuador

My neighbour sells his bananas through a middleman to the world market and he gets $1 for a 20 kg box of fruit. I sell my bananas to La Guelpa collective which is part of the fair trade market and I get $2.50 for every 20 kg box of fruit. This means I can have a much better standard of living.

The collective has invested its money into the village and farms. There is now clean water in all of the communities and we are trying to improve the health care and build more schools.

José from the Dominican Republic

My wife and I work a small farm, growing cocoa, and together with other farmers in the local farmers' co-operative (called CONACADO) we process, market and transport the cocoa. CONACADO sells the cocoa to UK fair trade chocolate, guaranteeing a better price for us all and enabling us to strengthen the co-operative. All my five children went to school and some to further training, although I cannot read or write.

▲ **Figure 30** Three stories of people who are benefiting from fair trade

Get Active

1 Use ICT to produce a graph or pie chart which shows the breakdown of the price of a cup of coffee in Figure 29.
2 Describe the main features of your bar graph or pie chart.
3 Suggest why the producing country receives only 11p of the total cost of the price of a cup of coffee.
4 What percentage of the price of a cup of coffee goes to the retailers?
5 Explain how retailers might justify their large profit margins.
6 Read the stories of Celestina, Luis and José. Explain how they benefit from fair trade.
7 Today our supermarkets sell an ever-increasing range of fair trade products:
   a Draw up a list of fair trade products.
   b Sort these products into different categories.
   c Why is the range of fair trade products in our shops increasing? Explain your answer from the point of view of: i) supermarkets and ii) consumers.

▲ **Figure 31** Divine chocolate supports the fair trade movement

weblinks

Some fairtrade links to explore:

www.fairtrade.org.uk
www.fairtrade.net/
www.fairtradefederation.org/

Benefits and problems of international aid

Types of aid

Aid is the giving of resources by one country or organisation to another country. Resources can be in the form of:

- money: loans or grants
- expertise: people who have skills and knowledge
- goods: food, technology and equipment.

Aid can be **bilateral** or **multilateral**. Bilateral (meaning two-sided) aid is when there are just two countries involved – the country giving the aid (the donor) and the country receiving the aid – the recipient. If the UK was to give aid to Kenya, that would be bilateral aid. This is the most common form of aid.

Multilateral (many sided) aid involves many different countries giving help. For example, the United Nations may give aid to a country. This aid will have been contributed by a number of countries, not just one.

Voluntary aid is also called charity aid. It is made up of money collected by agencies such as Oxfam, usually as voluntary donations from individuals. The money collected is then spent on various projects, usually in long-term development like combating soil erosion or improving education. Charities also collect emergency aid after a natural disaster.

Tied aid is when the donor country requires the country getting the aid to spend it on goods and services provided by the donor country. For example, a country might give aid for the building of a road network but require the recipient of the aid to employ companies from the donor country in the construction.

Alternatively, aid may be given on the understanding that military equipment is bought from the donor country. In this way the aid is not 'free', it is 'tied'.

Aid can also be subdivided into short- and long-term aid:

- Short-term aid is also known as emergency aid and is given in response to particular immediate need, for example after natural disasters such as tsunamis and earthquakes.
- Long-term aid is aid that usually takes years before it is of full benefit to a country, for example improved education or a tree-planting scheme.

Why is aid needed by some LEDCs?

LEDCs only need aid to help them to cope with the following:

- global inequalities due to differences in levels of development
- introducing sustainable methods of development
- the imbalance of trade which causes a trade deficit
- dealing with environmental disasters, for example earthquakes, tsunamis, floods
- recovering from people-made disasters such as civil war.

Reasons for providing aid

When shopping and someone approaches you with a collection box, what do you do? Many people give to charities in this way but what are the reasons why they do so?

Governments and individuals have different motives for giving aid. It can be a political decision. For example, Egypt is an important ally for the USA and in a strategic position in the Middle East. This friendship was an important one for the USA in the 2003 war with Iraq. There are many much poorer countries than Egypt, but the USA feels that it is important to keep its friends and so a lot of its aid goes to Egypt.

Countries also give aid for economic reasons. For example, many MEDCs see it as important to maintain links with LEDCs, many of whom are ex-colonies, because of the large market they provide. Many projects also require longer term assistance, for example the UK donated £100 million to build the Victoria Dam in Sri Lanka. Many UK companies and engineers were employed in this enormous construction project.

Many people may feel that they have a moral obligation to help countries who are facing difficulties or who have limited financial reserves.

▲ **Figure 32** Charity collection box

Comic Relief

Comic Relief is a well-known charity which uses comedy and laughter to support hundreds of groups, organisations and charities across the UK and Africa to tackle poverty and social injustice. It raises money from the public by involving them in events and projects that are innovative and fun. Comic Relief also seeks to inform and educate the public on issues relating to social change, working hard to make sure that the projects it supports are well thought through, well managed and will make a real difference to people on the ground. Comic Relief is committed to help end poverty and social injustice.

In the 2007 Red Nose Day, Comic Relief raised more than £67,250,099. Events such as this appeal to all ages and are a fun way of raising money for aid projects.

Two projects supported by Comic Relief are Asociación Coordinora Indigena y Campesina de Agroforesteria Comunitaria Centraamericana (ACICAFOC) and Bees for Development.

Asociación Coordinora Indigena y Campesina de Agroforesteria Comunitaria Centraamericana (ACICAFOC)

This association represents forestry and farming groups in a number of Central American countries such as Nicaragua, Belize, Costa Rica, Guatemala, Panama and Honduras. It has been given £239,200 by Comic Relief over 3 years.

Get Active

Comic Relief mixes local charities with international charities.

- Why do you think they do this?
- Do you agree that they should?
- Find out more about the work of Comic Relief: where your money goes and how your money helps. Check out the Comic Relief website: www.comicrelief.com.

1. List the areas of the world where Comic Relief provide support.
2. What kind of work does Comic Relief support?
3. Why are charities like Comic Relief vital in the provision of aid?
4. Why do you think Comic Relief is so successful in raising so much money for worthy causes?
5. Would it be better to leave the provision of aid in the hands of elected governments? Give reasons for your answer.

Why not get your school involved? You could organise fundraising events and your teacher can order a teaching pack. Check out the website for more details.

▲ **Figure 33** An example of aid: Comic Relief organises the Red Nose Day event

The association is for local groups to exchange experiences and knowledge as well as developing shared activities. Indigenous peasants and the population descended from African slave labour focus on forestry activities, and as a result develop different initiatives related to community forestry.

This is also partially supported by a project of the United Nations Food and Agriculture Organisation (FAO): Forest, Trees, and People Programme (FTPP). Activities concerning forest development in rural Central American communities have been organised.

Working with small-scale peasant farmers and the indigenous populations, the association encourages social and economic development. The leaders of the community recognise that, to achieve sustainable development of the forest ecology, local people must contribute to the solution of the problems of deforestation. It is the local people who live with the forest and have most to lose if it is destroyed.

It is also recognised that peasants need to be more involved in decision-making related to local resources and require more support from their governments and other organisations if they are going to adequately manage their resources and produce food more efficiently.

One view was that:

> '… it appears clearly that the best way to promote development is to organise the communities at communal and national level. Moreover, it is necessary to establish relationships outside our own borders, sharing experiences and supporting ourselves mutually.
>
> Maturity and confidence which characterise our peasant and indigenous populations is evident in the high interest …show[n] for recuperation, protection and management of natural resources. Concretely, one observes that in shared experiences and during the events, the organisations with very little support are able to manage and protect forest resources with a great deal of efficiency.
>
> Our interest is not only focused on showing mistakes, but also on finding solutions to problems affecting peasant forest development in the region.'

Bees for Development

The Bees for Development Trust has been given £100,000 by Comic Relief for a two-year project in Uganda.

Beehives not only produce honey but also wax and a number of other products used in health care. Just as with many products from LEDCs, African beekeepers face many difficulties when trying to market their products. The aim of this Comic Relief project is to help small-scale beekeepers in Uganda to increase their income and to strengthen their livelihoods from sales of honey and other bee products through fair and reliable markets.

▲ **Figure 34** The Bees for Development Trust aims to help beekeepers in Africa generate income and reduce poverty through advice, training and information

Training and information for beekeepers are enabling them to supply markets locally and regionally. Some groups will get fair trade and organic certification for their products.

ApiTrade Africa is a non-profit making, member-based company based in Kampala, the capital of Uganda. It was formed in 2005 to help to promote African bee products on the world market. The ApiTrade Africa network highlighted the need to increase people's awareness of African bee products. With the difficulties of exporting to restrictive European and other MEDC markets, they are shifting focus to the domestic and regional markets. Despite increased demand from beekeepers and increased consumer awareness, these markets have been largely underdeveloped. Developing the trade will help to stimulate regional investment.

Wide publicity has contributed to raising the profile of bee products in this part of Africa and this has also led to a growth in exports, particularly of fair trade certified honey, to Germany, USA and other places.

You can find out more about bees for development at: www.beesfordevelopment.org/.

Positive and negative outcomes of aid

As we have seen, aid can have many benefits for those countries which get it, promoting development and improvements in standards of living and the quality of life for many, while enabling people to help themselves.

However, it can also have negative outcomes. It does not always reach the people in most need and so differences between rich and poor widen even further. It can be used for over-ambitious schemes and some feel that it can lead to a country becoming dependent on the giver of the aid.

Figure 35 shows some of the problems associated with aid, which can lead to negative outcomes or the aid not being effective. Care must be taken to ensure that:

- aid programmes involve local people
- aid is appropriate to the situation
- we do not assume that all types of aid are useful in promoting development.

▲ **Figure 35** Problems with aid

Long-term aid has the advantage that it recognises that development is complicated and has many reasons behind it. A simple transfer of money from a rich country to a poor country may help to reduce some of the outward problems in the short term but, if it does not address the reasons for the lack of development, is unlikely to be of help in the longer term.

Get Active

1 Study Figure 35. Match the cartoons with the labels below:
- Aid doesn't reach the needy.
- Aid creates debt.
- Problems with the distribution of the aid.
- Problems with the use of the product.
- Aid is unsuitable.
- Aid is tied.
- Export earnings are needed to pay off debts.
- Aid undermines local producers.
- Aid creates dependence.

2 a What is the difference between tied and voluntary aid?
  b Give two examples each of short-term and long-term aid.
  c What are the benefits of long-term aid to an LEDC?
  d State fully three disadvantages aid can bring to an LEDC.

3 a Match the problems A–H overleaf with the solutions 1–8.
  b Suppose you had £20 to give to one of the solutions, which project would you select and why?
  c Read the whole story situations overleaf which correspond to the solutions 1–8 and list the ones which are appropriate types of aid.
  d Explain why some types of aid are inappropriate.

Aid problems:

Burkina Faso: A

Soil is being eroded from farmland as a result of fast flowing water.

Liberia: B

As a result of civil war many Liberians fled from their homes and lived in camps. They lacked many things including food.

Ghana: C

Babies that are born prematurely are more likely to die.

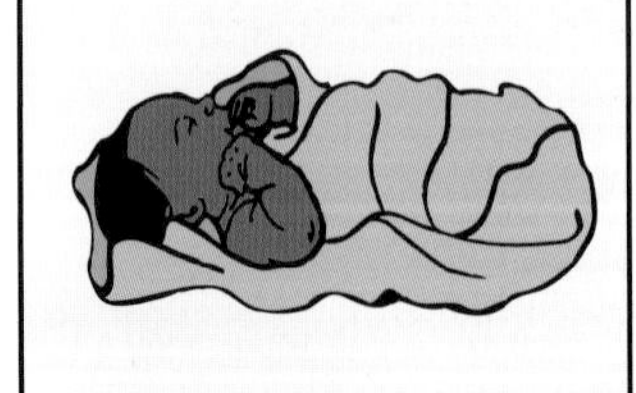

India: D

Children's education is suffering as there is a lack of textbooks in schools. There is a great need for secondary level science textbooks.

Guinea Bissau: E

There is a shortage of fresh water for local villagers.

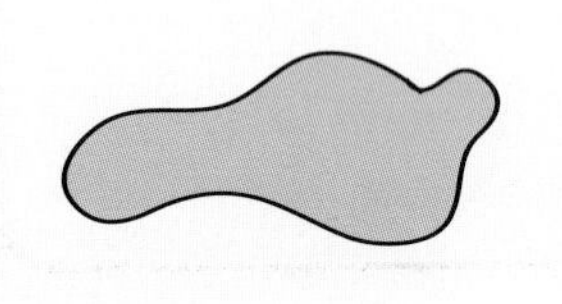

Guinea Bissau: F

Farmers have no way of transporting their produce to market. Public transport is too expensive and to carry it by hand is too difficult and takes too much time.

Nepal: G

There are many landslides which frequently block roads and destroy agricultural land.

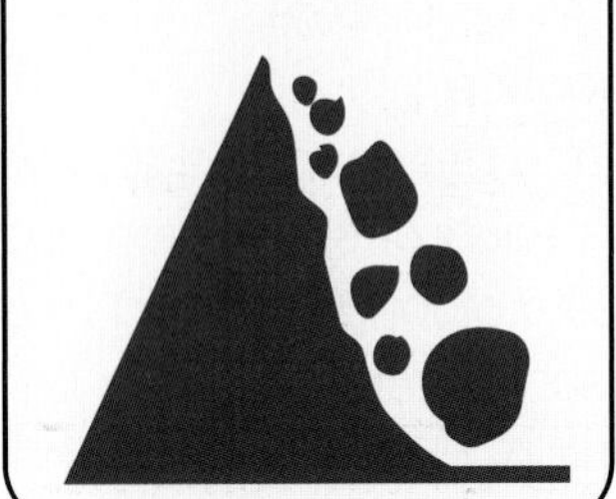

Tanzania: H

Coconut oil is an important income provider for many women. The graters used for producing the oil often don't work and are painful to use.

Aid solutions:

1

A baby incubator

2

A pump well

3

Donkey and cart

4

Sacks of wheat

5

Building stone banks

6

Planting trees and plants

7

Research for a new design of coconut grater

8

Science textbooks

Aid whole story situations:

1

The baby incubator cannot be used as the hospital's electricity supply is not constant. There also has been no training for African staff in how to use such a complex machine.

2

The pump wells were installed by the Japanese. The wells are made in Japan and therefore use Japanese parts. The pumps have broken down and the locals cannot get new parts to fix the pumps, as they were not involved in installing them.

3

The carts are made by a local tradesman and so can be repaired easily when necessary. The donkey and cart gets the farm produce to market while it is fresh and in good condition. This means a better price for the farmer.

4

The Canadian government sent wheat to Liberia which is a rice eating country. People did not know how to cook with wheat nor did they like it.

5

The women farmers were involved in building the stone banks that have saved water and stopped the soil washing away. The land has been reclaimed and harvests have greatly increased.

6

Local engineers are being trained by overseas engineers. The engineers work alongside local farmers who have the greatest knowledge about the vegetation. As a result the farmers learn how to save the soil and keep the roads clear.

7

Research has provided a new design of grater that is easy to use and increases coconut oil production. The grater is manufactured in a local workshop. The women can afford the new grater as they can pay for it in weekly instalments.

8

The textbooks were sent to a school in India by a school in the UK as they were no longer being used. The books are in English so only well-educated Indians can read them. Also, they are old and the information is badly out of date.

Sample examination questions

1 The development gap

Foundation Tier

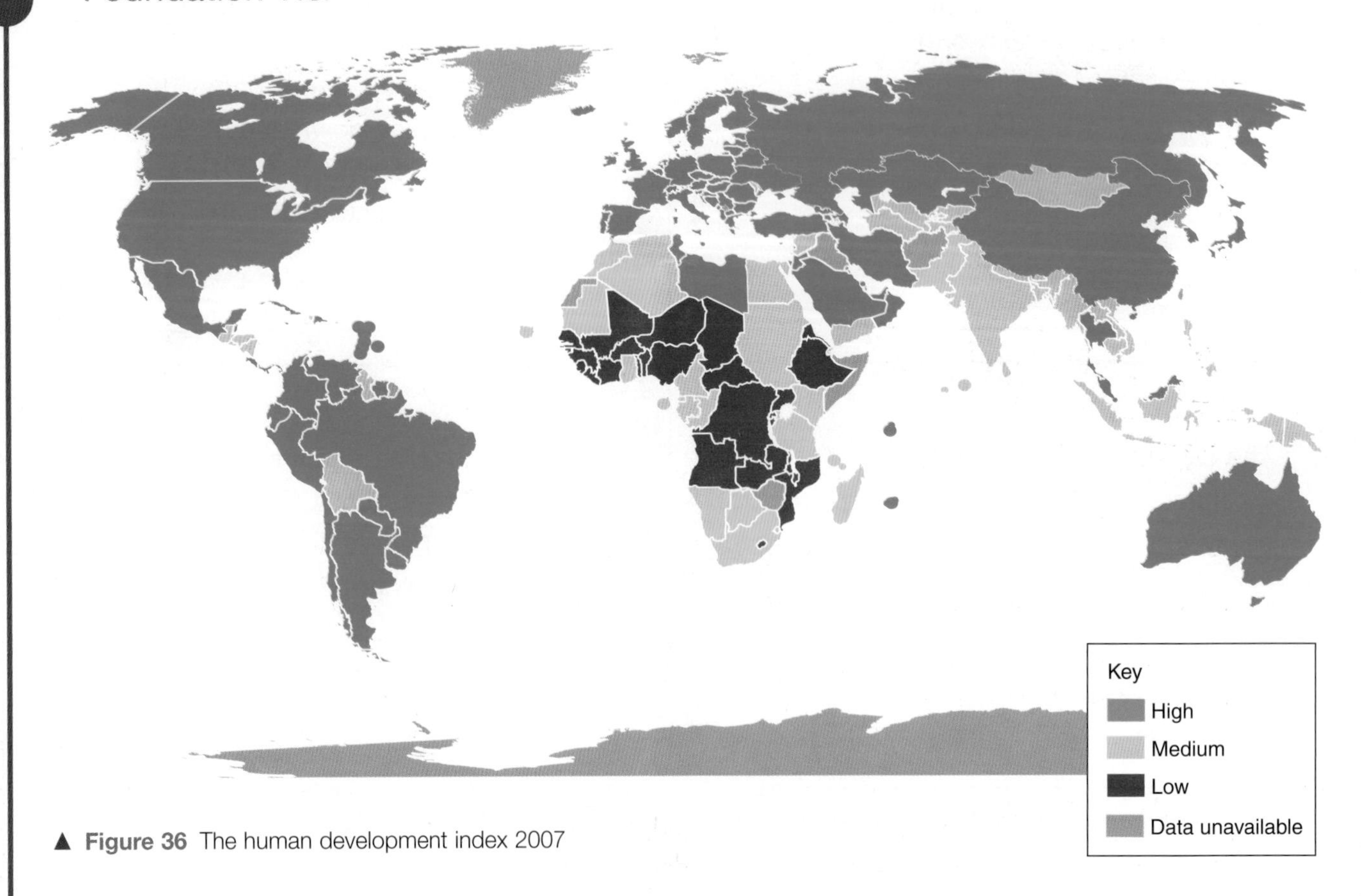

▲ **Figure 36** The human development index 2007

(i) Complete the following statements about the HDI figures for 2007:

- Australia has an HDI of high/low.
- MEDCs tend to have high/low HDI figures.
- Europe/Antarctica is the only continent with no data available at all. [3]

(ii) Describe how the HDI measures development. [3]

(iii) Suggest one reason why LEDCs find it hard to develop. [3]

Higher Tier

(i) Using the map shown above, describe how HDI figures from 2007 vary between continents. [3]

(ii) Explain why it is important to use both social and economic indicators when measuring development. [4]

(iii) Explain how debt and environmental factors can hinder the development of LEDCs. [6]

(iv) Describe and explain one strategy you have studied that is trying to reduce the global development gap. [8]

2 Factors contributing to unequal development

Foundation Tier

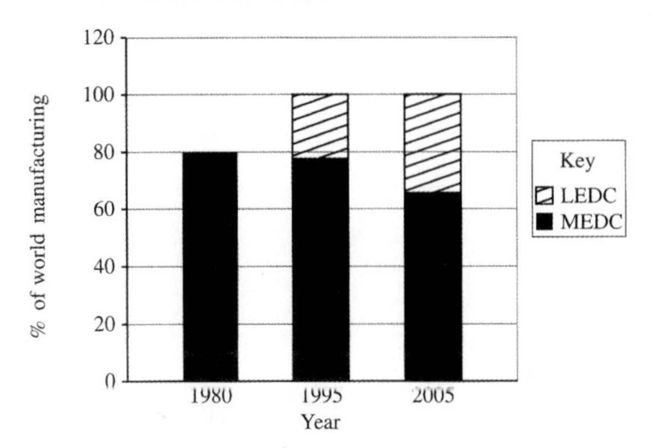

(i) Complete this graph by adding this information:

1980 20% LEDC

(ii) Describe how the percentage share of manufacturing in MEDCs has changed over time. [3]

(iii) For a named LEDC or NIC you have studied, explain how globalisation is helping it to develop:

- LEDC name. [1]
- Effect of globalisation. [4]

Higher Tier

(i) For a named LEDC or NIC you have studied, explain how globalisation is both helping and hindering development. [9]

3 Sustainable solutions to deal with the problems of unequal development

Foundation Tier

(i) State the meaning of appropriate technology. [2]

(ii) For a named project you have studied in an LEDC, discuss how appropriate technology has helped improve conditions within that country.

- LEDC. [1]
- How appropriate technology helped. [4]

The table below gives information about the price paid for coffee in 2007. Use it to help you answer questions (iii) and (iv).

	World market price (US cents per 500g of coffee)	The price Cafédirect pays (US cents per 500g of coffee)
Arabica Coffee	119	131

(iii) Explain how Cafédirect (a fair trade company) helps coffee growers. [3]

(iv) Explain why people in MEDCs would want to buy Cafédirect coffee rather than cheaper brands. [3]

Higher Tier

Study the information below about an aid organisation called Asha which works in the shanty town areas of Dehli, India. Use it to help you answer questions (i)–(iii).

Asha aims to improve the lives of 250,000 people in 30 shanty town areas of Delhi in different ways:

- Forming housing co-operatives to build new homes constructed by the local people.
- Training community health workers who link women and children to well-equipped clinics where treatment is cheap.
- In every Asha project only 20 households share a water tap, instead of nearly 150 in other shanty town areas.
- Asha organises rubbish collection and provides every 20 people with a toilet, instead of the usual average of one toilet for every 180 people in Delhi's slums.

(i) State the meaning of the term 'aid'. [2]

(ii) Match the type of aid provided by Asha on the left to each of the needs of people shown on the right. Write each out as a pair.

Sanitation	money to buy plots of land
Health care	toilets
Water supply	trained community health worker
Housing	water taps

(iii) State fully why the aid provided by Asha is considered to be sustainable. [3]

(iv) For a named project in an LEDC, describe and explain how appropriate technology has been used and evaluate the success of the project. [9]

(v) Explain how fair trade brings advantages to LEDCs. [4]

(vi) Discuss how aid can bring both benefits and problems to LEDCs.

UNIT TWO
Living in Our World

Managing Our Resources

Learning outcomes

In this theme you will learn:

- how population growth and increasing economic development lead to increased demands for resources
- how increasing use of resources impacts on the environment
- why strategies to manage resources are needed and how to evaluate them
- about sustainable solutions that deal with the problems caused by increased demands on resources.

Managing Our Resources

The impact of our increasing use of resources on the environment

What are resources?

Anything that we use and rely on can be called a **resource**. These include:

- fuels: e.g. natural gas, coal, oil
- metals: e.g. aluminium, iron, chrome
- bioresources: e.g. fish, trees, soil.

There are also other resources that might not immediately spring to mind. An unspoiled coastline or a rich culture is a resource, if you want to make money from tourism, for example.

How is the demand for resources changing?

Two main things are happening in the world which mean that we are using more and more resources.

The population is rising

The world's population did not reach a billion people (1,000,000,000) until the early 1800s. However, it has only taken until 1960 to reach three billion people and now the world's population is increasing by a billion people every 11 years. Each one of us consumes resources. The more people there are the more resources we need. By 2015 there will be over seven billion people in the world all requiring water and food. There is already pressure on soil and water resources to feed growing populations.

The increased population of the world will require more food than is currently being produced. This may lead to overcultivation and overgrazing, with the soils on which we depend for all of our food being damaged or destroyed. Ecosystems will also be damaged or destroyed with more land being brought into use for producing food, and this may cause extinction of species.

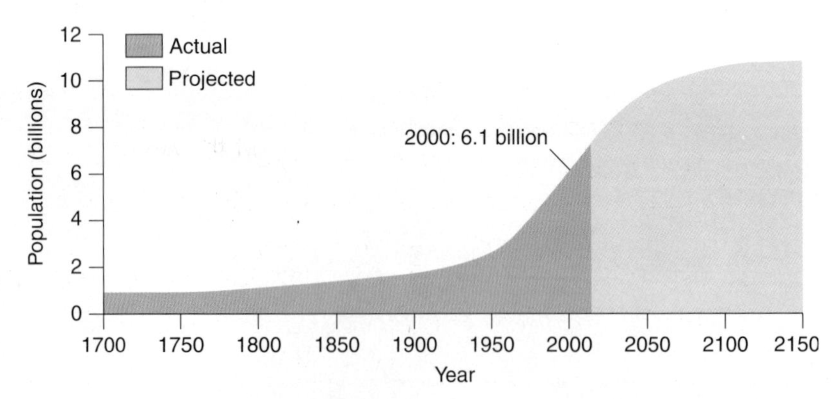

▲ **Figure 1** World population growth

Where wealth is increasing, people are consuming more

India, with a population of 1.1 billion, is one of the largest countries in the world. Its population is not just vast, it is getting richer and more able to afford to consume – to buy, buy, buy. As average incomes rise in India, the use of energy, food and other resources will also continue to grow. Consumer goods have shown a particular rise. In 2006 88% of Indian homes were said to have colour televisions, up from 65% in 2002. The numbers of air-conditioning units, digital cameras, refrigerators, cars and so on being bought has shown the same sort of growth. Each of these purchases, just like each of ours, has an impact on resources.

▲ **Figure 2** Consumption in India: shopping for a new home-cinema system

Get Active

1 To get some idea of how the population of the world is changing and how that population is consuming resources visit: www.worldometers.info:
   a What is the current population of the world?
   b By how many has the population of the world increased so far today?
   c Look at the information under the other headings. What facts stand out for you to support the view that the population of the world is consuming resources at a very quick rate?
2 Read the report 'India consuming double its natural resources' at: http://southasia.oneworld.net/todaysheadlines/india-consuming-double-its-natural-resources:
   a What do you understand by the terms 'ecological footprint', 'global hectare' and 'biocapacity'?
   b Quote figures from the report to support the view that India's natural resources are fast being exhausted under the strain of its growing population.
   c At what level is India's ecological deficit currently running?
   d Which two countries have a higher ecological footprint than India?

The human impact on the environment: carbon footprints

Using *any* resource has an impact on the environment. If we eat a can of beans there is a cost in growing the beans: natural vegetation removed to create the farmland, water used to irrigate the beans, chemicals used to reduce pests, power used to plough the soil and harvest the crop, power used in the processing, the mining to produce the steel and tin used in the metal containers, the energy used to make those, the transporting of the beans and the tins to the processing plant and the fuel used to transport those to your local supermarket. Add on the lights in the supermarket and the fuel you use to go to the shop and you have an idea of the total cost of using even the most basic of resources.

One of the best ways of working out how costly using a resource is to the environment is by working out the **carbon footprint**. This is a measure of the impact our activities have on the environment, particularly on climate change. The carbon footprint is a measurement of all the greenhouse gases that we each produce converted into the equivalent weight of carbon dioxide produced so that they can be compared.

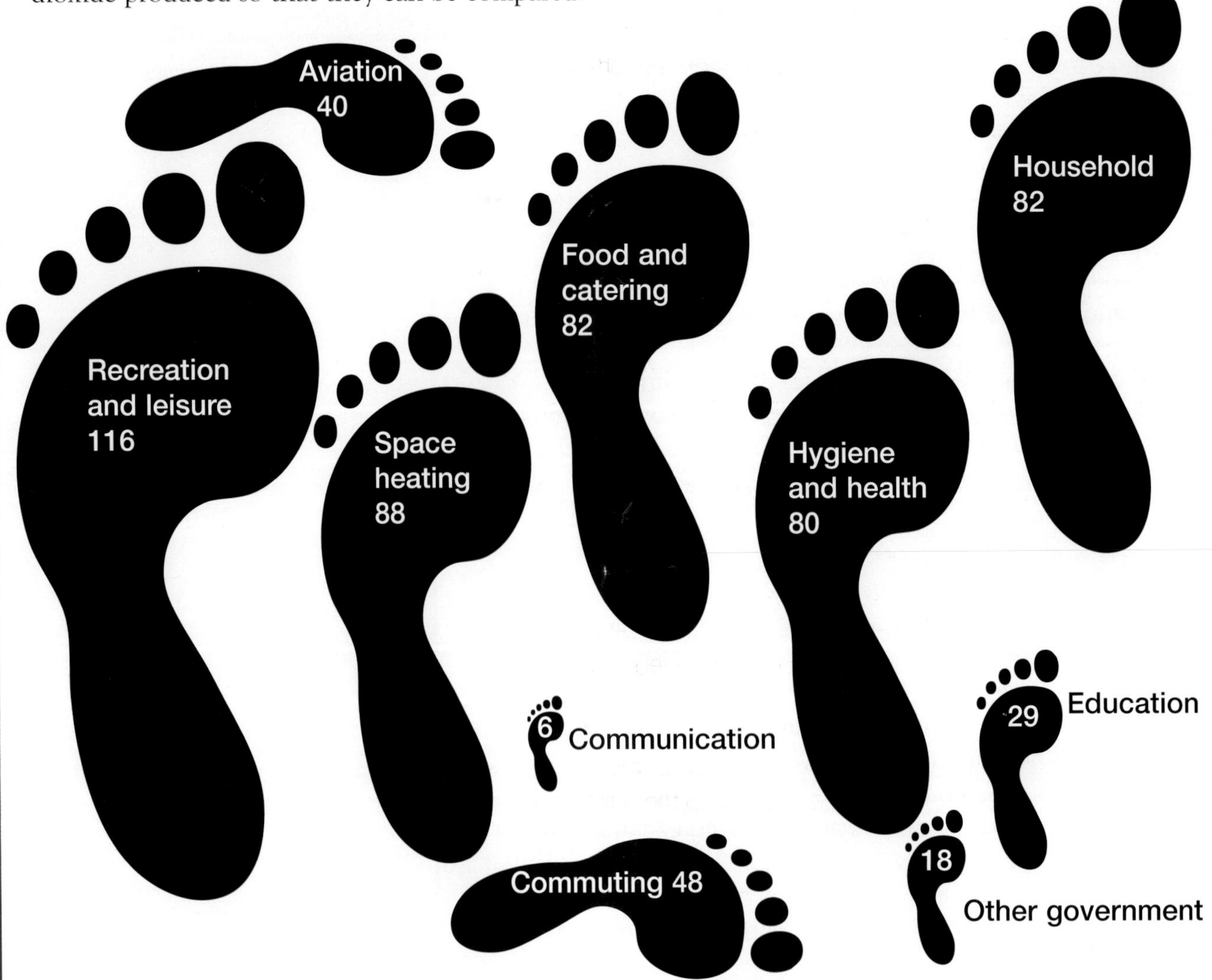

▲ **Figure 3** The UK's carbon footprint. The numbers represent millions of tonnes of carbon dioxide produced for each activity and the size of each footprint is roughly proportional to its output

Get Active

Have you ever considered how what you do in your life has an impact on the environment? The way we use the planet's resources makes up our ecological footprint. Measuring yours on the WWF Footprint Calculator, takes less than 5 minutes and could set you on a life-changing journey. Go to: http://footprint.wwf.org.uk/.

1 Calculate your footprint.
2 What is the breakdown of your footprint in terms of food, travel, home and stuff?
3 How many planets would it take to support your lifestyle? Do you think this is good or bad?
4 What were the top new eco-tips recommended for you? What do you think of these tips? Are they achievable for you? Why? Why not?
5 Scroll down the page where you found your footprint. Click on National Footprint Averages.
   - Which country has the lowest footprint?
   - Which country has the highest footprint?
   - How does the UK rate?
   - Where would you put your footprint on this chart? Which country comes closest to your footprint?
6 Having completed this activity is there anything that surprised or shocked you?

Get Active

The impact that different events have on the environment can also be calculated. Christmas is a time of the year when we increase our level of consumption.

1 Read the report on 'The carbon cost of Christmas' at: www.climatetalk.org.uk/downloads/CarbonCostofChristmas2007.pdf.
2 Quoting figures, outline the nature of the problem.
3 What could be done to bring about a low carbon Christmas in relation to: Christmas food? Christmas travel? Christmas lighting? Christmas shopping?
4 Can you think of any other events that lead to increased consumption? Make a list. Give feedback to the class. After hearing everyone's thoughts, agree a top three list of events.

A city within the European Union which is attempting to manage traffic in a sustainable way: Freiburg, Germany

Freiburg is a city in Germany with a population of over 200,000. In the early 1970s it was a city with major traffic problems; it is now heralded as a city which is close to 'car-free' living:

- The centre of Freiburg started to be pedestrianised from 1971.
- It had a network for cyclists planned from the same time.
- In 1972 it decided to retain its trams, something that other German cities were scrapping. The slogan for the tram company was 'faster than a sports car to the city centre'.
- From 1983 new tram routes were opened.
- Nowadays 70% of local journeys are made using the tram system.
- In the mid-1980s a pass was produced which provided cheap public transport for the whole city. Within the first year, the number of daily trips in Freiburg and the area around it increased by 26,400 journeys while the number of car journeys fell by 29,000.
- In the 10 years following the decision to issue the pass, the numbers using public transport doubled.
- Between 1976 and 1992 the percentage of car use fell from 60% to 46%.

Unlike many cities, the urban planners in Freiburg have not tried to make it car-friendly. The policy on traffic in the centre of the city was to give priority to public transport to help to preserve the historic city centre. In the 1980s traffic was further pushed out of the city. Even where cars could travel close to the city centre, in many areas speed was restricted to 30 km per hour and bicycle use was promoted. At many junctions bicycles have priority over vehicles! The main aim was to allow people to travel around more easily but to use cars less.

Controlling parking is a key feature of transport policy, and there is no free parking in the centre of the city. Commuters are encouraged to park and ride. In central residential districts there are resident-only parking zones, although even residents must pay for a parking pass. Many of Freiburg's streets are now free enough from traffic for children to play safely. Over 120 streets in the city are 'Play Streets' where the children take priority over the cars.

In just 20 years there were 4000 fewer cars using the city centre each day, even though the population of Freiburg had increased. In most

▲ **Figure 4** A tram in Freiburg

other cities the number of cars on the streets had risen rapidly in this period. By 2005 there were 3000 km of public transport lines in the Freiburg region. There are over 500 km of bicycle lanes and 5000 parking spaces for bicycles in the centre of Freiburg. Each tram stop is equipped with areas to leave bicycles as well, encouraging people to 'bike and ride'. Freiburg has grown with its increase in population but it has been kept as a compact city, avoiding urban sprawl. Many of the new buildings are five-storey apartments close to the tram. A total of 70% of the population of Freiburg now lives within 500 m of a tram stop. Why take a car?

The city continues to develop its **sustainable** traffic strategy. Its aims are:

- further reduction of car use
- continuous upgrading of the trams and other public transport network
- improvement in public transport services
- consideration of the impact on people as well as on the environment in terms of public transport
- taking public transport into account when planning other aspects of the city.

Get Active

Individually:

- What are the five cornerstones of the Freiburg transport concept? (To get ideas have a look at: www.unep.org/OurPlanet/imgversn/121/bohme.html.)

In groups:

- Your group is the board of directors of an ICT company that is just about to open a new factory in Freiburg. Your company is very supportive of the city's policies around traffic and transport. Your task is to think of ways in which your factory can show support for these policies. Draw up a list of things that your company will do to promote these policies.

Extension activity … extending your learning

Freiburg is a pioneer in planning and developing ecologically friendly suburbs, like Vauban in the south of the city. The planners and city authorities have set standards for traffic and public transport. You can read about these standards at: www.vauban.de/info/abstract4.html.

- What has been done to reduce traffic on the roads in the Vauban suburb and to encourage the use of public transport?
- What do you think of the idea of car-free living? Is it desirable?
- Could car-free living be developed in towns and cities in Northern Ireland?

Further information about Vauban in Freiburg can be found on the following websites:

- www.vauban.de/info/abstract.html
- www.cafebabel.com/eng/article/23545/eco-suburbs-vauban-freiburg.html
- http://uitp.org/mos/PTI//2007/05/09-en.pdf
- www.energie-cites.eu/IMG/pdf/Sustainable_Districts_ADEME1_Vauban.pdf.

You could also do a Google search (including an image search) on Vauban.

Increasing demand for resources in LEDCs and MEDCs

How population growth and economic development in LEDCs increase the demand for resources

If the population is growing in an area, and/or if economic development is increasing, the demand for resources will increase. We are used to increasing consumption in the rich part of the world where we live. The newest gadgets are must-haves. Whether it is a new mobile phone or a new mp3 player or this year's fashion, we consume large amounts of resources. Many LEDCs are now beginning to increase their consumption rapidly as well. It is for the same reasons: they may be increasing in population or the people of the country may be getting richer, or sometimes both of these things. Either way countries like this will be increasing the amount of the world's resources that they consume. This inevitably puts pressure on the environment as more mines are needed, more food needs to be grown, more trees have to be cut down, more water needs to be taken from rivers and more fuel has to be burned. In turn, this puts pressure on people as they increasingly see pressure on the environment and increased pollution, over-exploitation of natural resources and damage to ecosystems.

In addition, the richer a country gets, the more energy it needs. The energy is needed in the industries which are producing more 'stuff' for the newly affluent population. It is needed for the farms that are producing more foodstuffs for the people who are consuming more and more. New buildings consume energy and electrical goods and more vehicles will also consume electricity in their production and in their use.

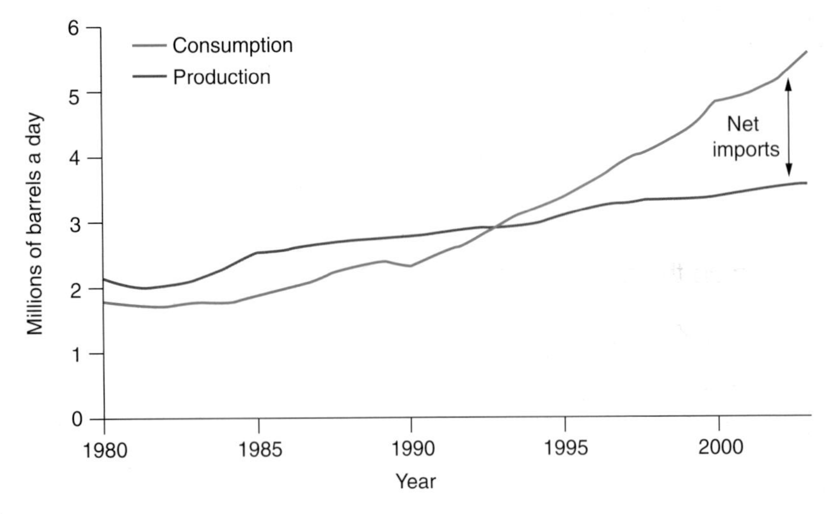

▲ **Figure 5** China's oil production and consumption for 1980–2003

Year	Earnings per person (US$)
1981	285
1986	275
1991	351
1996	667
2001	921
2006	1553

▲ **Figure 6** China's earnings per head in US dollars for 1981–2006

case study

The increasing demands for resources in one LEDC: China

One country where the population is vast and still rising is China. Even with the one child policy which limits family size, China is still growing by about one million people every month. Many of the 1.3 billion Chinese have become much wealthier too. With the Chinese economy growing at 9.5% each year, there has been an increased consumption of resources.

▲ **Figure 7** Fuelling the Chinese dragon

Of total world production, in 2005, China used:

- 26% of the steel
- 37% of the cotton
- 32% of the rice
- 47% of the cement.

China uses much of the world's steel and concrete and it will probably construct half the world's new buildings over the next 10 years. The enormous Chinese demand for imports is such that, when the country ran short of scrap metal in 2004, manhole covers went missing from cities all over the world as scrap metal prices rose – Chicago had 150 stolen in a month.

This may have benefited some producers, and has made some individuals very rich, but it has also pushed up the prices of basic products around the world and as a result many poor people have suffered. In the rich countries we have benefited from more affordable mp3 players, flat screen televisions and computers made in China, although our food and other basic prices have gone up too. In China there have been problems caused by the rapid increase in the use of resources.

case study

▲ **Figure 8** Pollution in Taiyuan, China

China has increasing levels of car ownership and new roads are being built to cope with these. The country is also investing heavily in ports and airports. If China ever gets to a ratio of three cars for every four of the population (the current US ratio), there will be 1.1 billion cars in the country. This will be more cars than in the whole world at present (800 million). To cope with this number of cars will be difficult and China would have to build roads, car parks and so on that would be equal in area to that part of China planted with rice now.

The number of consumer goods owned by Chinese people continues to rise too, particularly in the cities. These goods are available in vast shopping centres.

One of the largest shopping centres in the world can be found in Beijing: Golden Resources. With 230 escalators, 1000 shops and covering 550,000 square metres, it is enormous, and other shopping centres are being built across the country. Largely as a result of this increased consumption, China also generates waste on a vast scale. Each year four million refrigerators and five million televisions are thrown away.

▲ **Figure 9** Golden Resources shopping centre, Beijing, China

Year	Washing machines	Refrigerators	Colour TVs	Air-conditioning units	Ovens	Showers	DVD players	Computers
1986	65	18	29	0.1	–	–	–	–
1990	78	57	59	0.3	–	–	–	–
1995	89	66	90	8.0	–	30	–	–
2000	91	80	117	24	18	49	38	10
2003	94	88	131	62	37	67	59	28

▲ **Figure 10** Consumer items owned per 100 Chinese urban dwellers.

Get Active

1. Working with a partner, discuss what benefits and problems there might be for China, if Chinese citizens were ever to reach the income levels of their US counterparts?
2. Note what you agreed on.
3. Report back to the class.
4. Review and revise your notes after the feedback session.

So what is the impact of this growth of population and consumption on China's environment?

Air pollution

China itself accepts that two-thirds of the 338 cities for which air-quality data are available are polluted – two-thirds of them moderately or severely. The leading cause of death in China is respiratory and heart diseases related to air pollution. The **World Health Organisation** report that, each year, about 750,000 people in China die from respiratory problems. Some of this stems from the increasing number of coal-powered power stations needed to support the industrialisation and the increased wealth of the Chinese. Coal provides about 70% of China's energy production and consumption and it is likely that this will continue until 2020 at least. Looking forward to 2050, coal is still forecast to provide half of China's fuel needs. The use of coal has substantial environmental costs. For example, 80% of China's production of carbon dioxide, a gas that causes climate change, is as a result of burning coal.

Adding to this air pollution has been the increase in traffic on China's roads. For example, commuting times of 3 hours or more are not at all unusual in cities like Beijing, where streets not designed for cars but for pedestrians and bicycles are packed with more than a million vehicles. Sometimes rush-hour traffic moves at no more than 5 km an hour.

Much of this is because of the huge consumption of Chinese goods in rich countries like ours. 30% of greenhouse gases emitted by China are due to exports.

In addition to greenhouse gases, the power stations and vehicles add sulphur dioxide to the atmosphere which contributes to acid rain. Some estimates say that acid rain falls on 30% of the country.

▲ **Figure 11** Images showing the impact of growth of population and consumption on China's environment

Water pollution

About 300 million people in China are said not to have access to clean water. Another 400 million are said to have access only to poor quality water. Almost 90% of groundwater in cities is affected by pollution. Almost all of China's rivers are considered polluted to some extent. There is also a shortage of water and the Chinese government has had to start diverting water from the Yangtze River to cities in the north of the country, especially Beijing and Tianjin.

Efforts to protect the environment

China is making many efforts to combat these problems. In 2001, China set up a 'Great Green Wall' project, possibly the biggest ecological project ever known. The plan is to create a 4500-km 'green belt', starting with the restoration of 36,000 km^2 of forest, to be completed by 2010 at a cost of $8 billion.

There were 2349 nature reserves in China by the end of 2005. These covered 1.5 million km^2, about 15% of the landmass of China. It is claimed that these help to protect 85% of the different ecosystems of China, 85% of wildlife species, and 65% of the vegetation in China. A number of nature reserves and places of historical interest and scenic beauty have been included on the **UNESCO**'s World Heritage list and given other forms of international protection. Despite these efforts to protect the environment, China's environmental problems are enormous.

Ecology

China has a rich and diverse ecology. However, it would seem to be under threat. A study in Hunan Province has reported that the number of rare animals dropped dramatically. For example, South China tigers and leopards have not been seen for years. Even wolves and jackals, which used to be common in this part of China, have also disappeared. As a consequence, there are more pests such as mice because those animals, which previously kept their numbers in check, have declined. The main causes for the falling numbers of some animals are said to be poaching and damage to habitats. **Wetlands** are an example of a particularly vulnerable environment and many have been polluted, leading to a decline in the numbers of small aquatic creatures. In turn, the animals that depended on them for food decline in numbers.

Forests

From 1999 to 2004, China lost a million square kilometres of its forests, despite a ban on logging in 1999 because of the impact of deforestation on flooding and erosion along the River Yangtze. The head of the state forestry service, Lei Jiafu, said 'excessive logging is still a major problem'. Even though China's forests have increased recently from 16.5% in 1999 to 18.2% in 2004, these recently planned forests are immature and of limited wildlife value.

Soil

China's agriculture is changing. Since 1998, the area used to grow grain has fallen by 15%. China now has to import grain, as a result increasing the prices of grain around the world. The main reason seems to be China's rapid urbanisation. Cities are spreading rapidly as 500 million people now live in them – this is set to rise to 800 million by 2020. The farmland at the edge of cities is getting eaten up by this expansion.

City dwellers are willing to pay high prices for fruit and vegetables, while the prices for rice and wheat are capped, so farmers can make more money growing the more profitable fruit and vegetable crops instead. It has been estimated that, in 10 years, 13 million hectares have been converted to growing fruit and vegetables, an area about twice the size of the island of Ireland.

This has had an impact on the soils in these areas. Fields where vegetables are grown have been found to be more acidic, with average pH dropping from 6.3 to 5.4 in just 10 years. In addition there are four times the amount of nitrates in the soils, and 10 times as many phosphates. These changes are thought to be a result of farmers applying too much fertiliser to the soils in order to increase yields.

Get Active

In this activity you are going to think about the impact of population growth and consumption on China's environment.

1 Individually, read the following articles:
  a 'As China Roars, Pollution Reaches Deadly Extremes', *New York Times*, 26 August 2007: www.nytimes.com/2007/08/26/world/asia/26china.html?_r=1.
  b Fact file from the World Bank: http://alturl.com/9w9x.
  Individually, note the points you think to be important. You could print out both articles and use a highlighter to identify points that you think are important.
2 Join up with a partner, and think about the following statement: 'China is choking on its own success'.
  a List the points from the article that support this point of view.
  b List the points from the article that counteract this point of view.
  c On balance, which side of the argument do you support? Explain your reasons.
  d Give feedback to the whole class.
3 Consider everything you have heard from the different groups. Review and revise your initial notes. Write a response of about 250 words to the view that 'China is choking on its own success'.

case study

A renewable energy resource in an MEDC: wind power in Denmark

Denmark produces more of its electricity from wind power than any other country. The proportion of electricity from that source rose from 12.1% in 2001 to 19.7% in 2007. It aims to be over 50% by 2025. Much of this electricity comes from wind turbines located out at sea.

▲ **Figure 12** A helicopter lowers a technician to maintain the Horns Rev wind farm, Denmark

With wind generating about 20% of Denmark's electricity, the nation is a leader in turbine technology.

The largest wind farm in the world, as measured by the number of turbines, is Horns Rev, built 14 km from the Danish mainland in water between 6.5 and 12.5 m deep. One rather obvious difficulty with wind power is that when there is no wind there is no electricity being generated. Storing the electricity produced during windy times to release during calm times would be very expensive. One imaginative idea is to move to more electric vehicles. The recharging of these could use 'smart' systems which would charge the batteries when the power is plentiful and release the power back into the system when wind power is not available. If there were two million electric vehicles in total in the country, it is estimated that this could provide a standby storage of about five times the requirements of the whole of Denmark.

Eleven onshore wind turbines built in 2000 on the Danish island of Samsø were supplemented in 2003 by 10 offshore wind turbines. This and other **renewable energy** measures such as solar panels made this small island of 4124 people the largest carbon-neutral community on earth.

case study

There are a number of benefits of getting your electricity in this way.

Reduction of greenhouse gas production	Generating wind energy contributes no greenhouse gases to the atmosphere.
Sustainable method of producing power	Currently wind power provides 20% of Danish electricity consumption. The Danish government plans to increase this to cover more than 50% of electricity consumption in 2025, most of which will come from offshore wind farms.
Reduces dependence on imported fuels	Every megawatt of electricity produced by wind power reduces the need to import fuel. This will help to give Denmark security of supply, as they will not be depending so much on others for their energy needs.
Electric vehicles	Energy companies, in co-operation with 'Project Better Place' aim to establish an electric car-charging grid in Denmark. These have a number of advantages: • one 2-MW wind turbine provides enough electricity to run 3000 electric cars • owners will generally charge their cars at night when there is excess wind power production • electric cars are four times more energy efficient than hydrogen-powered cars, the other 'green' vehicles currently available.

Get Active

In small groups, research the Horns Rev project. Your task is to produce an informative PowerPoint presentation that you will share with the rest of the class and assess against previously agreed assessment criteria. Useful information can be found at:

- www.hornsrev.dk/index.en.html (general background information)
- www.mumm.ac.be/Common/Windmills/SPE/Bijlage/1%20%20Horns_Rev_brochure.pdf (brochure on Horns Rev)
- http://test7.scancommerce.dk/hornsrev/ (measurements at Horns Rev).

Before trying to put together the presentation, groups will need to agree on a number of things:

- content to be included
- visual materials to illustrate
- statistical information
- balance of text, statistics and visuals
- the number of slides
- roles and responsibilities of individual group members.

You will also, as a class, have to agree a list of criteria on which each presentation is to be assessed, e.g. broad headings, accuracy of information, subjectivity of the presentation, communication skills displayed, etc. There are many other criteria you may decide to include. When you have agreed the assessment criteria (product and process) write them out on a large flip-chart sheet and display them on the classroom wall for reference.

1 Carry out the research.
2 Make sense of the information you have gathered.
3 Prepare the group presentation.
4 Make the presentation to the whole class.
5 Assess the presentations.

Having seen and assessed all the presentations, think about the following question yourself and write your response: how would you weigh up the advantages and disadvantages of offshore wind power as exemplified by the Danish example at Horns Rev? In your opinion, do the advantages outweigh the disadvantages?

There may also be some problems.

Some harm may be caused to marine life while the wind farm is built	Marine animals such as seals and porpoises may be affected during the construction and operation of the wind turbines. The seabed is likely to suffer some damage but it is claimed that less than 0.1% of habitat would be totally lost.
Some people view wind farms as unsightly	The curvature of the Earth means that the turbines would be impossible to see from a distance of 45 km. However, at about 100 m high and 14 km from land, they will be visible. The shoreline closest to Horns Rev (Blåvands Huk) is made up of sandy beaches popular with tourists, both locally and from Germany. This may reduce earnings from tourism. For other tourists, a glimpse of one of the world's first offshore wind farms will be an attraction.
The wind turbines may harm bird life	Studies have shown that divers, common scoter and guillemots have avoided the Horns Rev area since the wind farm was established. On the other hand herring gulls, little gulls and Arctic/common terns seem to have become more numerous. The Danish government has made a total of 13,000 km^2 off limits for wind farms for bird protection reasons.
There is a cost to producing the turbines	While Horns Rev can generate enough electricity for 150,000 private homes, or nearly 2% of Denmark's total electricity consumption, the Horns Rev wind farm cost £245 million to build. There are some advantages here too as Danish companies make 40% of all wind turbines in the world and so this is big business for the country.
Other sources of fuel will be needed for when the wind does not blow	Denmark uses a range of renewable energy generation, not just wind power. These include the burning of waste products (biomass) in combined heat and power plants, solar electricity, and geothermal turbines powered by underground steam. Nevertheless, oil and gas remain a key element of Denmark's electricity production. In the North Sea, Denmark has 19 oil fields. While about 69,000 barrels were imported, 263,000 barrels were exported in 2003 (the most recent figures available) making Denmark a net exporter of oil. However, unless new oil fields are discovered, the oil is due to run out in the next 20 years.

Managing waste to protect our environment

Waste is not rubbish

Waste is a major issue in the UK and other parts of the world. The UK produces around 330 million tonnes of waste each year. Households and businesses produce about 25% of it and the remainder comes from sources such as building operations, sewage sludge and farming. Most of the waste produced ends up in **landfill sites**. It then generates methane as it rots. This gas is a greenhouse gas and contributes to climate change. Also a lot of energy is used up making new products to replace those thrown away. These new products later become waste themselves, contributing to further climate change. We are consuming natural resources at an unsustainable rate.

We are also running out of space to put our waste. Suitable landfill sites are filling up and it is difficult to find replacements. There is now a tax on disposing of waste. Active waste (waste that decomposes or is chemically reactive) is taxed more than inactive waste such as rocks, glass and concrete. In 2008–9 the tax was £32 for each tonne of active waste and is set to increase at £8 each year. Inactive waste is taxed at £2.50 per tonne.

▲ **Figure 13** A landfill site in Belfast

There are a number of reasons why dealing with waste is such a big issue in the UK:

- Shortage of landfill sites: landfill is when waste is dumped into the ground, sometimes in old quarries or in natural hollows. This is how most waste was disposed of in the past. However, suitable sites are now much rarer as the old ones get filled up. In addition, people do not want to live beside landfill sites as they fear smells, blowing waste and vermin such as rats and seagulls.
- Environmental and health concerns. There are many chemicals in waste, such as mercury contained in batteries. If these chemicals reached the water in the ground they could poison it, killing wildlife and possibly people. Diseases too could spread in places where waste was rotting down.
- The government has set targets to reduce landfill and to increase recycling.

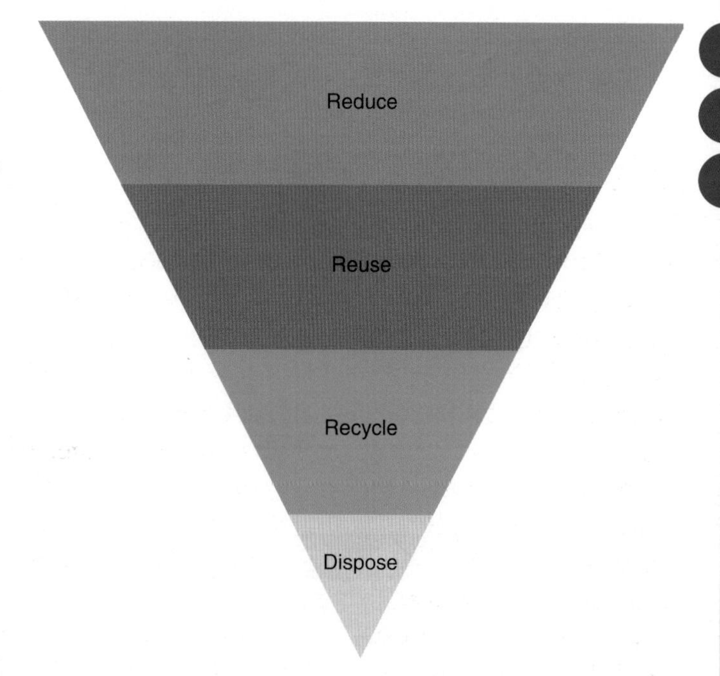

▲ **Figure 14** The waste hierarchy

'Reduce, Reuse, Recycle' is often the phrase you will see on the side of refuse lorries. What are each of these and why do you think they are in that order? This is called the **waste hierarchy**.

Waste prevention is where a lot of the effort is being placed. We need to reduce the waste that we produce and to reuse as much as possible to reduce the waste produced. Increased reuse and recycling are good for the environment – although not as good as reducing! Fewer resources and less energy are needed if reuse and recycling are done widely.

Get Active

- Think of your own household: how could your family reduce the amount of waste it produces? List all the things your family could do. Prioritise your list.
- What about your school? What sort of waste is produced and how could it reduce the waste produced? What schemes are currently in place in your school to reduce the amount of waste produced? How effective do you think these schemes are? Why do you say this?
- Pick a local business and consider if there any ways in which it could reduce the amount of waste it produces by reducing and reusing. Imagine you are employed by your local district council as an environmental health officer with a role to get local businesses to reduce and reuse. Write a letter to the managing director of your chosen local business outlining the rationale for reducing and reusing and proposing what you think this particular business could do to reduce and reuse.

After efforts are made to reduce the amount of waste produced, recycling and recovery are the next important activities. Recycling is common for paper, aluminium and glass and increasingly for plastics. These products can be turned into useful products for reuse. Organic material can be composted. This means rotting it down in a controlled way to create a material which is used to enrich soils. Some materials in waste can be burned to convert them into electricity. This is usually done on a large scale in what some people call waste-to-energy plants or what others call incinerators.

What is left then has to be disposed of in costly landfill sites. As well as the additional cost, putting waste into landfill is the worst option for the environment. We have seen how the resources within it are lost and how the decomposing waste produces greenhouse gases.

The targets that governments have set themselves and have been set by others to reduce landfill are challenging, as the table in Figure 15 shows.

Region	Recycling and composting target
Northern Ireland	35% by 2010 40% by 2015 45% by 2020
England	40% by 2010 45% by 2015 50% by 2020
Wales	15% by 2010 25% by 2015 40% by 2020
Scotland	25% by 2010 30% by 2015 55% by 2020

▲ **Figure 15** Recycling and composting targets by region

Get Active

If you were put in charge, what steps would you take to try to achieve the targets in Figure 15?

Without the help of everyone, the targets will not be met. Below is advice as to what members of the public can do.

- Minimise household waste.
- Undertake home composting where possible.
- Exercise purchasing decisions by choosing the most resource-efficient products.
- Actively participate in reuse and recycling initiatives, both at community level and individually.
- Build awareness in the community.

What things could *you* do to help to achieve these targets? What advice would you give a business to reduce its waste?

case study

A sustainable waste management approach in the Belfast area

Belfast produces a growing amount of waste each year. Figure 16 shows some of the amounts.

Eleven of the Councils around Belfast have joined together to form the Eastern Region Waste Management Group called ARC21. This covers an area from Ballymena in the north to Downpatrick in the south and from Antrim in the west to Portaferry in the east and including the city of Belfast. There are two other waste management groups covering the remainder of Northern Ireland.

All three waste management groups in Northern Ireland have to make sure that the use of landfills is reduced by about 80% by 2020. To do that, they have to use methods of waste disposal which are as affordable as possible. The councils in ARC21 managed to recycle or compost 24.8% of their waste in 2006–7 but this still meant that 434,649 tonnes of solid waste were sent to landfills. To cope with this, they manage a number of landfill sites including very large landfill sites, called 'superdumps' by some. These are Cottonmount, at Mallusk on the outskirts of Belfast, and Mullaghglass, in the Belfast hills above Lisburn.

Because of the economic and environmental costs of landfill, and because the councils will face large EU fines if they do not reduce the amount of waste going to landfill, they are also looking at alternative means of disposing of waste. They have plans to build the country's first ever **energy-from-waste** (EfW) and mechanical biological treatment (MBT) facilities. EfW plants remove any waste which will burn and then recycle or send the remainder to landfill. The burning of the waste is used to generate heat and electricity, possibly enough for over 20,000 homes. However, they are called 'incinerators' by their opponents and, while people may accept that they are necessary, they do not want them to be located next to where they live. Some people claim they cause pollution with dangerous chemicals and that they discourage recycling. The EfW plant is due to be built by 2011 and to be up and running by March 2014. In June 2009 Belfast City Council voted against the construction of an EfW plant (incinerator) on publicly owned land on the north foreshore of Belfast Lough

MBT is waste processing combining sorting of the waste and biological treatment, such as composting. MBT facilities are designed to process mixed household waste as well as waste from commerce and industry. The proposals will cost between £200 million and £500 million to design, build and operate two MBT facilities for processing 400,000 tonnes of waste each year, and will also pay for an EfW plant which can handle up to 370,000 tonnes a year. It is planned that two MBTs will be completed by 2011, and ready to sort and treat waste from 2012.

What Belfast gives out each year	Tonnes
Household waste	121,000
Sewage sludge	375,000
Commercial and Industrial wastes	150,000
Carbon dioxide	3,000,000
Sulphur dioxide	20,000
Nitrous oxides	14,000

▲ **Figure 16** Belfast's growing amount of waste

▲ **Figure 17** Local protest against location of an energy-from-waste plant

Get Active

1 Individually:
   a Why are landfill sites not seen to be the solution to getting rid of Northern Ireland's waste in the future? List a number of environmental, health and economic reasons.
   b By what percentage does the use of landfill sites in Northern Ireland have to be reduced by the year 2020?
   c Explain how an EfW facility operates.
   d What are the arguments for and against the construction of an EfW plant in Northern Ireland?

2 You are going to take part in a decision-making exercise where you will have to consider both sides of the argument as to whether an EfW plant should be constructed in Northern Ireland. Having considered both sides of the argument, you will have to make the decision that you think is correct.
   a Work with a partner to prepare a summary of the background to the issue for a local newspaper or radio station. Note: you should not make any decision at this stage – all that is required is a short summary of the issue under investigation so stick to the facts!
   b Begin to make your decision. Working with a partner, agree a good case why the EfW plant should be constructed. Note the key points of your argument.
   c Then working with a different partner, agree a good case why the EfW plant should not be constructed. Note the key points of your argument.
   d Now, working on your own, study carefully the two arguments you have prepared and decide which one you support. Remember that it is your opinion or view that counts, and not what the people around you think. If you were the government minister responsible for making the decision, would you allow the construction of the EfW plant to go ahead?
   e Two corners of the classroom will be identified – one for those who believe the construction of the EfW plant should go ahead, and another for those who believe that it should not go ahead. You are either for or against the construction project. No compromise is possible!
      - Go to the corner that has been identified for those who share your view about the construction of the EfW plant.
      - In your new groups, discuss why you think your decision is the right one. Elect a spokesperson who will argue the case (within a time limit, e.g. 2 minutes) for your group, and together agree on the points the spokesperson will make and be prepared to justify.
      - Elect a class chairperson and time-keeper and organise a 'public meeting' where the spokespersons from both groups can air the group opinions and be questioned.
      - Listen carefully to all the arguments, particularly those from the opposing side, and then take a class vote on the decision that should be made.
      - Note the result of the class vote. Did the class agree with your view?
      - Complete a short self-evaluation of this decision-making exercise.

Sustainable tourism to preserve the environment

Tourism growth

Tourism has grown very rapidly in recent years. Before that growth, most tourism in Northern Ireland, for example, was local and small scale. The tourist resorts of Bangor and Portrush grew up in Victorian times and were linked to the main cities by train. At that time most working people spent a one-week holiday in a seaside resort. Other holidays away from home were rare, and foreign travel even rarer, except by the very wealthy. This started to change in the 1960s.

A number of developments started then which have transformed tourism into mass tourism which has had an impact on the whole world. The changes included:

- *Increased leisure time.* People began to get longer holidays. For example, since the mid-1960s, the typical UK adult is now working almost 8 hours less per week, equivalent to between 7 and 9 weeks' holiday each year.
- *Increased disposable income.* Alongside shorter working weeks, in 2005 UK workers earned four times as much as they did in the 1980s. People therefore have a larger proportion of their salary available for their holidays.
- *Cheaper travel.* Travel is increasingly more affordable for more people. Cheap air travel has brought what were once faraway destinations into reach for many people. The internet has helped to bring down the cost of travel and holidays and more people are booking their holidays online.
- *Increased health and wealth of pensioners.* As people are living longer and healthier lives, in general, older people are now able to travel more than they could before. This has extended the season for many traditional summer resorts in the sun as pensioners take long holidays in the winter, avoiding the worst of the cold weather at home.

Tourism in the UK and Ireland is now characterised by mass foreign tourism. This is mainly to Spain, Greece and Portugal. However, there is some evidence of this pattern changing with tourists rejecting package holidays and increasingly travelling further. There is now nowhere on the globe which is out of reach of tourism and its impact.

▲ **Figure 18** Crowded beach in Albufeira, Algarve, Portugal

Impact of tourism

Tourism is an enormous industry growing at 6% every year. In terms of the numbers employed, it was estimated to be the biggest industry in the world in 2000. Over 200 million people work in the industry, and earn 11% of global earnings. The World Tourism Organisation calculated that there were 903 million tourists and that tourism earned £582 billion in 2007. In 1996 the earnings were just £258 billion. The number of international tourists is expected to double by 2020, reaching around 1.5 billion.

Tourism exploits the attractions of an area. Some of the attractions might be scenery, isolation, unspoilt natural beauty, wildlife or welcoming local people. The dilemma is that, when the tourism resources of an area have been consumed by large numbers of tourists, the original features which attracted people to the area have often been destroyed. Tourists will then move on to the next 'undeveloped' location.

Economic impact

We have seen that there are enormous amounts of money earned through tourism. It has a considerable economic impact in the areas where it is operating, and employment in tourism can generate a considerable income for local people, particularly if there are few alternative means of employment. This money can act as a stimulus to develop other forms of work and bring even more money into the area.

However, much of the money earned through tourism does not stay in the place where it is spent. If tourism is controlled by large companies not based locally, much of the money spent will go outside the area. For example, a visitor to Belfast might travel with a tour company which is run by a Spanish company, stay in a hotel owned by an American chain, eat in restaurants owned by an English firm and buy gifts which might be made anywhere in the world. If this were the case, very little of the cost of that holiday is left in Northern Ireland to stimulate economic growth. There is employment of course, but many of the often poorly paid workers involved in tourism, such as waiters, porters and maids in hotels, may be migrant workers, so even there much of the potential benefit may be lost. Also employment in tourism is often seasonal so jobs may only be available for a short tourist season.

Environmental impact

Tourism can improve the quality of the environment in an area. The money earned can be spent on improving roads and other transport links, and on building better houses and public buildings for example. It can also be invested in improving treatment plants for water supplies and for sewage. The features that tourists are coming to see – whether scenery or wildlife or historic buildings – are more likely to be conserved as a result of tourism.

However, tourism can also have negative effects on the environment. Water is a particular issue. Water is an important feature for tourists who require such things as swimming pools, golf courses and landscaped gardens. Water is also needed to support those industries which provide services for tourists, such as agriculture. Water also has to be of a reasonably high quality as tourists expect certain standards of purity for drinking, bathing and for recreational use. A survey in Zanzibar, a popular tourist destination on the east coast of Africa, showed that tourists, on average, used 685 litres of water each day; local residents use less than 50. Tourists staying in hotels rather than guesthouses used even more – an average of 931 litres each per day. Sustainable water management would suggest a limit to consumption of between 200 and 300 litres.

This has an impact on the environment as this water has to be removed from the ground or stored in reservoirs and treated before use. Often the water is also needed for agriculture and this may leave local people short of this precious resource.

Often tourism increases the pressure on local ecosystems. Massive numbers of tourists have a huge impact and put local habitats at risk. The tourists produce waste and pollution which can affect the local wildlife. Some tourist resorts feed sewage and other waste directly into the sea, damaging surrounding coral reefs and other sensitive marine habitats. To create open beach sites, important ecosystems such as mangrove forests and seagrass meadows are removed. Large numbers of tourists on beaches and lit-up seafronts have endangered marine turtles which rely on dark secluded beaches to lay their eggs. The increased popularity of cruise ships has also affected the oceans. With up to 4000 passengers and crew on board, these massive 'floating towns' are a major source of marine pollution. The waste produced on these cruisers is dumped overboard and sewage is discharged into the ocean, along with all of the other pollutants which large ships produce.

Cultural impact

Tourism can have a beneficial impact on the culture of an area, opening it up to other cultures and helping people to understand each other better. It can generate in local people a pride in their history and culture and in their buildings and environment. In some places tourism, preservation, heritage and culture are much more likely to overlap.

Tourism can also damage local cultures. Tourists may challenge the traditional attitudes to work, money and relationships. The restaurants, bars, discos and other entertainments provided to attract and entertain tourists can bring disturbing public behaviour, drunkenness, vandalism and crime. Young locals may copy the visitors' behaviour and this can result in social conflict.

Some people are encouraged to dress in their traditional costumes and perform rituals for tourists. This can devalue local customs and make real people with a very rich culture into something for tourists to photograph. In some cases what is left of the culture is so geared for tourism that most of the meaning of their lifestyles has been lost. One example is in Hawaii with, for example, the traditional greeting by 'hula girls' at Honolulu airport. The spiritual and sacred nature of traditional Hawaiian dancing has been lost. One writer quotes a native Hawaiian as saying: 'We don't want tourism. We don't want you. We don't want to be degraded as servants and dancers. I don't want to see a single one of you in Hawaii.'

Also see www.newint.org/issue245/aloha.htm.

Get Active

1. Describe the four factors that explain the growth in tourist numbers?
2. In what way have tourism trends changed most in the past 40 years or so?
3. What do you understand by the term 'mass foreign tourism'?
4. Quote some facts to support the opinion that 'tourism is the biggest industry in the world'.
5. What is the impact of tourism in terms of:
   - economy?
   - environment?
   - culture?
6. In your opinion, is the overall impact of tourism positive or negative. Give reasons to support your opinion.

▲ **Figure 19** Tourist encountering another culture: Maasai people meeting a Western tourist in Tanzania

The impact of one sustainable tourism project on the local community and the environment in an LEDC: Nam Ha, Laos

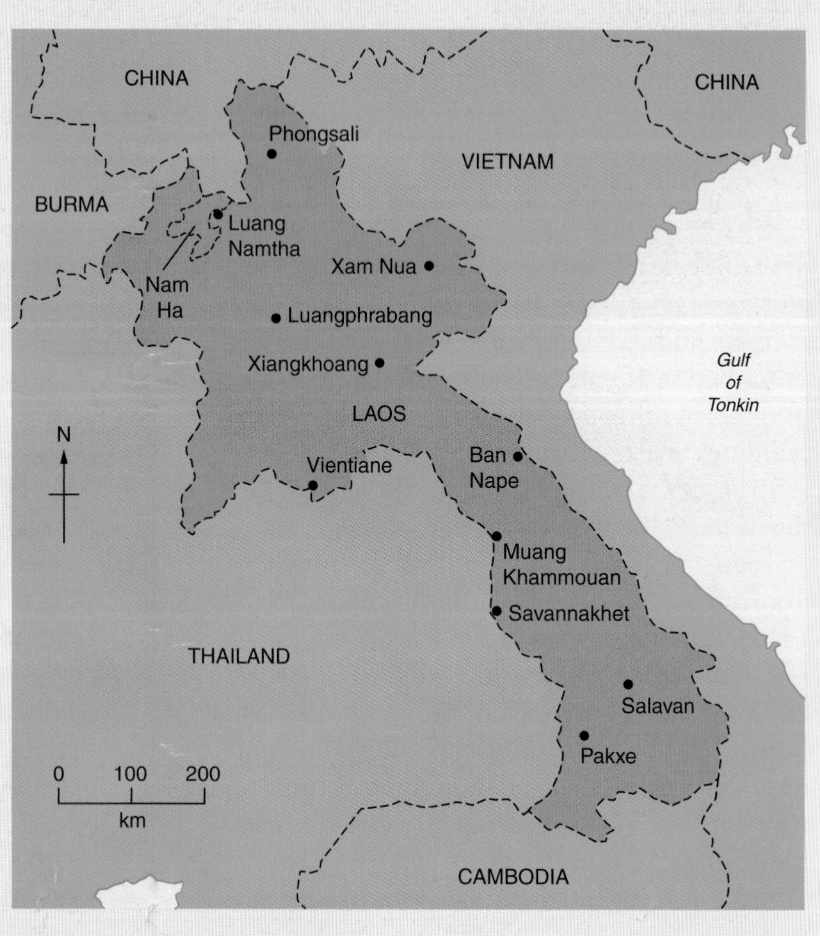

▲ **Figure 20** Map of Laos

Nam Ha is an area in the province of Luang Namtha in Laos, a country in South-east Asia. The official name for the country is Lao People's Democratic Republic.

Nam Ha covers 2224 km^2 from the lowlands of the Luang Namtha Plain to mountains of over 2000 m in altitude. The area was protected by being declared a National **Biodiversity** Conservation Area in 1993. Twelve years later it was declared a Heritage Park by ASEAN (Association of Southeastern Asian Nations). The park includes some of the largest and most important wilderness areas in Laos. Over 90% of the protected area is covered by dense mixed deciduous forest. Because of the variety of habitats, it supports a rich variety of plants and animals living in the wide range of ecosystems. This biodiversity is of national importance.

There are at least 37 larger mammal species found in the Heritage Park. Of these a number have been identified as especially important for conservation. They include large cat species such as clouded leopard, leopard and tiger, all of which are very rare. Leopards are hunted for their fur and suffer from loss of natural habit due to the spread of people in many parts of the world. The WWF has warned that the world's tigers are in danger of extinction, with numbers having fallen by half over the past 25 years. There are thought to be as few as 3500 left across the planet. There are many other rare animals too, such as gibbons and bears, and a small number of Asian elephants. Birdlife is

▲ **Figure 21** Some villagers in the Nam Ha region

▲ **Figure 22** An aerial view of the Nam Ha region

equally rich with at least 288 species recorded in the area. Of these, a number are very rare and need conservation, including types of pheasant, woodpecker and kingfisher. The smaller animals in the area have not yet been studied but it is likely that these too are rich and diverse.

An **ecotourism** project organised by UNESCO is currently working in Nam Ha. The Lao government's tourism authority is working closely with the Ministry of Agriculture and Forestry, the Department of Forestry Resource Conservation and the Ministry of Information and Culture. UNESCO provides some help in operating the project which is funded by grants from New Zealand, Japan and other sources. The area was identified by the Laos government as having a high potential for both cultural and nature tourism. The people who live in the area have rich cultures and are of interest to visitors. There are a range of activities ranging from boating on the Nam Ha and other rivers in the Park to trekking around the area. There are also caves in some areas which will attract tourists.

The project aims to make sure that the tourist industry in the Nam Ha area:

- contributes to the conservation of the natural and cultural heritage of Laos
- involves local communities in the development and management of tourism
- uses tourism as a tool to promote development in rural areas

▲ **Figure 23** A group of trekkers arrive in the Ban Nam Lai Akha village. This is one of the traditional villages participating in community-based tourism programmes in partnership with Green Discovery Laos. The objective is to develop a model of tourism to alleviate poverty, while at the same time provide tourists with a meaningful personal experience with rural villagers

- provides training and skills to local communities to help fight poverty
- produces tourism which is sustainable, both culturally and environmentally
- helps communities to establish cultural and nature tourism activities in and around Nam Ha.

The dilemma for the Laos government is how to promote tourism, with all the benefits that would bring for the inhabitants of Nam Ha and the whole of Laos, without damaging the wildlife and beauty of the area.

case study

The tourism industry in Laos is expanding rapidly. The number of international arrivals in 2000 was over 737,000, compared to just 38,000 in 1991. This rapid growth is a result of the Laos government actively encouraging tourism.

The number of tourist arrivals to Luang Namtha province increased from 4700 in 1995 to over 24,700 in 2000 and, to accommodate the growing number of visitors, many low-cost guesthouses and hotels have been built, often with attached restaurants.

Tourists stay in the area on average for 4 days and spend on average $9 each day. The main reason they visit is because of the people in the area (67.9%) and the nature and culture (66% and 50.4%). Many of the tourists that visit the park are independent travellers, backpackers for example. However, there are some package tourists as well. No matter what kind of tourist is involved, all trekking must be arranged through the Nam Ha Eco-guide Service. This ensures that the money made from trekking is reinvested in small-scale development in the area or to expand ecotourism.

In total the Nam Ha Eco-guide Service earned $34,400 in just over a year through providing trekking and river tours. While this sounds a small amount, it contributed up to 40% of total village income in the area and assisted the rural poor considerably.

Another advantage of ecotourism is that guides and tourists along trekking trails and along rivers deter outsiders who might otherwise use the area to hunt and fish illegally, threatening rare local wildlife.

There have also been considerable benefits to conservation as a result of the project. Two roads proposed for the area, which would have opened up some forests to logging and commercial trade in wildlife, were successfully argued against.

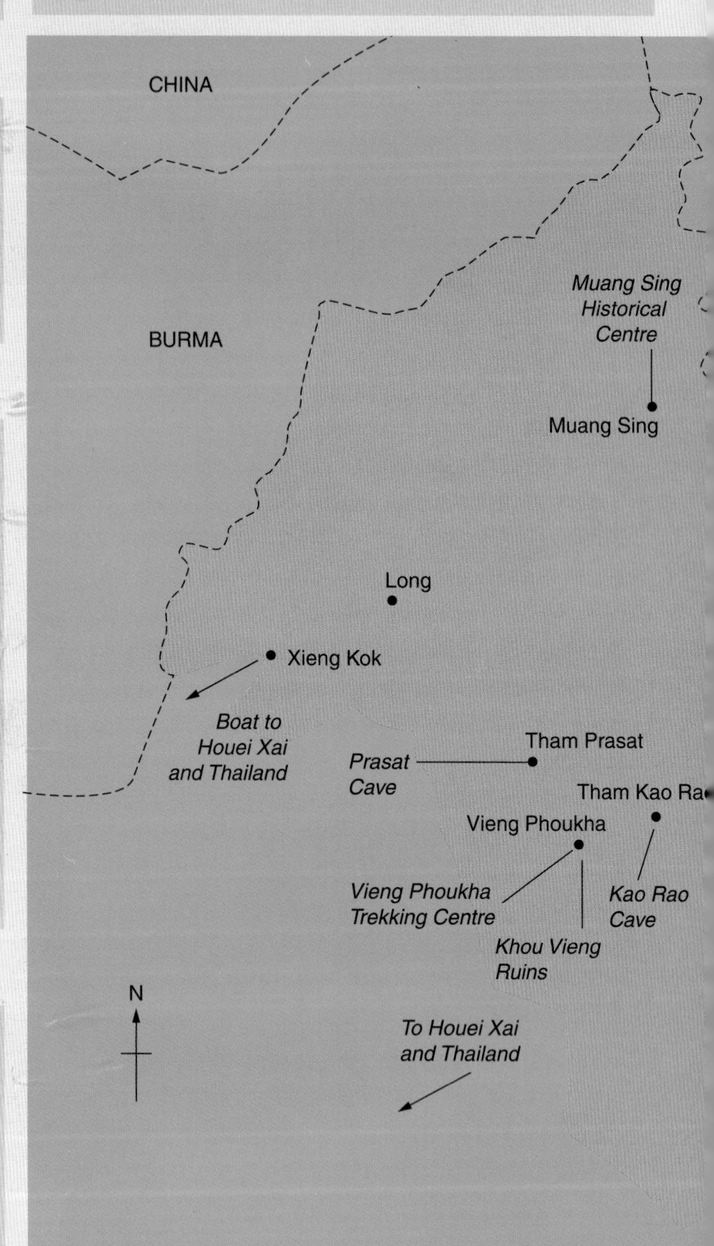

▲ **Figure 24** Tourism in Luang Namtha Province

To have long-term sustainability, local communities must have control of their own environment, and local people must be involved in the planning and the development of the tourism.

Earnings from tourism encourage the local community to protect and maintain wildlife in the short term. The local people can quickly see the benefit of conservation in terms of the earnings they can get from the ecotourism. Some villages have decided independently to impose fines to deter people from hunting. In the longer term, tourism interest easily shifts from one place to another so there is no guarantee that money will continue to be earned by local people. As a result, whether this protection will be maintained in the future is unclear.

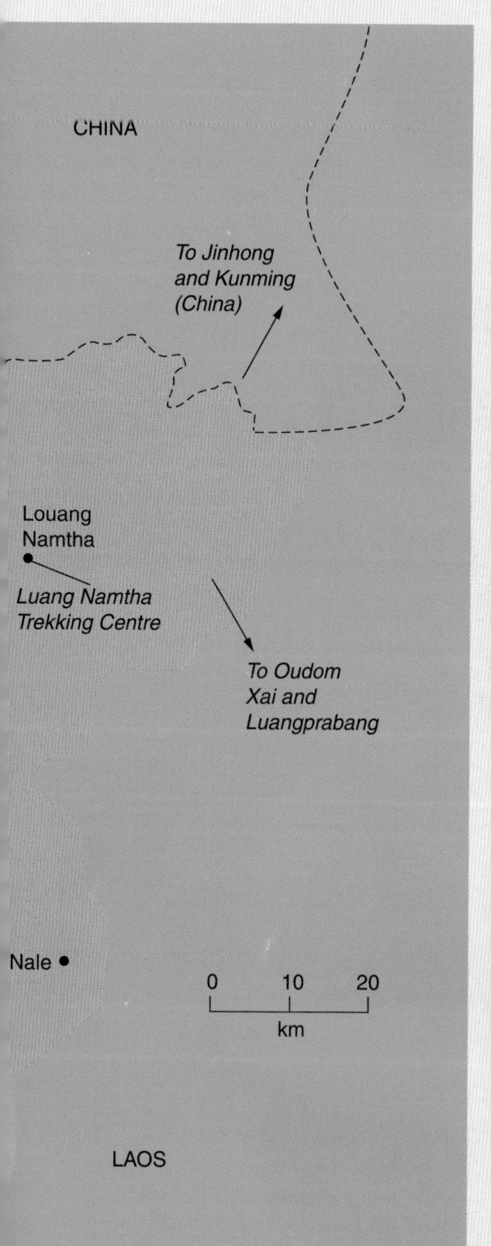

▲ **Figure 25** Village guides play an important role in managing visitor impacts. Here Pe-lo demonstrates his bird-calling skills to a group of trekkers. Pe-lo's tribe traditionally hunted birds, which is why he has these skills. Tourism is now a way that these skills can benefit the village in a sustainable way

Local people and the guides who lead the tours and the river trips are all more aware of the environment than before and this has led to an emphasis on conservation which did not previously exist. However, some areas should not be developed for ecotourism as any disturbance might damage fragile ecosystems.

Get Active

In groups, think about the following question: 'In an LEDC, like Laos, how might the government promote ecotourism in a region like Luang Namtha province, with all the benefits that it would bring for the people that live there, without damaging the wildlife and beauty of the area?'

You might find useful information at the following websites:

- www.ecotourismlaos.com/namha.htm
- www.unescobkk.org/index.php?id=486
- www.wcs.org/globalconservation/Asia/laos/laossitebasedconservation/namha.

You could complete a Google search (or use any other search engine) using prompts such as: ecotourism in Laos; Nam Ha, Laos, etc.

Prepare a PowerPoint presentation to present the views of your group to the rest of the class. It is important to include visual information such as location maps, photographs, graphs, sketches and diagrams as well as text and statistics to support the arguments that you make.

Sustainable tourism projects also exist in MEDCs. One such example is the North York Moors National Park in England.

Extension

Working in groups, your task is to find out as much as you can about how the North York Moors National Park promotes sustainable tourism and then present your findings to the rest of the class.

As a group, you need to decide:

- the main focus of your presentation
- content areas that need to be researched
- type of visual material needed
- how to present research findings
- roles for group members.

A good starting point is: www.northyorkmoors.org.uk/content.php?nID=413. You could use a search engine to find other websites relevant to sustainable tourism in the North York Moors National Park.

Sample examination questions

1 The impact of our increasing use of resources on the environment.

Foundation Tier

(i) State the meaning of the term 'carbon footprint'. [2]

(ii) Complete each of the following statements by writing either the word 'smaller' or 'larger'. One has been completed for you:

- Flying to France on an aeroplane creates a **larger** carbon footprint than using the ferry.
- Walking to work creates a ________________ carbon footprint than driving to work.
- Buying locally produced food creates a ______________ carbon footprint than buying imported food.
- Leaving all the lights on in your house at night will create a _______________ carbon footprint than if you turned them all off. [3]

(iii) For a city that you have studied, describe two traffic control measures which are in place. Remember not to use a city from within the British Isles.

- city [1]
- measures. [4]

Higher Tier

(i) State the meaning of the term 'carbon footprint' and explain how to reduce the size of your own carbon footprint. [6]

(ii) Explain what the cartoon is telling us about China's carbon footprint.

(iii) Describe and evaluate two traffic control measures in place within a city you have studied. Remember not to use a city from within the British Isles. [9]

WHY CHINA'S CARBON FOOTPRINT IS SO LARGE

2 Increasing demand for resources in LEDCs and MEDCs.

Foundation Tier

(i) For an LEDC you have studied, explain how population growth has put pressure on the environment. [4]

(ii) For an MEDC you have studied, explain how renewable energy is helping with energy production. [4]

Higher Tier

(i) For an LEDC you have studied, describe and explain how population growth has caused demand for resources and has put pressure on the environment. [7]

(ii) For an MEDC you have studied, evaluate the benefits and problems associated with renewable energy production. [9]

3 Managing waste to protect our environment

Foundation Tier

(i) Explain why waste management is now an important issue in the UK. [4]

Use the diagram below to help you to answers questions (ii) and (iii).

(ii) Name the least common type of waste found in bins. [1]

(iii) Name three waste items which could be recycled. [3]

(iv) Explain the concept of reduce, reuse and recycle. [3]

What's in your bin?

Make our city more sustainable!
RECYCLE!!!

%
43.8% Materials that will rot down
17.2% Paper and card
8.6% Plastic
7% Glass
3.4% Metal
1.3% Clothing
18.7% Other

Higher tier

(i) Explain why waste management is now an important issue in the UK. [6]

(ii) Explain how the concept of reduce, reuse and recycle could help ease the problems of waste disposal. [4]

(iii) Using one case study area, explain why a range of waste management approaches is needed. [7]

4 Sustainable tourism to preserve the environment

Foundation Tier

(i) Explain why the tourism industry has grown so rapidly since 1960. [4]

(ii) Describe two positive impacts that tourism can bring to an area. [4]

(iii) Using one case study country, describe how sustainable tourism is having a positive impact. [5]

Higher Tier

Study the diagram below which shows information about a holiday to India. Use it to help you answers questions (i) and (ii).

(i) Name the type of tourism promoted. [1]

(ii) Explain two advantages this type of holiday might have for the local area. [6]

(iii) Evaluate the positive and negative impacts tourism can cause to any area. [6]

(iv) Using one case study area, assess the impact of a sustainable tourism project. [8]

INDIAN TIGER CONSERVATION HOLIDAY

Learn about this unique jungle ecosystem when you help a ranger and experience wildlife and conservation first hand.

During your holiday you will learn about the unique habitat and how to identify many of the species resident in the Reserve.

You meet one of the local rangers when you help them to track and document the day in the life of a tiger.

We only use local accommodation, food and services. We also plant enough trees to offset the carbon dioxide emissions from your flight.

Glossary

Unit 1: Understanding Our Natural World

Theme A: The Dynamic Landscape

Abrasion/corrasion (1) The grinding of rock fragments carried by a river against the bed and banks of the river. (2) A process of erosion which occurs when a wave hits the coast and throws pebbles against the cliff face. These knock off small parts of the cliff causing undercutting

Attrition A process of erosion where transported particles hit against each other making the particles smaller and more rounded

Confluence The point where two rivers meet

Constructive wave A wave with a strong swash and weak backwash which contributes deposition to a beach

Deposition The dropping of material on the Earth's surface

Destructive wave A wave with a strong backwash and weak swash which erodes a coast

Discharge The amount of water in a river which is passing a certain point in a certain time. It is measured in cumecs (cubic metres per second)

Drainage basin An area of land drained by a river and all of its tributaries

Erosion Wearing away of the landscape by the action of ice, water and wind

Flooding A temporary covering by water of land which is normally dry

Groundwater flow Water which is moving through the bedrock

Hard engineering A strategy to control a natural hazard which does not blend into the environment

Hydraulic action (1) A form of erosion caused by the force of moving water. It undercuts riverbanks on the outside of meanders and forces air into cracks in exposed rocks in waterfalls. (2) The process whereby soft rocks are washed away by the sea. Air trapped in cracks by the force of water can widen cracks causing sections of cliff to break away from the cliff face

Infiltration The movement of water into the soil

Interception The process whereby precipitation is prevented from falling onto the ground by plants. It slows run-off and reduces the risk of flash flooding

Long-shore drift The process whereby beach material moves along a coastline, caused by waves hitting the coast at an angle

Mouth The end of a river where it meets the sea, ocean or lake

Percolation The movement of water from the soil into the bedrock

Saltation The bouncing of medium-sized load along a river bed or the seabed

Soft engineering A strategy to control a natural hazard which does blend into the environment so is often sustainable

Solution/corrosion The process by which water (in river or sea) reacts chemically with soluble minerals in the rocks and dissolves them

Source The starting point of a river, it may be a lake, glacier or marsh

Surface run-off/overland flow Water which is moving over the surface of the land

Suspension The transportation of the smallest load, e.g. fine sand and clay which is held up continually within river or seawater

Through-flow Water which is moving through the soil

Traction The rolling of large rocks along a river or seabed

Transportation The movement of material across the Earth's surface

Tributary A stream which flows into a larger river

Water cycle The continuous circulation of water between land, sea and air

Watershed The boundary between drainage basins, it is often a ridge of high land

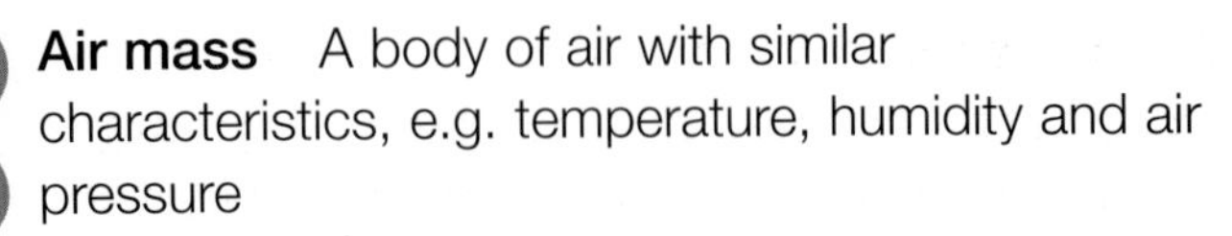

Theme B: Our Changing Weather and Climate

Air mass A body of air with similar characteristics, e.g. temperature, humidity and air pressure

Anemometer An instrument which is used to measure wind speed

Anticyclone A weather system with high pressure at its centre

Atmospheric pressure The weight of a column of air measured in millibars

Barometer An instrument used to measure air pressure

Climate The average weather conditions of an area over a long period of time, e.g. 35 years

Cloud cover The amount of sky covered by cloud, measured in oktas

Cold front The zone where cold air comes behind warm air. The cold air undercuts the warm air forcing it to rise cool and condense

Depression A weather system with low pressure at its centre

Fossil fuel Any resource found in the Earth's crust which contains carbon and can be burnt to release heat, e.g. coal, oil or gas

Front The zone where two types of air mass meet

Global warming The warming of the atmosphere, i.e. the increase over time in average annual global temperature. This is probably related to human activity through the release of greenhouse gases

Greenhouse effect A natural process where our atmosphere traps heat. Some of the insolation that is absorbed by the Earth's surface is re-radiated to the atmosphere where it is held by the greenhouse gases – carbon dioxide, methane, nitrogen dioxide, CFCs and water vapour

Maximum thermometer An instrument used to measure the hottest temperature reached in a place

Millibar the unit used to measure air pressure

Minimum thermometer An instrument used to measure the coldest temperature reached in a place

Precipitation A form of moisture in the atmosphere, such as rainfall, sleet, snow and fog

Rain gauge An instrument which catches and measures precipitation

Satellite image A photograph taken from space

Synoptic chart A weather map which shows the weather as symbols over an area

Temperature The hotness or coldness of the air in relation to weather. It is usually measured in degrees Celsius

Warm front The zone where warm air comes behind cold air

Weather The day-to-day condition of the atmosphere. The main elements of weather include rainfall, temperature, wind speed and direction, cloud type and cover and air pressure

Wind The movement of air within the atmosphere

Wind direction The geographical direction (compass point) from which a wind blows

Wind speed The speed at which air is flowing. It can be measured in knots

Theme C: The Restless Earth

Convection current Repetitive movements set up in the mantle due to heating by the core. These currents make the crust move

Core The centre of the Earth, found below the mantle. It is extremely hot and may be made of metal

Crust The upper layer of the Earth on which we live. It is solid but is split into sections called plates

Earthquake A tremor starting in the crust which causes shaking to be felt on the Earth's surface

Epicentre The first place on the Earth's surface to feel shockwaves from an earthquake. It is directly above the focus

Fault line A weak line in Earth's surface, where crust is moving, causing earthquake activity

Focus The point of origin of an earthquake under the Earth's surface

Lava plateau This is a flat, wide surface that is formed when lava comes out of the ground and spreads out quickly

Liquefaction The process of solid soil turning to liquid mud caused by shaking during an earthquake bringing water to the surface

Mantle The layer above the Earth's core. It makes up 80% of the Earth's mass. It behaves like liquid rock

Mid-ocean ridge Where two plates made of oceanic crust move apart, the magma of the mantle rises to fill the gap, causing the crust to rise and form a ridge

Ocean trench A feature of a destructive plate margin which involves oceanic crust. Where the oceanic crust is forced down into the mantle it sinks below its normal level to create a deep trench in the ocean

Plate margin/boundary A zone where two plates meet. Plate boundaries may be described as constructive, destructive, conservative or collision

Plates Sections of the Earth's crust which are constantly moving due to convection currents set up in the mantle

Richter scale A scale between 0 and 9 which measures the strength of an earthquake

Rock types Geologists divide rocks into three rock types, depending on how the rock was made: igneous, sedimentary and metamorphic

Seismograph An instrument designed to measure the energy released by earthquakes

Subduction zone An area where crust is being forced down into the mantle

Tsunami Large waves caused by underwater earthquakes

Volcanic plug A landform made from the hardened vent material from inside a volcano. This material is exposed when the surrounding volcano is eroded away

Volcano A cone-shaped mountain built up from hardened ash and lava, from which molten material erupts onto the Earth's surface

Unit 2: Living in Our World

Theme A: People and Where They Live

Aged dependency The proportion of people aged 65 or over in a population

Birth rate The number of live births per 1000 of a population per year

Central business district (CBD) The part of a town (or larger settlement) which is dominated by shops and offices and is usually close to its centre

Counterurbanisation The movement of people away from towns and cities to smaller towns, villages or areas in the countryside

Death rate The number of deaths per 1000 of a population per year

Emigration The movement of people away from one country to another

Function of a settlement The main reason why a settlement is there

High order function A good or service which is used infrequently, maybe because it is expensive

Immigration The inward movement of people to a country from another

Low order function Goods or services which are used regularly

Migration The permanent or semi-permanent movement of people from one place of residence to another. Migration can be classified, for example into *forced*, e.g. due to war or famine, or *voluntary*, e.g. looking for better work

Natural increase The positive difference between the birth rate and the death rate. For example, birth rate = 41 and death rate = 20, then natural increase = 21 per thousand

Population structure The way in which a population is made up of males and females of different ages

Pull factor Any attractive/positive aspect or quality of a place which attracts (pulls) migrants to it

Push factors Any negative aspect or quality of a place which causes people to leave it

Range The maximum distance which people are prepared to travel to get to a good/service

Rural–urban fringe An area on the outskirts of a city beyond the suburbs where there is a mixture of rural and urban land uses

Settlement A place where people live

Settlement hierarchy The arrangement of settlements in order of importance from small to large, eg ranging from an individual farmstead to a megalopolis

Shanty town A characteristic of LEDC cities; an area within them of unplanned poor quality housing which lacks basic services like clean water

Site The physical characteristics of the land on which a settlement is located, e.g. wet point, bridging point or defensive site

Sphere of influence The area served by a settlement

Threshold of a product or service The minimum number of people needed to support a good/service

Urban sprawl The unplanned growth of a city into the nearby countryside

Urbanisation An increase in the proportion of a country's population who live in urban areas

Youth dependency The proportion of people aged 15 or under in a population

Theme B: Contrasts in World Development

Appropriate technology Technology which is suited to the level of development in the area where it is used

Bilateral aid Resources are given directly from a rich 'donor' country to a poorer 'recipient' country. If conditions are placed on the way in which the money is used, then this becomes tied aid

Development The level of economic growth and wealth of a country. The use of resources, natural and human, to achieve higher standards of living. This includes economic factors, social measures and issues such as freedom

Development gap The division between wealthy and poor areas, in particular the disparity between LEDCs and MEDCs

Economic indicators Figures relating to the wealth and economy of a country

Fair trade A type of trade where producers in a poor country get a fair living wage for their product and which promotes environmental protection

Globalisation The way in which countries from all over the world are becoming linked by trade, ideas and technology

Human development index (HDI) A measure of development which combines measures of wealth, health and education, thus mixing social and economic indicators

LEDC A less economically developed country, often recognised by its poverty and a low standard of living

MEDC A more economically developed country, often recognised by its wealth and a high standard of living

Multilateral aid MEDCs give money to an international organisation, like the World Bank, which then redistributes the money to LEDCs

Newly industrialised country (NIC) A country which experienced rapid economic growth since the 1980s, e.g. South Korea

Primary activity An activity which uses the Earth's resources as a way of making money, e.g. farming fishing, agriculture, mining

Quality of life A measure of a person's emotional, social and physical well-being

Quaternary activity An activity which focuses on the research and development of products

Secondary activity An activity which involves the manufacturing or building of a product which is sold to make money. The processing of a raw material

Social indicators Figures relating to the quality of life within a country

Tertiary activity An activity where a service is provided

Tied aid When conditions are placed by the 'donor' on the way that money or resources are used by the 'recipient' country

Trade The business of buying, selling and distributing goods and services

Voluntary aid The general public in MEDCs give money to voluntary organisations like Oxfam, which use the money to fund development projects

Theme C: Managing Our Resources

Biodiversity Biodiversity is the variation of life forms within an ecosystem

Carbon footprint A measure of the amount of carbon dioxide produced by a person, organisation or country in a given time

Ecotourism Otherwise known as green tourism. A sustainable form of tourism which involves protecting the environment and local way of life at the destination

Energy-from-waste plant Sometimes called incinerators, these use the parts of waste that burn to generate electricity

Landfill site A large hole in the ground into which rubbish is dumped

Renewable energy A sustainable source of electricity production such as wind, solar or biofuels

Resource Anything that we use and rely on. A renewable resource is a sustainable resource which can be used over and over again without running out. Resource depletion is when a resource is used at a faster rate than it is being replaced, causing it to run out. A non-renewable resource is a resource which cannot be replaced in geological time once it has been used

Sustainable A way of using resources so that they are not destroyed but remain available for others to use in the future

UNESCO The United Nations Educational, Scientific and Cultural Organisation (UNESCO) is part of the United Nations. It promotes peace and security through international collaboration in education, science, and culture

Waste hierarchy The arrangement of waste disposal options in order of sustainability

Wetlands Marshes, bogs and lakes which provide rich habitats

World Health Organisation The World Health Organisation (WHO) is an agency of the UN (United Nations) that coordinates public health around the world, with its headquarters in Geneva, Switzerland

Index